Straßer • Wahl
Graphics and Robotics

Wolfgang Straßer
Friedrich Wahl

Editors

Graphics and Robotics

With 128 Figures,
some in Colour

Springer

Prof. Dr.-Ing. Wolfgang Straßer
Wilhelm-Schickard-Institut für Informatik
Graphisch-Interaktive Systeme
Universität Tübingen
Auf der Morgenstelle 10, C9
D-72076 Tübingen, Germany

Prof. Dr.-Ing. Friedrich Wahl
Institut für Robotik und Prozeßinformatik
Technische Universität Braunschweig
Hamburger Straße 267
D-38114 Braunschweig, Germany

ISBN 3-540-58358-0 Springer-Verlag Berlin Heidelberg New York

Library of Congress Cataloging-in-Publication Data
Graphics and robotics/Wolfgang Strasser, Friedrich Wahl. p. cm.
Includes bibliographical references and index.
ISBN 0-387-58358-0 (U.S.: acid-free paper)
1. Robotics. 2. Computer graphics. I. Strasser, Wolfgang, 1941- .
II. Wahl, Friedrich.   TJ211.G72 1995 629.8' 9266-dc20-95-36099 CIP

Cover Design: Konzept & Design, Ilvesheim
Typesetting: Camera-ready by authors   Printing: Mercedesdruck, Berlin
Binding: Lüderitz & Bauer, Berlin Prod. Editor: Peter Straßer, Heidelberg
Printed on acid-free paper   SPIN 10057326   33/3140 – 5 4 3 2 1 0

Preface

This book is a result of the lectures and discussions held during the international workshop on "Graphics & Robotics", which took place at Schloß Dagstuhl, FRG, April 19-22, 1993. The event brought together leading experts from both disciplines to identify common scientific problems, to present new solutions and to discuss future research directions in graphics and robotics.

The papers included in this book were written after the workshop and reflect the exchange of ideas and experiences during the workshop. The final selection was made after a careful reviewing process.

The organisation of the papers:

Since the availability of reasonably priced graphical workstations, robot designers and researchers have used these devices to anticipate the kinematic/dynamic behavior of robots before actual construction and application. Nowadays, simulation and offline programming constitute indispensable tools in modern production engineering. Nevertheless, there are still many efforts needed to further the knowledge of efficient graphical representations and computer graphics algorithms to build artificial robot worlds. A state-of-the-art introduction to the principles of robot simulation is given in the first paper by Laloni et al. The contribution by Brunner et al. outlines new simulation concepts in the framework of teleoperation such as space applications. The papers of Müller and Purgathofer et al. deal respectively with path planning strategies and collision detection techniques for environments with obstacles.

To extend the possibilities of virtual experimentation and artificial imagination, worldwide investigations towards virtual reality are in progress. The paper by Wachsmuth et al. outlines research in this direction and presents first results.

There are many international efforts to achieve task-level programming and/or automated programming of robots/assembly stations on the basis of product descriptions like CAD data for assemblies. These tasks need powerful modeling techniques and geometric representation schemes and thus again are a common research area for graphics and robotics people. The papers by Gutsche et al., Caracciolo et al., and van Holland et al. stress this interesting field of active research. Advanced modeling techniques for objects with curved surfaces are treated in the papers by Seidel and Greiner. The paper by Klein shows how to integrate various surface representations into one object-oriented programming environment and demonstrates the elegance and power of object-oriented implementations.

Certainly one further area of close interrelations between graphics and robotics is the field of robot vision. It would have been beyond the scope of this workshop to host this subject extensively – there are many events especially devoted to this topic. In these proceedings there are four papers touching the area. The paper by Kroll et al. outlines an interesting new approach for depth or range data acquisition, which may be used for automated model-generation as described in the paper by Winzen et al. The paper by Ehricke deals with the visualization of 3-dimensional data and presents new and intuitive mechanisms for their quick interpretation.

The last paper of the book, by Gagalowicz, can be considered as the quintessence of the workshop: his vision system for a domestic robot makes use of advanced theories and techniques from both disciplines and defines the most challenging research task, which will be solved by joined efforts of both scientific communities to free us from housework and to leave – finally – housecleaning to the robot.

Wolfgang Straßer, Tübingen   Fritz Wahl, Braunschweig

June 1994

Table of Contents

Principles of Robot Simulation and their Application in a PC-based Robot Simulation System

C. Laloni and F. M. Wahl

Institute for Robotics and Computer Control, Technical University of Braunschweig
Hamburger Str. 267, D-38114 Braunschweig, Germany

Abstract

This paper addresses some fundamental topics which have to be regarded during the design, implementation and usage of graphical robot simulation systems.

After a short summary of robot simulation system purposes, we derive the basic requirements, which have to be satisfied, in order to obtain a useful simulation system. We show, that different modeling steps are necessary to build up an internal representation of a robot arm and the robot work cell, which can be used to simulate and visualize the execution of robot tasks. The main parts of such a model are the geometrical and the kinematical representation. Different geometrical representations and possible modeling techniques are presented. In addition, general considerations about the computation of the robot kinematics and its inverse, which plays an important role in off-line robot program development, are made. An affixment technique which is used to combine the kinematical and the geometrical model is introduced and the working principle is demonstrated with the help of a modeled example world.

Finally we focus on some special aspects of robot simulation such as the graphical visualization and the different interpretations of time within a simulation system; in addition, we outline the main software modules, which are more or less incorporated in each graphical robot simulation system.

Many of the discussed principles of graphical robot simulation are illustrated by means of a PC-based graphical robot simulation system. This system was designed and implemented at our institute and is currently used to teach students some principles of robotics within practical courses.

1 Introduction

The simulation of robots and robot work cells is one of the main aspects in the field of robotics research. To understand the importance of graphical robot simulation, it is helpful to consider the various aspects why and where graphic robot simulations are used. During the design of new robot arm structures and work cell layouts the functionality of the robot and the work cell can be tested without building expensive prototypes. In addition, existing robot work cell layouts can be optimized easily; thus, e.g., the optimal position of the robot arm, tools or workpieces can be determined within the simulated work cell.

A fundamental advantage in industrial applications is the usage of simulation systems for off-line program development; due to this, it is not necessary to interrupt the work of the real world robots which usually are integrated in a complex production line. This saves money, because the factory production need not to be hindered. The verification of robot trajectories and the possibilities of early object collision detection within simulation systems provide a higher security and prevent serious damages. Even the coordination of multiple robots, which usually requires more careful planning can be tested without any danger to man and machine. Finally, the use of robot simulation systems should not be underestimated in the fields of research and education. New control algorithms, e.g., can be tested long before the corresponding hardware is available and students can be taught the principles of robotics on simulation systems inexpensively and safely.

To obtain this wide range of functionalities, it is clear that a robot simulation system has to satisfy a variety of requirements. In the following, some of the basic requirements are discussed and the associated techniques which are used to fulfill these requirements are presented.

First of all, the robot arm and each component of the robot work cell has to be modeled. As we will show in section 2, this modeling consists of various steps, depending on the type of objects which have to be modeled, or the purpose of the simulation. The main modeling steps, which are discussed in more details in this paper are the geometrical modeling (section 2.1) and the kinematical modeling steps (section 2.2).

To achieve a 3d graphical animation capability, the previously defined graphical model of the objects or object parts and the kinematic model have to be combined. This is done in robot simulation systems by using the so-called *affixment* data-structures, which are presented in section 3. As we will show, with these affixments a simulated world can be completely modeled and even object relationships such as *'object A is mounted to object B'*, or *'object C is gripped by the robot's hand'* can be expressed.

Subsequently, the main software modules, constituting a typical robot simulation system and their organization is described in section 4. Simultaneously we consider some additional aspects which have to be regarded during the simulation. Thus, a variety of tools like a robot program editor and interpreter are necessary to achieve a comfortable simulation environment with off-line robot programming capabilities. In addition we show, how virtual cameras can be used (see also section 4), to enhance the visual output and to give the user an optimal visual feedback during fine positioning tasks. Further, we explain the importance of the term time within a graphical robot simulation system. Especially, if the simulation computation only can be done off-line and the simulation time is not identically with the simulated time, it is necessary to get correct information about elapsed times, if the simulated actions should be executed in a real world environment.

Finally we summarize the main topics of this paper and give a a short conclusion.

2 Modeling of Robots and Components

If we consider a typical robot work cell or robot environment, we basically can distinguish different components which have to be modeled within the robot simulation system. Usually, the main component is the robot arm itself. In addition to this, there are grippers and tools, such as welding guns or screw drivers, which are used by the robot. In contrast to these components, belonging directly to the robot, there are the components of the robot environment. These components can be divided into two main classes – dynamic and static environment components. The class of dynamic environment components consists of all objects, which are able to perform autonomous actions or which can be activated by external applied forces. Typically, part suppliers, feeders or conveyer belts belong to this class. The remaining environment objects, such as walls, desks, control units etc. are constituting the class of the static environment components.

Each of these components has to be modeled; depending on the type of object, different modeling steps have to be performed.

Usually the first modeling step is the definition of a *geometrical model*. This model is necessary for the visualization of the simulated work cell during the simulation period. The various representation forms, which can be used are outlined in section 2.1. To build up such a graphical representation, special graphical editors (e.g. CAD systems) can be used. Some basic and simple object construction methods, which were implemented within our PC-based simulation system [Schlorff88, Laloni+91] are explained in section 2.

In addition to this, a *kinematic description* (section 2.2) is necessary for all mechanical parts, which are able to perform any kind of motion; typical examples are the complete robot arm or any other mechanical device such as a part feeder. Such a kinematical description is necessary, regardless if the motion is caused by actuators belonging to the object, like in the case of the robot arm, or if the motion can be caused by forces applied to the object from outside (e.g. to a crank). The technique which is usually used to derive and to describe the kinematics, bases on the *Denavit-Hartenberg-Notation* (section 2.2). In addition to the robot arm kinematics it is very useful during off-line robot program development, to have the relationship between the cartesian coordinates within the robot work space and corresponding joint variables. This relation is known as the *inverse kinematics problem* (see section 2.2.2) and offers the possibility to specify robot movements relative to a user defined cartesian coordinate system.

Depending on the purpose of the simulation and the desired simulation accuracy the dynamic characteristics of the objects have to be modeled; suppose, e.g., if a control problem has to be simulated. With the additional use of a *dynamic model* of the robot arm, the robot simulation can be improved and even critical effects such as overshots can be simulated correctly. Generally the dynamic model consists of a set of *dynamic equations* which can be obtained from known physical laws and which relate forces and torques to joint positions, velocities and accelerations. For a more detailed discussion of the dynamic modeling problem, which is not part of this paper, we refer to [An+88, Craig89, Featherstone87, Spong+89].

Finally, object specific *device functions* have to be modeled. If, e.g., an ultrasonic sensor or even a simple switch is included in the simulation, the functions of these devices, such as the output signals have to be modeled. Moreover, even the effect which is caused by the application of a work cell object has to be modeled; suppose, e.g., a welding gun, which causes a welding seam or a spray gun, which causes an air brush and changes the color of other objects.

Consequently, we can summarize the following basic modeling steps:

- Graphical representation

- Kinematical representation

- Dynamical model

- Device functions

2.1 Geometric Modeling

The shape of an object or the geometric model can be represented by various techniques. The most frequently used forms are the *wire frame representation, the surface or boundary representation* and the *solid model representation.*

2.1.1 Wire Frame Representation

In the so-called wire frame representation an object is represented only by its vertices and the edges, connecting the vertices (see figure 1).

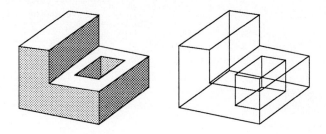

Figure 1: Original object (left); wire-frame representation (right)

The main advantage of the wire frame representation is, that the creation and postprocessing, such as the computation of a visual transformation, can be done very fast without using specialized graphics hardware, due to the simple representation form. Unfortunately, this representation has to cope with several disadvantages. Due to the lack of information about the surfaces of the represented objects, wire frame models offer only poor visualization capabilities and a nonunique interpretation; an open box, e.g., can not be distinguished from a closed one, because both objects are represented by the same wire frame model.

2.1.2 Boundary Representation

The surface or boundary representation (B-rep) of an object consists of a set of planar curves or plane equations forming a polygon mesh of the object shape (see figure 2).

If in addition cubic pathes or splines are allowed to define the boundaries of an object; even free-form shaped objects can be represented. Depending on the complexity of the resulting polygon mesh, it has to be taken into account, that the processing complexity of the algorithms working on these objects increases drastically. In contrast to the wire frame representation mentioned above, the explicit representation of object boundaries leads to good visualization possibilities; hidden-line or hidden-surface and shading algorithms can be applied to the surfaces to enhance the quality of the graphical output. However, the information about the in- and outside of the object, which is very helpful e.g. in collision detection algorithms, can not be derived directly from the object model, but has to be computed explicitly.

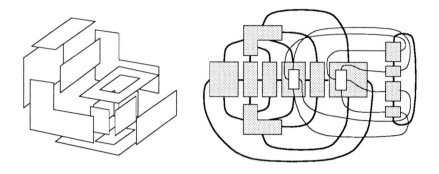

Figure 2: Boundary representation; boundaries (left); polygon mesh (right)

2.1.3 Solid Model Representation

In the solid model representation a modeled object is represented by primitive solids or previously modeled solids, which are combined to more complex ones, with set operations, such as union or intersection (see figure 3).

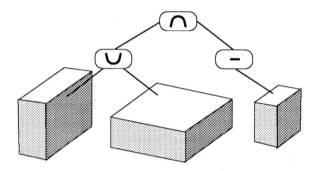

Figure 3: Representation with primitive solids and a CSG-tree

Typically the set of primitives consists of cubes, cones, spheres etc., with variable characteristic parameters, such as the diameter or the height. The representation of a composed solid object is done by the so-called constructive solid geometry (CSG) tree. Each node of the CSG-tree represents a set operation, with additional transformations for the relative positioning of the objects. A leave of the CSG-tree represents a primitive with specified parameters. Such a CSG-tree always represents a valid 3d object which can be interpreted unambiguously, but one object can be represented by different CSG-trees. Due to the fact, that solid objects are modeled, it is easy to distinguish between the in- and outside of objects, which is a big advantage, with respect to the implementation of collision detection algorithms.

As the CSG-tree has to be evaluated each time the object is processed, such a representation leads to a high computational complexity; thus, often specialized hardware is required to deal with solid modeled objects.

For a more complete discussion of the advantages and disadvantages of the various geometric representation forms we refer to [Mortenson85, Mäntylä88, Straßer+89]. Within our PC-based robot simulation system, we have used a wire frame representation, with additional surface information, taking into account the limited computational resources of a PC. Thus, we have combined the advantages of a simple wire-frame representation with the better visualization capabilities of the B-rep representation; the graphical output can be enhanced, by applying fast back face culling algorithms for the visualization of the objects.

2.1.4 Object Modeling Techniques

The definition of the object models or representations, can be done either by a textual specification of the object parameters (e.g. the coordinates of the vertices, linkage of vertices to edges, etc.), or interactively by using a graphical editor. Due to the more convenient modeling possibilities and the direct visual feedback, graphical editors are usually preferred. Depending on the selected object representation, the modeling techniques used within such graphical editors are different. Generally we can distinguish surface and volume oriented modeling systems, which are corresponding to the boundary or solid representation techniques.

In our simulation system, we have implemented three different modeling procedures, providing a comfortable object geometry specification to the user [Laloni88, Künne90]. The basic idea of these modeling techniques is the construction of a 3d object from an arbitrary user defined 2d polygon. The most simple form of extending a 2d polygon to a 3d object is the translation of the polygon along a previously defined translation vector. In addition to this, the user defined polygon can also be rotated around a rotation axis lying in the plane of the polygon, to obtain a 3d object. With a previously specified rotation angle and the number of subdivisions of the rotation angle, the object is computed automatically. These two techniques allow the creation of a variety of simple objects or object parts; example objects (single components) created with these techniques are shown in the figures 10, 11 and 13.

The third modeling technique is similar to the generalized cylinder approach which is well known in the field of computer vision and was introduced by [Agin+76] (see also [Kashipati+92]). Again one (or more) arbitrary user defined 2d polygons are used; but in addition, a user defined polyline (spine) (figure 4b) is needed. To obtain a 3d object, the polygons can be positioned and oriented at the vertices of the polyline (see figure 4c). The vertices of subsequent polygons along the polyline are then connected automatically or manually. With these connections, additional planes specifying the object shape are formed.

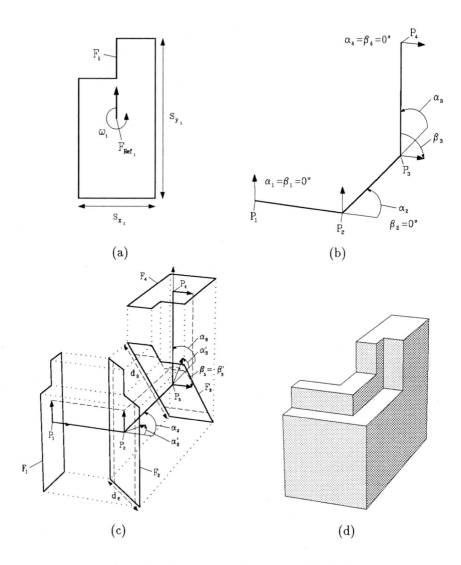

Figure 4: Construction of a generalized cylinder

Various build-in tools allow the modification of the polygon geometry at each specified position. Thus, it is possible to extend e.g. the length of the distance d_2 (figure 4c) with respect to the angle α_2. Such a modification is necessary, if a right angled object like it is shown in figure 4d is modeled. Figure 5 shows some example objects modeled as generalized cylinders within our simulation system.

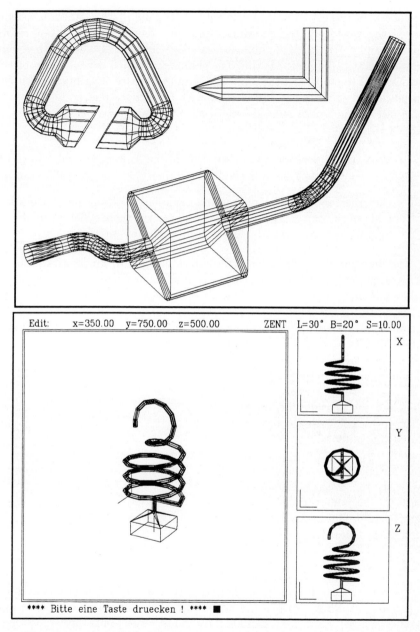

Figure 5: Examples of generalized cylinders (top)
Modeling environment of the PC-based system with generalized cylinder (bottom)

2.2 Kinematic Modeling

Kinematics generally deals with the study and representation of the geometry
of the motion of a mechanical device with one or more joints and links. This

is done with respect to a fixed reference coordinate system, which is usually called the world or base coordinate system. Kinematics does not regard masses and forces and/or moments causing the motion. Thus, the robot arm kinematics only regards the joint parameters which define the geometric structure of the links and the joint angles and velocities describing the spatial displacement of the robot end-effector with respect to time.

In the field of robot arm kinematics the following two questions play an important role.

- What is the position and orientation of the end-effector relative to the base coordinate system for a given manipulator and given joint angles?

- Can the robot arm reach a given cartesian position and orientation, and which joint angles have to be used? Are there different joint configurations, which satisfy these condition?

The first question is known as the direct or forward kinematics problem. The second one is called the inverse kinematics problem. As we will see, a symbolic solution of the direct kinematics problem can be found easily, using the *Denavit-Hartenberg* notation [Denavit+55] to describe the robot arm kinematics (see also [Fu+87, Paul81]). In contrast to this, the computation of a symbolic solution of the inverse kinematics problem is more complicated and sometimes even impossible.

The figure to the right shows the relationship between the direct and the inverse kinematics. The direct kinematics computes for given joint angles and link parameters the position and the orientation of the end-effector, whereas the inverse kinematics delivers the joint variables for a given link parameters set and an end-effector position.

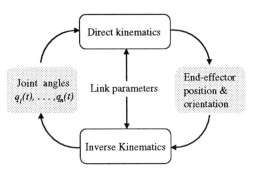

2.2.1 Kinematic Representation (Direct Kinematics)

If we consider a robot arm, we can state that often such a mechanical manipulator can be modeled as an open-loop chain, consisting of several rigid bodies (links), which are connected by joints. The joints, either prismatic or revolute, are driven by actuators and each joint constitutes one degree of mechanical freedom. One end of this open loop-chain is fixed to the robot base, whereas the other end is usually free and attached to the end-effector.

To describe such a structure Denavit and Hartenberg [Denavit+55] proposed a systematic and generalized approach using homogeneous transformation matrices; this approach leads to the Denavit-Hartenberg (D-H) notation.

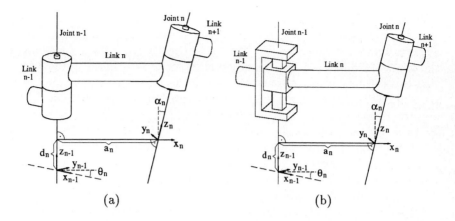

Figure 6: Assigning link coordinate systems to revolute and prismatic joints

Each matrix describes the spatial relationship or the transformation between two adjacent links. The successive application of these transformations to all links of the robot arm leads to an equivalent homogeneous transformation matrix, which describes the spatial placement of the end-effector with respect to the base coordinate system of the robot arm. Thus, this transformation matrix constitutes the solution of the direct kinematics problem.

To obtain the homogeneous transformation matrix between two adjacent links, a link coordinate system or link frame has to be assigned to each link according to the following three rules (see also figure 6); assume, we intend to assign a coordinate system to link n:

- The origin of the coordinate system of link n is set to be at the intersection of the common normal between the axes of joint $n-1$ and n with the axis of joint n. In the special case, where both axes are parallel the origin can be set on an arbitrary position on the axis of joint n.

- The z-axis z_n of the coordinate system of link n is aligned to the joint axis of joint n.

- The x-axis x_n is aligned with the common normal and is directed from joint $n-1$ to joint n.

With these rules, the coordinate system of link n is completely defined, because the direction of the axis y_n can be derived from the right hand coordinate system rule.

After having assigned link coordinate systems (frames) to each link, the relationship between two adjacent links (link coordinate systems) can be expressed by four elementary transformations. Thus, e.g. the transformation from link $n-1$ to link n can be derived as follows:

With a rotation of the coordinate system of link $n-1$ around the z_{n-1} axis, the x_{n-1} axis can be aligned with the x_n axis of frame n. The rotation angle is noted in figure 6 as θ_n. The subsequent two transformations move the origin of frame $n-1$ into the origin of frame n. We can see in the figure, that this can be done by a translation along the z_{n-1} axis and an additional translation translation along the common normal or the common x-axes (x_n and the rotated x_{n-1}). The translation distances are noted as d_n and a_n. Now the origins of the transformed frame $n-1$ and frame n and their x-axes coincide. The last transformation completes the transformation of frame $n-1$ into frame n, by aligning the z-axis of the transformed frame $n-1$ with the z-axis of frame n. This is done by a rotation of the transformed frame $n-1$ around its x-axis about the angle α_n.

Consequently, the relationship between two adjacent links can be described with four homogeneous transformations with four transformation parameters θ_n, a_n, d_n and α_n. These parameters are called *D-H parameters*. The θ_n is a variable parameter in the case that a revolute joint is modeled (figure 6a), and is called the *joint variable*. In the case of a prismatic joint (figure 6b), d_n is called the joint variable. In both cases, the other D-H parameters are called *link parameters*, because they describe the geometrical structure of the link.

If we apply this technique to all n links of a robot manipulator, we obtain n D-H parameter sets for a robot with n degrees of mechanical freedom.

Each of the four transformations, which are necessary to transform the frame of link $n-1$ into the frame of link n can be expressed by a corresponding homogeneous transformation matrix. The product of all four transformation matrices leads to an equivalent homogeneous transformation matrix, which is called the *A-matrix* or *D-H transformation* matrix. The generalized form of such an A-matrix is

$$
\begin{aligned}
A_i \;=\; & Rot(z_{i-1}, \theta_i)\, Trans(z_{i-1}, d_i)\, Trans(x_i, a_i)\, Rot(x_i, \alpha_i) \\[4pt]
=\; & \begin{pmatrix}
\cos\theta_i & -\sin\theta_i\cos\alpha_i & \sin\theta_i\sin\alpha_i & a_i\cos\theta_i \\
\sin\theta_i & \cos\theta_i\cos\alpha_i & -\cos\theta_i\sin\alpha_i & a_i\sin\theta_i \\
0 & \sin\alpha_i & \cos\alpha_i & d_i \\
0 & 0 & 0 & 1
\end{pmatrix}
\end{aligned}
\tag{1}
$$

The index i indicates, that the transformation matrix A_i represents the transformation of frame $i-1$ into frame i.

If we build the product of all successive matrices A_i we obtain an equivalent homogeneous transformation matrix, called $^{R}T_H$ matrix.

$$
\begin{aligned}
^{R}T_H \;=\; & A_1\, A_2\, A_3 \cdots A_n \\[4pt]
=\; & \begin{pmatrix}
n_x & o_x & a_x & p_x \\
n_y & o_y & a_y & p_y \\
n_z & o_z & a_z & p_z \\
0 & 0 & 0 & 1
\end{pmatrix}
= \left(\begin{array}{ccc|c}
\Big[\vec{n}\Big] & \Big[\vec{o}\Big] & \Big[\vec{a}\Big] & \Big[\vec{p}\Big] \\
0 & 0 & 0 & 1
\end{array}\right)
\end{aligned}
\tag{2}
$$

This matrix equation delivers 12 non trivial equations. The rotational submatrix of the $^R\mathbf{T}_H$ matrix consists of the $\vec{n}$ (normal), $\vec{o}$ (open) and $\vec{a}$ (approach) vectors. They define the orientation of the last coordinate frame of our robot arm, which is usually the hand coordinate frame, with respect to the robot base coordinate system. The $\vec{p}$ (position) vector defines the position of the hand coordinate frame relative to the base coordinate frame. Thus, the $^R\mathbf{T}_H$ matrix specifies the position and orientation of the endpoint of the robot arm with respect to the robot base coordinate system. Consequently, the $^R\mathbf{T}_H$ matrix constitutes the solution of the direct kinematics problem.

2.2.2 Inverse Kinematics

The second main problem in the field of robot arm kinematics is the inverse kinematics problem (IKP). Usually the definition of the position and orientation of the robot hand is much more convenient for a robot programmer, if it can be specified relative to the cartesian world or base coordinate system or relative to a user defined system, instead within the joint variable space. Thus, if such a cartesian programming is desired within the robot simulation system, the solution of the IKP is necessary.

To solve the IKP, various numerical approaches have been developed (see also [Siciliano90, Nakamura91]). In contrast to analytical approaches, numerical techniques are always able to compute iteratively the joint variables corresponding to a given position and orientation of the robot hand coordinate frame for robot arms with arbitrary kinematical structures. But as the numerical approaches usually require long computation times and because they often have to deal with convergence problems in the neighborhood of singularities or in case of degenerate arm kinematics, it is desirable to use the analytical solution, if it can be found.

Regarding the example of the simple three-axes robot arm (shown in the figure on the right hand side) the direct kinematics solution can be directly formulated. It is obvious, that the p_z component of point P depends only on d_1. In addition it can be stated, that the p_x and p_y components are depending from θ_2 and the length of d_3.

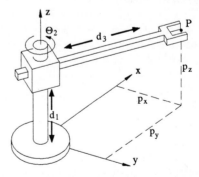

Consequently, we obtain the following direct kinematics equations for the three-axes manipulator.

$$
{}^W\mathbf{T}_P = \begin{pmatrix} p_x \\ p_y \\ p_z \end{pmatrix} = \begin{pmatrix} d_3 \cos\theta_2 \\ d_3 \sin\theta_2 \\ d_1 \end{pmatrix}
$$

These direct kinematic equations, can be used to derive the inverse kinematic equations. Thus, d_1 depend directly from p_z, and the solution of d_3 can be obtained by squaring and adding the direct kinematic equations of p_x and p_y. θ_2 can be computed using the arctan function of p_x and p_y. The solution of the IKP can be stated as follows:

$$d_1 = p_z \qquad d_3 = \pm\sqrt{p_x^2 + p_y^2} \qquad \theta_2 = \arctan(\frac{p_y}{p_x}) \ [+\pi]$$

Regarding the inverse kinematics equations we can note, that the equations for the joint variables θ_2 and d_3 have two mathematical solutions. Generally, multiple mathematical solutions of the inverse kinematics equations indicate, that a desired position can be reached by different geometrical configurations of the robot arm, corresponding to the different joint variables solutions. In the example of the three-axes arm, two sets of joint variables satisfy the inverse kinematics condition:

$$(d_1, \theta_2, d_3)_1 = (p_z, +\sqrt{p_x^2 + p_y^2}, \arctan(\frac{p_y}{p_x})) \qquad (3)$$

$$(d_1, \theta_2, d_3)_2 = (p_z, -\sqrt{p_x^2 + p_y^2}, \arctan(\frac{p_y}{p_x}) + \pi) \qquad (4)$$

If we regard the kinematical structure, we can immediately verify these two solutions. The first configuration reaching P is illustrated in the figure. But in addition to this the point P can be reached, if we turn the robot around the z axis (rotation about angle π) and translate d_3 in the negative direction.

To compute the inverse kinematics solution for robot arms with more degrees of freedom, we have integrated in our robot simulation system a symbolic kinematics inversion program (SKIP) [Rieseler+90, Rieseler92]. This module uses an efficient technique to derive the inversion of robot arm kinematics based on a receipe previously proposed by Paul [Paul81]. Similar to the example shown above the direct kinematics solution equations ($^R T_H$ matrix) are used to solve the IKP. In addition the matrix equations which can be obtained by premultiplying the inverses of the A_i matrices are used. The matrices on the right hand side are functions of the elements of the $^R T_H$ matrix and the first joint variables. The elements on the left hand side are either zero or constant or functions of the remaining joint variables. By postmultiplying the inverse A_i matrices, additional matrix equations are obtained. Thus, for a robot arm with n variable joints, $2n - 1$ matrix equations, each with 12 non trivial single equations can be found.

Within this set of $12(2n - 1)$ equations, SKIP searches for those equations, which can be used to solve the IKP for a joint variable. The equations (5) - (7) are typical results of such an automated computation of the inverse kinematics solution, generated by the SKIP; the equations represent the inverse kinematics solution for the first three joint variable of the Manutec robot arm, shown in figure 7.

$$\theta_1 = \arctan\left(\frac{p_y - d_6 a_y}{p_x - d_6 a_x}\right)[+\pi] \tag{5}$$

$$\theta_2 = \arctan\left(\frac{\dfrac{\langle\mathrm{Arg}_1\rangle}{2a_2}}{\pm\sqrt{\langle\mathrm{Arg}_3\rangle}}\right) - \arctan\left(\frac{\langle\mathrm{Arg}_2\rangle}{p_z - a_z d_6 - d_1}\right) \tag{6}$$

$$\langle\mathrm{Arg}_1\rangle = (a_2^2 + \langle\mathrm{Arg}_2\rangle^2 + (p_z - a_z d_6 - d_1)^2 - d_4^2))/(2a_2)$$
$$\langle\mathrm{Arg}_2\rangle = p_x c_1 + p_y s_1 - (a_x c_1 + a_y s_1)d_6$$
$$\langle\mathrm{Arg}_3\rangle = \langle\mathrm{Arg}_2\rangle^2 + (p_z - a_z d_6 - d_1)^2 - \langle\mathrm{Arg}_1\rangle^2$$

$$\theta_3 = \arctan\left(-\frac{p_x - a_x d_6 - a_2 c_1 c_2}{c_1(p_z - a_z d_6 - a_2 s_2 - d_1)}\right) - \theta_2 \tag{7}$$

Similar to the three-axes robot, the IKP of the Manutec arm offers two mathematical solutions for the first joint variable θ_1. These two solutions correspond to 'shoulder left' and 'shoulder right' configurations shown in the figures 7 (a+b) and (c+d) respectively. For each solution of θ_1, the equation of θ_2 offers two additional solutions, corresponding to the 'arm up' and 'arm down' configuration in figure 7 (a+d) and (b+c) respectively. The solution of θ_3 depends on θ_2, such that for a given 'arm up' configuration of θ_2, θ_3 provides a 'forearm down' position and vice versa. Consequently, we can obtain four possible solutions of the IKP for a given hand position and orientation for the first three links of the Manutec arm, if we neglect joint angle limitations.

The multiple solutions of the IKP are often very important during robot programming in the real world as well as in the simulated one. Assume, e.g., that a desired end-effector position can not be reached due to a collision of the robot arm with the environment. In these cases, maybe another collision free arm configuration can be found among the multiple solutions.

3   Representation of Composed Worlds

After each part of the robot and each object of the work cell is geometrically modeled and after the kinematical structures are defined, both representations have to be combined to obtain a useful graphical simulation capability. In addition, the components of the robot work cell have to be arranged within the simulation world and their relationships such as *the workpiece is lying on the table*' or *'part A is attached to object B*' have to be modeled. For that purpose, similar to the specification of the robot arm kinematics, homogeneous transformation matrices within the so-called *affixment data structure* is used. An affixment defines

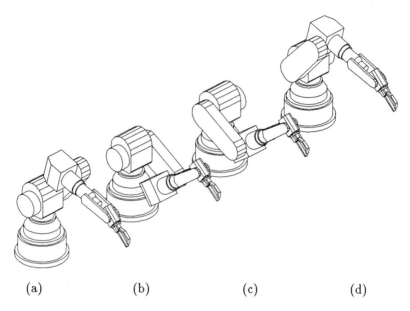

(a)   (b)   (c)   (d)

Figure 7: Multiple solutions of the inverse kinematics problem

- a fixture between two objects. Thus, an object A which is affixed with an object B, has to be moved if the position of B changes.

- the relative position and orientation between two object coordinate systems (frames) by means of homogeneous transformation matrices. Thus, the relative position of two subsequent robot links, e.g., can be expressed by an affixment with a variable transformation matrix (the corresponding A_i matrix).

In the following the principle data structures used within the affixment concept are are shown:

```
struct object { NAME      name;        /* name of the object       */
                FLAG      updated;     /* for processing purpose   */
                FRAME     objectframe; /* absolute object position */
                AFFIX     *affixment;  /* pointer to affixmentlist */
                GEOMETRY  *represent;  /* pointer to representation */
                OBJECT    *next;       /* pointer to next object    */
              }


struct affix  { OBJECT    *affixed;    /* pointer to affixed object */
                TRANSFORM relative;    /* transformation to object  */
                AFFIX     *next;       /* pointer to next affixment  */
              }
```

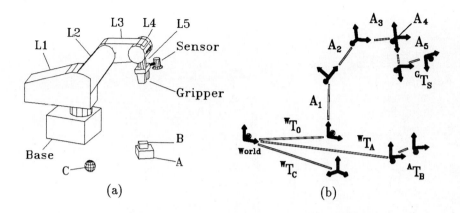

Figure 8: Example world to illustrate the affixment technique

Basically we can distinguish the **OBJECT** data structure, containing all object specific information and the **AFFIX**ment data structure, defining relationships between objects. The **OBJECT** data structure usually provides a pointer to the geometrical object representation (**GEOMETRY**) and contains the object position and orientation (**FRAME**) relative to the world coordinate system of the simulated world. Additional fields, such as the object name (**NAME**) and an additional flag (**FLAG**) are used during modification and update procedures. To concatenate all objects of the modeled world the **OBJECT** structure contains a corresponding pointer to the next object. The relationships to other objects are defined by a list of affixments structures which are concatenated to the **OBJECT** structure by the **AFFIX** pointer.

The **AFFIX**ment data structure contains a pointer to the affixed **OBJECT** and a **TRANSFORM**ation defining the position and orientation of the affixed object relative to the current object. As one object can have relationships to multiple other objects, the corresponding **AFFIX**ment structures can be concatenated within a list using the next affixment pointer.

To explain the principle of the affixment technique, in the following a robot arm within a simple environment is modeled (figure 8). The robot arm of the example world consists of a *base*, five variable links (*L1-L5*) and a *sensor*, which is firmly connected to the *gripper*. In addition three workpieces *A*, *B* and *C* are lying in the workspace of the robots arm. In figure 8a the geometric representations of the single objects are shown; figure 8b shows the positions and orientations of the objects, either defined relative to other object frames or relative to the world coordinate system. Each transformation is expressed by a homogeneous transformation matrix. The matrices A_i, which have been discussed in section 2.2 are representing the variable transformation matrices between the successive robot arm links. A matrix ^iT_j specifies the constant transformation which leads from object i to object j.

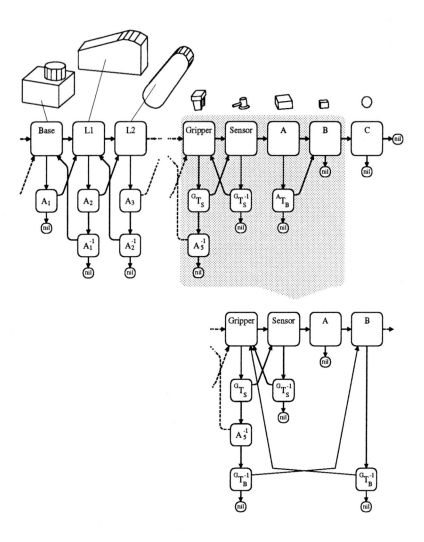

Figure 9: Data structures

The corresponding object-affixment data structure representing the example world is shown in figure 9. Each object of the world is represented by a corresponding OBJECT structure which is concatenated within a linear list of OBJECT structures. To each OBJECT structure the AFFIXment list, corresponding to the relationships of the objects is attached. Thus, e.g., the object *base* has only one affixment, because only the link *L1* is affixed to the *base*. The transformation which leads from the frame of *base* to the frame of *L1* is denoted as the variable homogeneous transformation A_1 (figure 8b). In contrast to *base*, object *L1* has a relation to two other objects – the *base* and $L2$. Consequently two affixments are attached within an affixmentlist to $L1$. The first affixment specifies that object $L2$ is connected to $L1$ with the relative transformation A_2; the second one defines the connection of $L1$ to the *base* using the inverse of the transformation which leads from the *base* to $L1$, denoted here as A_1^{-1}.

The following objects $L2$-$L5$ are represented in the same way, each with two affixments with variable transformations, because they are connected to the previous and the successive link by by variable joints. Such an affixment structure defines a relationship between two objects which can be expressed by '*object1 is connected to object2 by a variable transformation and vice versa*'.

In contrast to this, the affixment list of the *gripper* structure consists of one affixment with a variable transformation and a second one with a constant transformation. The variable transformation A_5^{-1} defines the variable connection to the last link ($L5$) of the robot; in contrast to this the constant transformation $^G T_S$ leads to the object *sensor* which is firmly connected with the *gripper*. Due to the fact, that the *sensor* is also firmly connected with the *gripper* by a corresponding affixment with a constant transformation, we have defined a relationship '*object1 is firmly mounted to object2 (and vice versa)*' between the *gripper* and the *sensor*.

Regarding objects A and B, we notice that object A has an affixment with a constant transformation, pointing to B, but B has no affixment pointing to A. With such a structure, relationships like '*object B is lying on A*' can be expressed.

With such an object-affixment structure a robot movement can be simulated very easy; assume, e.g., link $L1$ is moved by changing the joint variable of the joint between the *base* and $L1$. This can be expressed by changing the corresponding joint variable within matrix A_1, which specifies the position and orientation between the *base* and $L1$. Consequently the new position and orientation (**FRAME**) of $L1$ can be computed by multiplying the frame of *base* with the new transformation matrix A_1. After the frames of all objects which are either directly or indirectly affixed to $L1$ are also updated; the object-affixment structure represents the actual state of the simulated world. If the position of $L1$ is changed, e.g. by an external force applied to $L1$, all successive links, connected directly or indirectly by an affixment to $L1$ will get a new position; in addition, even if the *base* is moved, because it is also affixed to $L1$. This is a correct result of the object-affixment structure and corresponds to the movement of the complete robot, by a force applied to $L1$.

In contrast to this, the relationship expressed between objects A and B is different, because only B is affixed to A. Similar to the example above, a motion of A causes a motion of B, but if B is set to a new position, the position of A is left unchanged.

Even changes of the relationships between objects can be simply represented by the object-affixment structure. Assume a situation in which the robot arm has gripped object *B* and lifted it from *A*. This is equivalent to the new relationship '*the gripper and B are vice versa firmly connected*'. In addition the relationship '*object B is connected to or lying on A*' expressed by the single affixment of *A* pointing to *B*, has to be eliminated. Thus, the grey marked portion of the object-affixment data structure shown in figure 9, has to be changed accordingly to the structure shown below.

Due to the structure of the object-affixment representation, usually a recursive update procedure is used to update the internal representation after any change within the object configuration. The example **update_object()** procedure shown below, updates the frames of all objects, which are either directly or indirectly affixed to the current object. Due to the recursive update procedure and the object-affixment structure, which may contain closed reference loops, the **updated** flag inside the object structure is necessary to prevent wrong multiple updates and to guarantee procedure termination.

```
update_object( op )
OBJECT *op;
{
  AFFIX   *ap;          /* actual affixment of affixmentlist of 'op'  */
  OBJECT *op_next;      /* object, referenced by 'ap'                 */
  ap=op->affixment;     /* let ap point to first element of affixlist */

  while( ap!=NULL )
  {
    op_next = ap->affixed;                                    /* [1] */
    if( !op_next->updated )                                   /* [2] */
      { /* object was not actualized until now */
        op_next->updated    =TRUE;                            /* [3] */
        op_next->objectframe=op->objectframe * ap->relative;  /* [4] */
        update_object( op_next );                             /* [5] */
      }
    ap = ap->next;
  }
}
```

To combine the graphical model and its kinematical description and to arrange the objects within the simulation world, usually a graphical editor is used. The definition of the object positions and orientations can be done relative to other objects, previously defined feature coordinate systems or relative to the world coordinate system. Further, additional modeling commands allow the modification of the internal object-affixment representation of the world.

Figure 10 shows a typical modeling sequence of a Mitsubishi RM-501 manipulator within the graphical world modeler of our PC-based robot simulation system [Plank89]. In the first figure the kinematical structure of the robot arm, is represented as a skeleton. In the following figures, the previously geometrically modeled links are subsequently positioned and oriented with respect to the link coordinate systems which are defined by the robot kinematics. Simultaneously the internal object-affixment data structure is built up.

In figure 11 the complete modeled RM-501 robot inside the PC modeling environment is shown, and a complex robot work cell, consisting of two robots, various environment objects and a conveyor belt is shown within the simulator environment [Schlorff88].

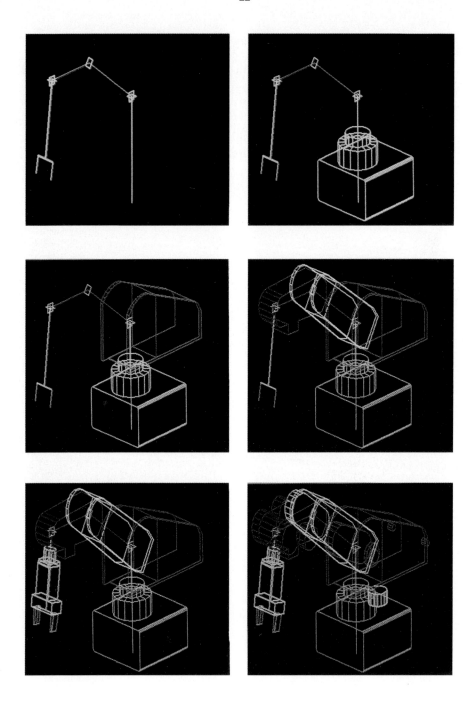

Figure 10: Modeling sequence of a Mitsubishi RM-501 manipulator

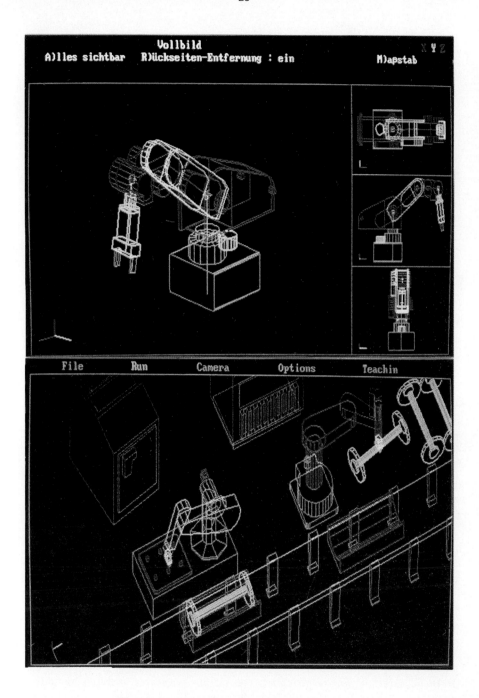

Figure 11: Modeling of a robot work cell

4 Simulation System Modules

In this section a short overview about the software modules, which are typically involved within a graphical robot simulation system is given. In addition their principal organization is shown. Figure 12 presents a basic structure of a graphical robot simulation system, with its various input and output databases and their associated programs and modules. In a practical realization of a simulation system, the modules shown in the figure are not necessary physically separated; moreover the diagram represents the various functionalities which are needed. The implementation of these modules can vary between single subroutines within a large software system, stand-alone programs and even hardware modules, e.g. in the case of the graphic module.

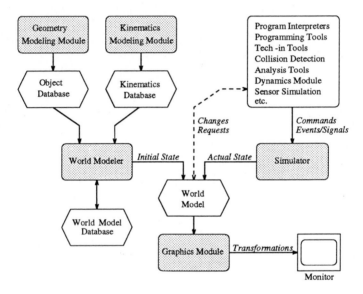

Figure 12: Principal modules of a graphical robot simulation system and their organization

As we have seen in section 2 various modeling steps have to be performed to prepare a graphical robot simulation. Usually these modeling steps are done by using specialized software modules/programs to create the different models. Thus, a CAD modeling program can be used to define the geometrical structure and to create the geometrical representation of all objects belonging to the simulation. The resulting representations are stored within a geometry data base. This allows the comfortable integration of single modeled objects within multiple simulation environments.

To define the kinematic structure and other related data such as joint limitations and the maximum joint velocities of mechanical parts and especially the robot arm, a kinematic modeling module is integrated. The resulting kinematic descriptions are stored within a kinematics data base.

The combination of geometrical representations, kinematic descriptions (and further models) and the arrangement of the different objects within the simulated world is done by a world modeling system. Usually the definition of a robot work cell is an iterative procedure including the modules mentioned above, to achieve an optimal work cell layout. The output of such a modeling system are either completely modeled work cells or submodules of work cells, both stored in a work cell database.

The main module of the simulation system is the simulator. The task of the simulation module is the computation of the actual state of the simulated robot work cell with respect to certain instructions defined e.g. within a robot program or events and signals, generated by other objects, such as simulated sensors. The interpretation of a robot program or the simulation of sensor signals can be done either by the simulation module itself or by specialized external modules. During the computation of the new state of the work cell model, the simulation module has to take into account the parameter time to compute the time varying state or behavior of the simulation components. We generally have to distinguish the terms *simulation time* and *simulated time*. The simulation time is the stretch of time, which is consumed during the computation of the simulation. As usually no requirements for a real time simulation are made, the simulated time which specifies the time which is simulated within the simulation is more important. As simulations are mainly used for off-line programming or robot program optimization, it is very important that the stretch of simulated time which is consumed during a certain robot movement within the simulation corresponds to the stretch of real time needed in the real world for the same action. In addition, the actions, signals and events within the simulation system must occur at the same time instant within the simulated time and the real time, to produce a useful simulation.

Closely related to the simulation module are a variety of input/output, analysis and control modules. Thus, a robot program editor/debugger and the integration of various programming techniques, such as the cartesian teach-in or the position specification by user defined frames provide comfortable off-line programming. In addition, an automated or visual collision detection is necessary to enable the development of error free robot programs and robot movements. Figure 13 (top) shows an example of an optical collision detection, within our PC-based simulation system, using *virtual cameras*. The virtual camera technique allows the free specification of positions, orientations and camera parameters of virtual cameras relative to world coordinates or relative to other objects within the robot work cell. In figure 13 (top), one camera is mounted in the robots hand looking in gripping direction; a second camera is placed such, that the pallet can be seen from side view. The images produced by those two virtual cameras, enable the programmer to perform the gripper positioning without any collisions with environment objects.

Additional analysis tools allow robot program optimization. The quality of the robot's arm movement e.g. can be better judged if the arm trajectory is displayed (see figure 13 (bottom)) or if the corresponding arm positions and orientations can be stored within a protocol file.

The graphic module is responsible for the visual transformations of the actual simulated work cell and the graphical visualization on a display device; this provides a direct visual feedback. Depending on the desired quality, the output of the graphic module can vary between a simple wire frame representation and photorealistic images. As the computational complexity of the algorithms, which are used, e.g., to perform a hidden surface removal or ray tracing usually is very high, the quality of the visualization is often limited due to limited computaional resources. During the last years, more and more specialized software systems have been designed for the graphical visualization of 3d objects/worlds, e.g. PHIGS (see [Howard+91]) and even specialized hardware components have been developed. In figure 14 the same robot work cell is shown within the environment of the robot simulation system running on a Sun Sparc Workstation with specialized graphical hardware. The simulation system shown here, is a ported version of the PC-based robot simulation [Glave+90].

5 Conclusion

Although we could only discuss a few aspects of robot simulation within this paper, we have presented some fundamental aspects, which have to be taken into account during the design, development and practice of graphical robot simulation systems. We have shown, that a robot work cell typically consists of a variety of different objects, which have to be modeled within different modeling steps. The basic modeling steps – geometrical and kinematical modeling – have been discussed in more details. We have summarized the main geometric representation forms and we demonstrated three simple modeling techniques. With the help of our PC-based robot simulation system we have shown, that the resulting geometrical modeled objects are sufficient to model even complex robot work cells.

The definition and computation of the forward kinematics, which has to be solved for the robot and objects with a mechanical structure has been derived. The principle problems during the computation of the inverse kinematics especially the multiple solutions of the inverse kinematics problem and their interpretations have been discussed. The internal representation of the modeled world has been shown and the affixment concept with its corresponding object-affixment data structure has been introduced. Finally, the basic modules constituting a robot simulation system, their organization and special aspects of simulation and off-line programming have been summarized.

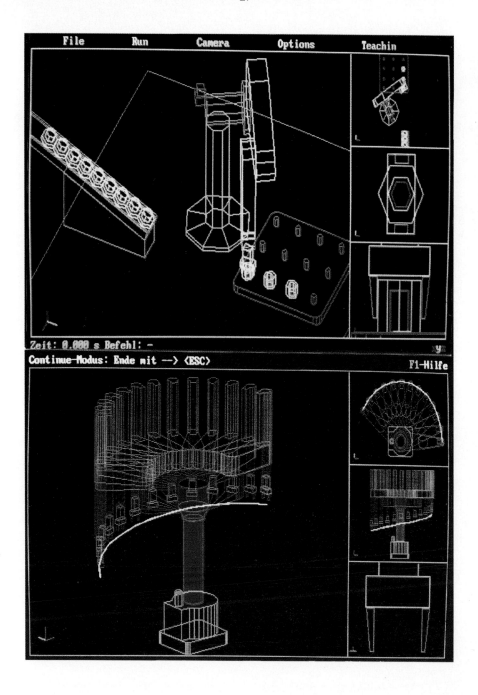

Figure 13: Visualization of robot work cell during simulation

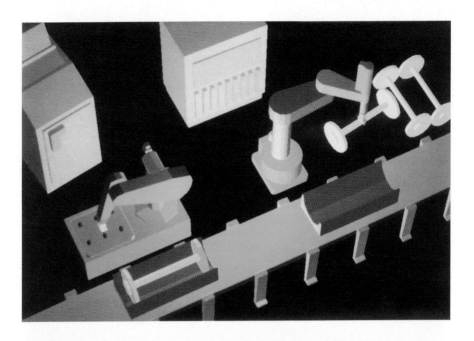

Figure 14: Graphical display on a Sun Sparc Workstation with specialized graphics hardware

References

[Agin⁺76] G. J. Agin and T. O. Binford: Representation and description of curved objects. *IEEE Transactions on Computers*, 25:439–449, 1976.

[An⁺88] C. H. An, C. G. Atkenson and J. M. Hollerbach: *Model based Control of a Robot Manipulator*. The MIT Press, 1988.

[Craig89] J. J. Craig: *Introduction to Robotics Mechanics and Control*. Addison-Wesley Publishing Company, 1989.

[Denavit⁺55] J. Denavit and R. Hartenberg: A kinematic notation for lower pair mechanisms based on matrices. *Journal of Applied Mechanics*, 22(2):215–221, June 1955.

[Featherstone87] R. Featherstone: *Robot Dynamics Algorithms*. Kluwer Academic Publishers, 1987.

[Fu⁺87] K. S. Fu, R. C. Gonzales and C. S. G. Lee: *Robotics: Control, Sensing, Vision, and Intelligence*. McGraw-Hill, 1987.

[Glave⁺90] V. Glave and A. Waltke: Implementierung des Robotersimulators URSI auf Sun-Workstations. Studienarbeit (in German), Institute for Robotics and Computer Control, Technical University of Braunschweig, Germany, 1990.

[Howard⁺91] T. L. J. Howard, W. T. Hewitt, R. J. Hubbold et al.: *A Practical Introduction to PHIGS and PHIGS PLUS*. Addison-Wesley, 1991.

[Kashipati⁺92] R. Kashipati and G. Medioni: Generalized cones: Useful geometric properties. In L. Shapiro and A. Rosenfeld, editors, *Computer Vision and Image Processing*, pages 185–208. Academic Press, Inc., 1992.

[Künne90] N. Künne: PC-basierte Modellierung verallgemeinerter Zylinder. Studienarbeit (in German), Institute for Robotics and Computer Control, Technical University of Braunschweig, Germany, 1990.

[Laloni88] C. Laloni: Graphisch-interaktiver Polyedermodellierer. Studienarbeit (in German), Institute for Robotics and Computer Control, Technical University of Braunschweig, Germany, 1988.

[Laloni⁺91] C. Laloni, G. Plank, H. Rieseler et al.: PC-basierte Modellierung und Simulation zur OFF-line-Programmierung von

Industrierobotern. In D. W. Wloka, editor, *Robotersimulation*, pages 121–152. Springer-Verlag, Berlin, Heidelberg, New York, 1991.

[Mäntylä88]   M. Mäntylä: *An Introduction to Solid Modeling*, Volume 13 of *Principles of Computer Science Series*. Computer Science Press, 1988.

[Mortenson85]   M. E. Mortenson: *Geometric Modeling*. John Wiley & Sons, Inc., 1985.

[Nakamura91]   Y. Nakamura: *Advanced Robotics, Redundancy and Optimization*. Addison-Wesley Publishing Company, 1991.

[Paul81]   R. P. Paul: *Robot Manipulators: Mathematics, Programming, and Control*. MIT Press, Cambridge, Massachsetts, USA, 1981.

[Plank89]   G. Plank: Entwicklung eines menügesteuerten, grafischen Robotermodelliersystems (RMS). Studienarbeit (in German), Institute for Robotics and Computer Control, Technical University of Braunschweig, Germany, 1989.

[Rieseler$^+$90]   H. Rieseler and F. M.. Wahl: Fast symbolic computation of the inverse kinematics of robots. *IEEE International Conference on Robotics and Automation, Cincinnati, Ohio*, May 1990.

[Rieseler92]   H. Rieseler: *Roboterkinemtik - Grundlagen, Invertierung und Symbolische Berechnung*, Volume 16 of *Fortschritte der Robotik*. Vieweg & Sohn, Braunschweig/Wiesbaden, 1992.

[Schlorff88]   U. Schlorff: Off-line Programmierung und kinematische Simulation von Industrierobotern. Diplomarbeit (in German), Institute for Robotics and Computer Control, Technical University of Braunschweig, Germany, 1988.

[Siciliano90]   B. Siciliano: Kinematic Control of Redundant Robot, Manipulators: A Tutorial. *Journal of Intelligent and Robotic Systems*, 3:201–212, 1990.

[Spong$^+$89]   M. W. Spong and M. Vidyasagar: *Robot Dynamics and Control*. John Wiley & Sons, 1989.

[Straßer$^+$89]   W. Straßer and H.-P. Seidel, editors. *Theory and Practice of Geometric Modeling*. Springer-Verlag, Berlin, Heidelberg, 1989.

Graphical Robot Simulation within the Framework of an Intelligent TeleSensorProgramming System

Bernhard Brunner, Klaus Arbter and Gerhard Hirzinger

German Aerospace Research Establishment (DLR), Oberpfaffenhofen,

Institute for Robotics and System Dynamics, D-82230 Wessling, Germany

1 Abstract

Up to now robot task execution is limited to move the manipulator on the joint or cartesian level from one position into another one. We propose the so-called TeleSensorProgramming concept that uses sensory perception to bring local autonomy onto the manipulator level. This approach is applicable both in the real robot's world and in the simulated one. Beside the graphical offline programming concept the range of application lies especially in the field of teleoperation with large time delays. The feasibility of graphically simulating the robot within its environment is extended by emulating different sensor functions like distance, force-torque and vision sensors to achieve a correct copy of the real system behaviour. These simulation features are embedded into a task-oriented high-level robot programming approach. Sensor fusion aspects with respect to autonomous sensor controlled task execution are discussed as well as the interaction between the real and the simulated system.

2 Introduction

Today the most significant problems in the field of automation and robotics arise in the *uncertainties* given by the robot inaccuracies and an unknown, unstructured or vague environment. Mechanical inaccuracies at the manipulator level and uncertainties in the environment cannot be compensated automatically by the system itself. Local adaptations on path generation level have to be done via teach-in commands by human operator. Even small deviations in position, orientation and shape of all the objects to be handled are not allowed because the task execution will fail in an uncertain environment. Graphical simulation of robot tasks and downloading the generated commands to the real robot is limited to the joint or cartesian motion level. This approach is only useful if geometrical consistency of real environment and the simulated one can be guaranteed. This is a demand that cannot be met with available programming systems.

To solve these problems there is the necessity for the robotic system to work with intelligence to a certain degree. The goal is to handle given tasks with full autonomy to get a successful execution of the desired job. But today there is no way to achieve this aim of such a high intelligent behaviour because of the lack of an adequate artificial intelligence. The first step to increase autonomy on the execution level is the feasibility of *sensory perception*. The processing of sensory data is the most important requirement for achieving autonomous behaviour. Without information about the actual surroundings no decisions can be made for further actions because successful task execution can be considered as impossible in an uncertain environment. High level planning facilities for task scheduling as well as intelligent error handling mechanisms are required for full autonomy but state-of-the-art techniques are insufficient to provide the adequate tools. Presently full autonomy is not reachable.

Therefore we favour a *shared autonomy* concept that distributes intelligence to man and machine [1]. Presuming that the necessary information about the actual environment is available from the sensor systems partial tasks can be executed independently on the machine level. Specifications and decisions on a high task planning level have to be done by human beings. Local sensory feedback loops are executed by the robot system, global task level jobs have to be specified interactively by a human operator. Coarse planning activities have to be done on a task-oriented level by human intelligence, fine path planning on manipulator level takes place on a sensor based control level with predefined artificial intelligence [2].

For this shared control approach we have coined the term *TeleSensorProgramming*. This means a new way for robot programming on a task oriented level. The teach-in of a robot system occurs not on the joint or cartesian manipulator level but on a high language level, i.e. the operator plans activities on a level which can be worked off by the robotic system independently from human intervention. In figure 1 we see two corresponding control loops with local autonomy at the simulaton as well as at the remote system. On the local control loop the robot can successfully execute the predefined tasks with the aid of his own sensory information both in the simulated and in the real system. The communication between the two loops runs via a common model data base which delivers a priori knowledge for the execution on the remote level and a posteriori knowledge for the update of the model on the simulation level.

In other words TeleSensorProgramming (TSP) means teaching by showing typical situations including nominal sensory patterns with the aid of sensory refinement in a completely simulated world on a task-oriented level. For such an intelligent programming system different tools are needed to implement the required functionality. First a sophisticated simulation system has to be provided to emulate the real robotic system. This includes the simulation of sensory perception within the real environment. Beside this sensor simulation the shared autonomy concept has to provide an efficient operator interface to setup task descriptions, to configure the task control parameters, to decide what kind of sensors and control algorithms should be used, and to debug an entire job execution phase.

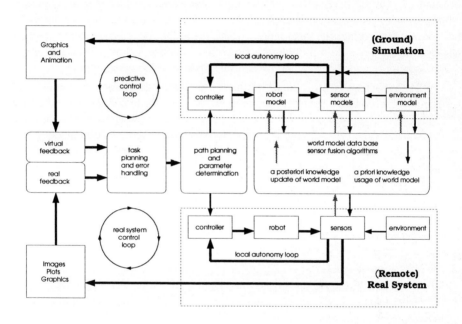

Fig. 1: The TeleSensorProgramming Concept

Two applications in the field of robotics can be found that can be handled with the proposed TeleSensorProgramming approach. First the *graphical offline programming* concept is extended by the processing of simulated sensory data and by the introduction of local autonomy on the task description level. This means that not only the joint and cartesian information is gathered by graphically guiding the robot during the offline programming task, but also the simulated sensory information to store them offline as nominal patterns for subtask execution on a local feedback loop level. The fine motion control loop to handle uncertainties takes place independently of any human intervention both at the simulation side and the real one.

Second the field of *telerobotics* with large time delays especially in space and subsea applications seems to be a good experimental area for this sensor based task oriented programming approach [3]. Direct visual feedback in a control loop, where a time delay of a few seconds is inherent, is not feasible for the human operator to handle the robot movements in a suitable way. Predictive simulation — graphical and functional — is the medium for the operator to telemanipulate the remote system online [4]. The operator has only to guide the robot in a rough manner through the task space and to activate specific sensor control phases. After sending these gross commands to the remote system the real robot will be able to execute the desired task with its own local autonomy after the delay time has elapsed. On the basis of the online requirement realtime power is an important aspect with regard to simulation facilities. The main feature of our telerobotic concept is to replace the time-delayed visual feedback by predictive stereo graphics with sensor simulation providing a supervisory control technique that will allow to shift more and more autonomy and intelligence to the robot system.

The *main focus* of this paper lies on the geometric model based simulation of robot, workcell and a set of typical sensors. We are able to emulate laser distance and force-torque sensors under task specific realtime constraints. Stereo vision is simulated by the tools of graphical animation as the framework for a model based vision approach. These different kinds of sensors can be used to develop and test new types of sensor fusion algorithms to provide efficient control schemes and to verify the proposed TeleSensorProgramming approach.

3 Graphical robot simulation

First we will talk about the graphical robot simulation. The most important demand at a simulation system is the request for a natural emulation of the real world as far as possible. This means in our context that the operator can work within a virtual environment close to the real one. As state of the art in the field of graphical robot simulation can be considered a *gouraud-shaded visualization* of the geometrical environment with the possibility of defining different light sources as well as *three dimensional stereo* views especially for online teleoperation modes. In contrary to these topics is the realtime facility for visualization of complex workcell scenes. Commercial robot simulation systems have an update rate up to 5 Hz, but online mode requires about 20 Hz for a jerkless motion. The bottleneck lies both in the complexity of most of the workcell environments and in the inefficiency of internal model representation [5].

To overcome this problem we use a *hierarchical geometric model* structure based on an efficient polyhedron description for visualizing gouraud-shaded objects in realtime [6]. First we use system features as backface removal and z-buffering for eliminating non-visible surfaces. Second we calculate for each view the three dimensional viewing area to eliminate non-visible objects. Objects out of the viewing area are not taken into account for drawing the perspective view. Especially for viewing on a local area of interest this approach increases the screen update rate significantly. Stereo animation is very helpful in operating the robot in the telemanipulation mode. Three dimensional visualization becomes available by hardware facilities as the shutter technique. Software tools have been written to determine different stereo angles or viewpoint displacements.

To move the robot on the cartesian level we use a six degree of freedom input device [7]. All the translational and rotational movements in the 3D-space can be activated simultaneously by handling an optoelectronic force-torque sensor device mounted into a ball-like housing. This *sensor- or controlball* is also used to move the view of the whole workcell into the desired aspect. The viewing matrix of the actual view is respected on calculating the incremental cartesian motion commands because the sensorball values have to be interpreted in the actual display coordinate system.

4 Sensor simulation

To achieve local autonomy on the fine motion level the simulation system has the ability to emulate all the sensor functions available in the real environment. We distinguish between *tactile and non-tactile* sensors. The last can be emulated by calculating simple interference or projective functions, but tactile sensors as force-torque sensors cause dependencies between sensor stiffness and gripper placement which has to be considered in the emulation of the real sensor behaviour. First of all we have to achieve realtime power for simulating the local sensory loops in a real manner. This means for a complex workcell description to build a hierarchical model description for a fast object feature access and model update.

4.1 World model description

On the geometrical level we use the boundary representation model from the graphical simulation. Polyhedral objects are modeled via flat polygons whose edges are ordered in a counterclockwise manner for a correct orientation. All the object features can be accessed by their *logical relationships* (see figure 2). Surfaces, edges and vertices are stored in lists with additional pointers to the corresponding features. For instance an edge representation field contains the pointer to the bounding vertices as well as to the neighbouring faces. For computational aspects it is often very helpful to have the logical access to a desired feature instead of the need for an expensive search through the entire feature list.

Sensor simulation can be considered as an application of collision detection, e.g. the interaction between a force-torque sensor and the touched object can be recognized as a collision detection and quantification problem. Traditional methods like the octtree representation are to inefficient especially in a dynamic changing world. We have implemented another approach based on a geometrical index structure, the so-called *cell tree* [8].

This method partitions the workcell space in a recursive way similar to the binary space partitioning or the octtree approach. The difference lies in the quantification of the knots, whose extension is not predefined but depends on the convex hulls of the occupied objects in the particular subtree. The advantage can be seen in a fast yet very precise search for actually interesting objects. One application of this geometrical representation is the computation of object intersection. Of course a fast restriction of the interesting regions to a minimal number of polyhedrons is desired. The leaves of the cell tree characterize the *interesting regions*. Because the cell tree is specified only for convex polyhedrons the knots passed during object selection consist of the convex hulls of the objects involved. In the leaves of the cell tree, i.e. after the object selection, a relation is evaluated which assigns the real areas of a concave object which might occur to the areas of the convex hulls. This area relation is generated during construction of the geometric world model. Intersection and interference checks preceded by a corresponding object selection are thus realizable in an efficient way for convex as well as for concave objects.

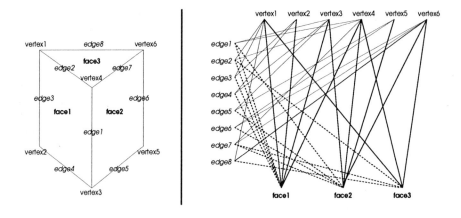

Fig. 2: Logical Object Relationships

This geometrical data base approach delivers a high efficiency in searching interesting areas and implementing interference algorithms. The complexity of interference calculations is reduced from exponential to logarithmical order [8]. But the time consuming generation of the cell tree has to be done every time the environment has changed. Therefore this method is only applicable in a static world. For that reason we favour a *bounding sphere* approach for a fast object exclusion. Both sensors and objects are wrapped in a sphere which represents the maximal expansion of each of them. The simple sphere representation via center and radius allows the fast detection of that objects that can be reached by the desired sensor in the actual configuration. We assume that the sensors can be mounted on a moveable part e.g. the robot gripper which means a permanent change in the sensory perception during robot actions.

4.2 Simulation of range finder distance sensors

To emulate the behaviour of a laser distance sensor we have to calculate the interference between the sensor beam and the nearest object surface. The real sensor works in the triangulation mode which delivers very accurate results in the predefined working range [3]. We assume that the optical features of the object surfaces are negligible. Therefore we do not consider the reflection properties of the objects but calculate the simple *geometrical interference* between a directed straight line and an oriented plane. First of all we have to find the face which reflects the sensor beam. To increase the search speed for the reflecting plane we apply methods of computational geometry. Backface removal is done by comparing beam direction and surface orientation. To determine whether the intersection point lies within the surface boundaries we use a fast algorithm for the so-called star-shaped polygons [9]. The fact that only these objects are considered whose bounding spheres lie within the working area of the distance sensor is described in the previous section. For computational speed increasing additional redundant information as surface normals is explicitly stored in the world model data structure.

4.3 Simulation of force-torque sensors

In the field of robotics with sensory feedback a few approaches have been published in the simulation of force-torque sensors. In [10] a method is proposed for contact force calculation based on a static force-torque equilibrium. With this approach it is possible to determine the contact type. We consider point-to-face, line-to-face and face-to-face contacts as possible contact types. To derive exact values especially when multiple contact types are found or in the case of a kinematically closed loop further assumptions have to be made as virtual displacements. All the other methods [11] are based on the principle of d'Alembert which requires a complete dynamic model of the workcell that is mostly not available and furthermore very time consuming to calculate the necessary motion equations.

We have followed an approach which is based on the *deformation of a flexible element* [12]. This flexible element emulates a force-torque sensor about the artificial deformations which can be derived from the violation of given constraints. The method converts information about the geometrical contact type into motion and force constraint equations. These data together with the description of the sensor stiffness and the assumption of a force-torque equilibrium contain sufficient information to calculate the virtual contact forces.

Compliance of environment as well as friction is not taken into account so far. Due to low motion speed in our range of application we even neglect the robot's dynamics and base our computations on the virtual interference of the sensor and the colliding objects. Motion and force constraint equations are derived from the interference data. The simulated force and torque values are calculated from these constraint equations and the known sensor stiffness characteristics. The formula for calculating forces F and moments M is

$$\begin{bmatrix} F \\ M \end{bmatrix} = K * \begin{bmatrix} \Delta \\ \delta \end{bmatrix} = K * J^{-1} * D,$$

where K represents the sensor stiffness matrix in the sensor frame, Δ the differential translational deformations of the sensor and δ the rotational one. $\begin{bmatrix} \Delta \\ \delta \end{bmatrix}$ can be expressed by $J^{-1} * D$, where D are the deviations in the contact space, i.e. the local motion constraint violations. J has the meaning of a Jacobian matrix that defines the transformation of the deformations from the sensor system into the contact space. In the case of an overdetermined equation system, $K * J^{-1}$ has to be replaced by its pseudoinverse.

$$K * J^{-1} \Rightarrow J^T * (J * K^{-1} * J^T)^{-1}$$

In the calculation of the *motion constraint conditions* we distinguish between the free collision of the robot with the environment and the constraints given by kinematical dependencies. In the first case for example the robot is approaching a part of the workcell.

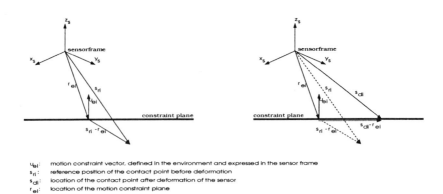

u_{ei}:   motion constraint vector, defined in the environment and expressed in the sensor frame
s_{ri}:   reference position of the contact point before deformation
s_{di}:   location of the contact point after deformation of the sensor
r_{ei}:   location of the motion constraint plane

Fig. 3: Motion Constraint Conditions

The force-torque sensor mounted on the robot end effector delivers measured values, when the gripper is colliding or touching the part. For the computation of the simulated sensor value the geometrical sensor part, e.g. the gripper is virtually penetrating the touched object. In general, relative motion constraints between robot end effector and the environment are violated (see figure 3). After detection and exact determination of the contact type the force-torque sensor deformes in order to comply with the motion constraints.

The constraint equation for the translational motion constraint is

$$u_{ei} * (s_{ri} - r_{ei}) + \begin{bmatrix} u_{ei} \\ s_{ri} \times u_{ei} \end{bmatrix}^T * \begin{bmatrix} \Delta \\ \delta \end{bmatrix} = 0$$

The first term $u_{ei} * (s_{ri} - r_{ei})$ represents the translational constraint violation before deformation of the force-torque sensor and is an element of D. The second $\begin{bmatrix} u_{ei} \\ s_{ri} \times u_{ei} \end{bmatrix}^T * \begin{bmatrix} \Delta \\ \delta \end{bmatrix}$ represents the correction due to this deformation necessary to compensate this constraint violation and is an element of the Jacobian J.

In the second case kinematical dependencies between the environment and the robot gripper are detected, for instance if the robot has grasped a part which is connected to a fix mounted object for the present. In contrast to the first case the virtual differences between the desired task frame and the simulated one represent the motion constraint violation. Rather the deviation between the cartesian tool center point frame of the robot and the task frame that is identified as the ideal position for grasping the part than the virtual interference between colliding parts is used for deforming the sensor element.

For selecting the constraint equations it is necessary to check the linear dependencies of the detected motion constraints. The interference algorithm reduces the found intersection data to an independent set of motion constraint information. For details on deriving forces and torques from given constraints see [13].

4.4 Simulation of stereo vision

For the simulation of vision the two control loops, shown in figure 1, have to be considered. First in the outer loop, including the human operator, the needs for the global handling of the system have to be respected. Both in telemanipulation and in offline programming modes the operator uses the camera views to get the correct orientation within the workcell environment. Information about the actual configuration, especially about the depth information must be available to the operator for handling the robot in all degrees of freedom. Hence we think stereo vision simulation is inevitable for our application. Second in the inner local autonomy loop the controller needs specific sensor information which is used in the different elemental moves. Each control phase uses the sensor information to achieve the correct control behaviour. This sensor information is based on a *feature based level* as input data for the control algorithm.

Therefore in a sensory feedback simulation system a sophisticated model of a vision camera is not required for the emulation of the desired sensor data. In a detailed model all the internal and external camera parameters have to be known as well as the optical properties of the surfaces and the geometric description of the light sources [14]. In our context not the physical behaviour or the exactly calculated pixel values are important but the interpretation of them. The system has only to emulate the output data of the real system. If the real picture processing system works at a feature based level, the simulation has to deliver the appropriate values. Hence the sensory data from the vision system can be derived from the geometrical data model without respect to the light sources and the optical surface properties as reflectance or refraction.

We consider points, lines and surfaces as object features following the geometric world model. The projection from the 3D space to the camera plane is done with respect to the predefined camera parameters. The result is the corresponding feature in the projection plane. Especially for the acquisition of stereo vision data this feature based method has the advantage that the correspondence problem has not to be solved. Corresponding object features in the different camera views can easily be detected by using the same geometric world model interface.

5 Task level simulation

One of the main principles of our TeleSensorProgramming concept is the task-oriented robot programming approach. A complete robot task can be composed of so-called "elemental moves", which represent the different subtasks of the whole job in a descriptive manner.

5.1 Elemental moves approach

For each elemental move the *constraint space configuration* (CSC) has to be defined. This means the description which degree of freedom (DOF) in the cartesian 3D-space is position or sensor controlled. For instance a contour following task in the xy-plane can be described by the position controlled DOFs z_{trans}, x_{rot}, y_{rot}, z_{rot} and the sensor controlled x_{trans} and y_{trans}. Beside this declaration of the CSC information several control parameters have to be configured for interpreting all the incoming robot and sensor data in an adequate way. In other words the a priori knowledge about the CSC is used to assign the control parameters with the appropriate values. Furtheron each subtask is essentially described by the initial as well as the final state of the corresponding elemental move. For the position controlled subspace the desired start and end position is fixed, for the sensor controlled the nominal sensor pattern in the initial and final subtask state. A plausibility check has to run to look for the congruence between the end conditions of the subtask and the start conditions of the following one that the consistence of the subtask sequence is ensured within the entire robot task. As described above the term "teaching by showing" means essentially that the goal conditions of an elemental move are shown by the graphical simulation of the robot, the sensors and the interaction with the environment. The transition from one subtask to the following, i.e. the recognition that the goal state of the elemental move has been reached is done by a heuristical method, but we have also examined the applicability of neural networks on this topic [15].

5.2 Sensor controlled subspaces

For the handling of the sensor controlled subspaces we outline a method for *estimate the motion parameters* by the known sensor values to achieve the predefined goal state of the robot's pose (cartesian position in translation and orientation or joint angle position). In other words we have to find a control sequence that transduces the robot end effector from a pose x_0 into the nominal pose x^* which is described by its corresponding sensor values y^*. x^* is assumed to be unknown or uncertain. The motion parameters relative to the sensed environment are expressed by the vector increment Δx_k, the actual sensor values by the vector y_k. In the training phase, i.e. the teaching by showing, the nominal sensor values y^* can be derived by a function f from the actual interaction between robot, sensor and environment in the nominal robot's pose x^*.

$$y^* = f(x^*)$$

In the subtask execution we want to find a controller sequence that is able to reach the teached goal state dependent on the nominal sensor value vector. Starting from a pose x_0 we calculate stepwise the motion parameters Δx_k in order of the actual and nominal sensor values, i.e. we apply a linear controller of the form

$$\Delta x_k = C * (y_k - y^*).$$

The optimal controller coefficients, in the sense of least square estimate, are expressed by the pseudoinverse

$$C = \left(J^T J\right)^{-1} J^T,$$

where the elements of J are the partial derivatives of the sensor values y to the motion parameters x.

$$J_{i,j} = \frac{\partial y_i}{\partial x_j}\Big|_{x^*}$$

The teaching process is implemented in an efficient way because the nominal sensor values y^* can be easy derived from the simulation or the real system. The controller design, i.e. the construction of J is also implemented in a simple manner by experimentally estimating the Jacobian J, i.e. moving the simulated or real robot by increments, using the difference quotients

$$J_{i,j} \approx \frac{\Delta y_i}{\Delta x_j}\Big|_{x^*}$$

This approach allows us the implementation of an efficient *sensor fusion* algorithm. To the elements of the measurement vector y all the sensor values can be assigned which are applicable in the desired sensor controlled subtask. To get better estimation results, it is often helpful to use redundant sensor information. We have implemented it to combine stereo vision (2 cameras) data with laser range data (4 distance values) and have observed fast as well as wide convergency.

For the implementation of such a *sensorimotion* approach we have applied other methods as PID control or neural networks [16]. At the time we are working on a comparison between this different approaches.

6 Conclusion

We have described the simulation facilities within a graphical robot programming system on the basis of the new TeleSensorProgramming concept. First we have introduced this new approach with respect to the application areas of time delayed teleoperation and graphical offline robot programming. Second an efficient model was described to emulate the robot workcell including the perception and processing of sensory data. The robot's kinematics and the sensor information of laser distance, force-torque and vision sensors are simulated in real time. Third the task oriented level within the framework of the TeleSensorProgramming approach is outlined especially with respect to the teaching-by-showing concept and to sensor fusion aspects under control considerations.

End of April 93 a small multisensory robot based on these concepts was flying in space with a 10 day-space shuttle mission (spacelab D-2 mission on shuttle COLUMBIA, flight STS 55). This robot technology experiment ROTEX was very successfull and showed that with these sensor-based concepts even present-day space robots are able to perform different prototype tasks in a variety of operational modes, that include automatic (reprogrammable) operation, on-board teleoperation and on-ground teleoperation using human and/or machine intelligence. Thus the concepts outlined in this paper (e.g. the unified treatment of sensor-based teleoperation and sensor-based offline-programming) are no longer just ideas or proposals, but they have proven their efficiency in real space flight.

ROTEX was Europe's first active step into space robotics. It proved that already today complex multisensory space robot systems can be successfully operated in the most different modes with fast transients between these modes allowing to quickly adapt to different situations. For example during the flight when the robot was supposed to move back from an arbitrary contactless situation into its standby position automatic path planing was applied, while when in contact with the environment a more cautious ground teleoperation was chosen. We clearly state that two key issues were crucial for making ROTEX a unique event and a big success:

1. the multisensory gripper and, tightly connected, the local sensory feedback concept based on shared autonomy.
2. the predictive stereographics simulation based on world models that include sensory perception and feedback.

Delays of up to 7 seconds were thus compensated without causing problems. The ROTEX control structures are thus that in the future the human operator may step more and more towards even higher on-board autonomy without changing the loop structures. However we feel that for a number of years remotely operating robots will show up limited intelligence only, so that human "anytime" intervention will remain important for a long time to come. In the future we want to improve the high level operator interface towards a general purpose system and to extend the tools for the simulation of sensor data processing.

References

[1] G. Hirzinger, J. Heindl, K. Landzettel, and B. Brunner, "Multisensory shared autonomy — a key issue in the space robot technology experiment rotex," *Proc. of the IEEE Conf. on Intelligent Robots and Systems (IROS), Raleigh,* 1992.

[2] T. Sheridan, "Human supervisory control of robot systems," *Proc. of the IEEE Conf. of Robotics and Automation, San Francisco,* 1986.

[3] G. Hirzinger, J. Dietrich, and B. Brunner, "Multisensory telerobotic concepts for space and underwater applications," *Proc. of the Space and Sea Colloquium, Paris,* 1990.

[4] A. Beiczy and W. Kim, "Predictive displays and shared compliance control for time-delayed telemanipulation," *IEEE Int. Workshop on Intelligent Robots and Systems, Ibaraki,* 1990.

[5] B. Ravani, "World modeling for cad based robot programming and simulation," *in: Ravani B. (ed.), CAD based Programming for Sensory Robots, NATO ASI Series F50, Springer, Berlin,* 1988.

[6] U. Kuehnapfel, "Grafische realzeitunterstützung für fernhandhabungsvorgänge in komplexen arbeitsumgebungen im rahmen eines systems zur steuerung, simulation und off-line-programmierung," *PhD Thesis at Universität Karlsruhe (in German),* 1992.

[7] J. Heindl and G. Hirzinger, "Device for programming movements of a robot," *U.S. Patent No. 4,589,810, May 20,* 1986.

[8] O. Guenther, "Efficient structure for geometric data management," *Lecture Notes in Computer Science 337, Springer Berlin,* 1990.

[9] F. Preparata and M. Shamos, "Computational geometry," *Springer, New York,* 1985.

[10] R. Desai, J. Xiao, and R. Volz, "Contact formations and design constraints: a new basis for the automatic generation of robot programs," *in: Ravani B. (ed.), CAD based Programming for Sensory Robots, NATO ASI Series F50, Springer, Berlin,* 1988.

[11] A. Goldenberg, "Modeling the interaction between robot and environment," *in: Casals A. (ed.), Sensor Devices and Systems for Robotics, NATO ASI Series F52, Springer, Berlin,* 1989.

[12] P. Simkens, J. de Schutter, and H. van Brussel, "Force-torque sensor emulation in a compliant motion simulation system," *Proc. of the CSME Mechanical Engineering Forum, Toronto,* 1990.

[13] P. Simkens, "Graphical simulation of sensor controlled robots," *PhD Thesis at KU Leuven (Belgium),* 1990.

[14] J. Raczkowski, K. Mittenbuehler, and C. Fohler, "Simulation of vision in robot applications," *IFAC Symposium on Robot Control (SYROCO), Karlsruhe,* 1988.

[15] O. Beran, "Classification of robot assembly states for the activation of robot control phases with neural nets," *Master's Thesis, Technical University Munich (in German)*, 1993.

[16] G. Wei, G. Hirzinger, and B. Brunner, "Sensorimotion coordination and sensor fusion by neural networks," *submitted to the IEEE Int. Conf. on Neural Networks*, 1993.

Using Graphics Algorithms as Subroutines in Collision Detection

Heinrich Müller*

Abstract

In the field of raster graphics, numerous efficient algorithms – in software as well as in hardware – have been developed in order to meet the requirements of interactivity. We investigate how to apply these algorithms to motion planning problems. It turns out that in particular the z-buffer algorithm is helpful for a rasterized implementation of the retraction approach known from literature, and for cell decomposition methods. The reason lies in the fact that calculation of Voronoi diagrams can be reduced to the calculation of visible surfaces.

1   Introduction

The speed of the basic operations is crucial for interactive computer graphics. For this reason considerable research has been performed in optimizing algorithms and transferring them into efficient implementations in soft- and hardware. The question arises whether these results and techniques are restricted to computer graphics, or whether they can be used in other fields, too. We will discuss this question for the problem of collision detection and motion planning.

The usefulness of graphics in motion simulation is obvious when thinking for instance of the simulation of an optical sensor by visible surface calculation. A further example is the use of the z-buffer algorithm of computer graphics for simulation of range sensors. We will briefly sketch these immediately apparent applications in the third chapter of this contribution.

The main part is devoted to less straightforward applications of graphics operations. The basic idea is to use rasterizing techniques for path planning purposes in configuration space (C-space). This idea was followed by [Lengyel et al., 1990] who applied fill algorithms of raster graphics to obtain a rasterization of C-space. This work is summarized in sect. 2.1.

In practice, the approach of Lengyel et al. is limited to C-spaces of only low dimension, up to 3 or 4. The main difficulty is the storage requirement

---

*Universität Dortmund, Informatik VII, 44221 Dortmund, Germany
e-mail: mueller@ls7.informatik.uni-dortmund.de

of the graph that must be searched. This difficulty can be diminished by *retraction*. The retraction approach was described by [O'Dúnlaing et al., 1987] in a classical geometric setting. We will show how graphics algorithms, in particular the z-buffer algorithm, can be used to obtain a rasterized version of retraction (sect. 2.2). The resulting graph can usually be expected to be smaller than that of the previous approach.

The way how retraction is obtained is to perform a cell decomposition of C-space and choosing the one-dimensional cells as basis for a network of paths. The approach how cell decomposition is obtained in our case let it seem to be even more efficient to use the full-dimensional cells instead of the one-dimensional ones for path planning. The resulting graph is small, although some additional work is necessary for path finding within the cells. We will see that the size of the graph and the complexity of the cells can traded in some sense against each other. Within the framework of rasterization this approach of *C-space partitioning* is the most efficient one (sect. 2.3). Its advantage is relatively small storage requirements.

Many ideas presented in this report are preliminary and need refined investigations and analysis.

2   Path Planning

The problem of path planning can be stated as follows:

Input. A scene S in 2- or 3-space, an object O.

Output. For two arbitrary locations l_1, l_2 of O, is there a path of O between l_1 and l_2 in S? Report a path, if one exists.

S consists of obstacle space and free space. O is not allowed to intersect the obstacle space, it has to lie completely in free space.

There are two basic versions of this problem. In the *query version*, S is preprocessed into a data structure. The data structure is designed so that for arbitrary pairs l_1, l_2 the question can be answered more efficiently than without. In the *immediate version* the problem is solved for just one pair l_1, l_2, and nothing than the answer is retained. The methods we present in the following can be applied to both versions.

2.1   Path Planning in Rasterized C-space

The idea of C-space is to represent a location of O in S by a d-dimensional vector [Lozano-Perez, 1983]. The set of all vectors representing locations of O is called *C-space*. d is the number of degrees of freedom the object O has. For example, if an object is allowed only to move translational in the plane, each location obtained can be described by two values, for instance the coordinates of one of its points, eg. its center. The special point is called reference point.

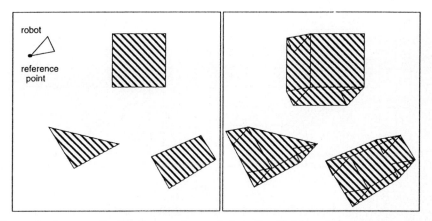

Figure 1: A scene S with three polygonal obstacles (left) and the corresponding C-space for a triangular moving object O (right).

If the object is additionally allowed to rotate, its angle with respect to a fixed direction, eg. one of the coordinate axes of S, is added as a third value. The translational case leads to a two-dimensional C-space, whereas C-space is three-dimensional when rotation is added. Figure 1 shows a space S consisting of three polygonal obstacles. O is a triangle. The reference point used is the vertex with the sharpest angle.

Obstacle space and free space transfer into C-space. A location vector belongs to free space if O at the corresponding location in S lies completely in free space. Otherwise, the vector lies in an obstacle. The right part of Fig. 1 shows the corresponding C-space of S.

Path-planning in rasterized C-space as proposed by [Lengyel et al., 1990] consists of three steps:

1. Calculate a voxel representation of C-space.

2. Calculate a C-space navigation function.

3. Determine the shortest path from any voxel start position to the target if there is a viable solution.

It is the first step where raster graphics is used. Consider the example of Fig. 1. The C-space is represented by a raster image. The C-space obstacles are drawn into this raster image and filled with a color different from background color. Drawing of filled polygonal regions is a standard operation of today's raster graphics processors, allowing to perform this step very efficiently. The polygonal boundary is obtained by calculating its vertices from the vertices of the original polygon and the triangle of O by applying an operation called *Minkowski sum*. The Minkowski sum of two sets A and B is defined by

$$A \oplus B := \bigcup_{\mathbf{a} \in A} (\mathbf{a} + B) = \{\mathbf{a} + \mathbf{b} \mid \mathbf{a} \in A, \ \mathbf{b} \in B\}.$$

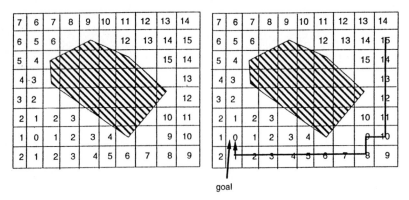

Figure 2: Example of a navigation function.

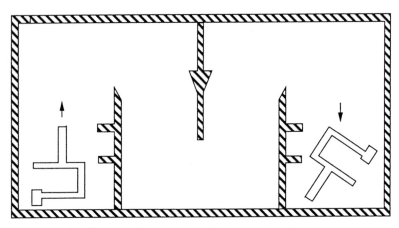

Figure 3: Motion simulation in the plane.

In our case, we have to take $S \oplus (-O)$.

The navigation function of step 2 is represented by labeling the free space voxels. Starting with location l_1, which is labeled 0, the rest of the voxels is labeled in breadth-first manner with the distance to this voxel, eg. the minimum number of voxels that have to be traversed in order to reach voxel l_2. Figure 2 shows an example for a C-space consisting of one polygonal obstacle.

Finally, the labeling constructed in step 2 allows to find a shortest path, if any, from an arbitrary l_2 to l_1 by following a sequence of voxels with monotonously decreasing labels. Thus the solution can be seen as a semi-query version in which a data structure is established for fixed l_1 which allows to find a path quickly for arbitrary l_2.

Concerning the efficiency, this solution requires $O(m^d)$ space for the labeled raster, in case of a d-dimensional C-space and a resolution of m intervals in each axis.

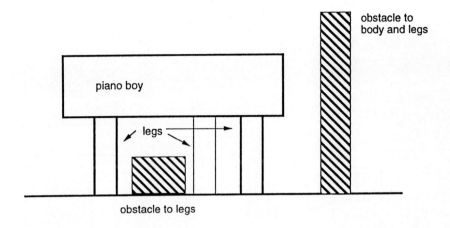

Figure 4: Composition of the C-space of a piano from the C-space of the legs and the C-space of the body by a boolean *or*.

In practice, the following results were obtained by Lengyel et al. for the scene shown in Fig. 3:

C-space size:	$256 \times 256 \times 120$
C-space calculation:	22.6 s
navigation function:	44.1 s
shortest path:	0.11 s

The calculation times were measured on a HP 835 Turbo-SRX.

Rasterizing allows the composition of complex C-spaces from more simple ones by bitblt operations, eg. composition of pictures by bit operations, like eg. the boolean operations *and*, *or*, or *exor*, which are applied to the corresponding pixels of two or more given pictures. The example shown in Fig. 4 again goes back to Lengyel et al.. The C-space of the piano is obtained by a boolean *or* of the C-space of the legs and the C-space of the body.

This can be even taken further by building up the C-space of the three legs by a boolean *or* of three C-spaces, one for each leg. In fact, since the C-space for all three legs is the same, only that one is required to be constructed from scratch. From this C-space, the two others are obtained by translation of each layer of orientation. Figure 5 shows an example.

2.2 Path Planning by Retraction

Path planning by retraction is based on the concept of Voronoi diagrams.

Given. A set M of points in d-space.

Voronoi diagram. The set V of points in d-space with equal minimum distance to at least two points of M.

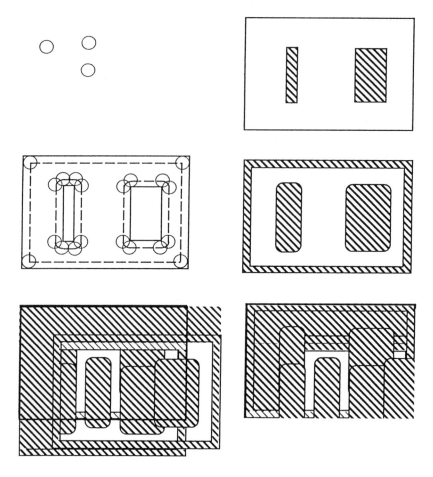

Figure 5: Composition of the C-space of three legs from that of one.

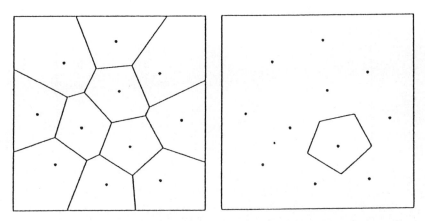

Figure 6: A point Voronoi diagram (left) and a single Voronoi cell.

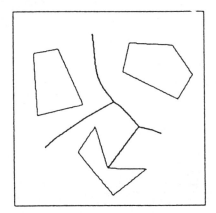

Figure 7: A polygonal region Voronoi diagram.

An important special case is M consisting of a finite set of points. Figure 6 shows an example. A Voronoi diagram of this type is called *point Voronoi diagram* (PVD). The PVD partitions the space into disjoint cells each containing just those points in space which are closer to one of the given points than to all the others, cf. Fig. 6 (right).

A second important case is M consisting of polygonal regions as shown in Fig. 7. This sort of diagram is called *polygonal region Voronoi diagram* (polygonal RVD or RVD, for short).

Interesting about both sorts of Voronoi diagrams is that RVDs can be approximated by PVDs, cf. Fig. 8 [Geiger, 1993].

Now, the retraction approach can be sketched as follows [O'Dúnlaing et al, 1987]:

1. Construct the Voronoi diagram in C-space of S.

2. Construct a network N of curves on the Voronoi diagram so that

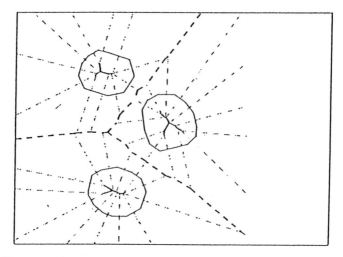

Figure 8: Approximation of a RVD by a PVD [Geiger, 1993].

(a) each point of free space can be moved (in free space) onto N

(b) there is a path between two points in free space iff the corresponding points are in the same connected component of N.

3. Calculate the projection of the two given points onto N.

4. Find a path in N between the projected points, if one exists.

The crucial point is the network N which has to be constructed efficiently and which has to allow an efficient projection of arbitrary points in free space. [O'Dúnlaing et al.] have shown that this works immediately with the RVD of a disk moving in polygonal obstacles in the plane. The network N is just the edges, i.e. the 1-d cells of the cell decomposition induced by the RVD. In configuration spaces of more than two dimensions, the 1-d cells of the RVD usually do not allow an easy enough projection. An exception is the point Voronoi diagram since this diagram partions the space into convex cells in which projection is immediate. In general, the network of 1-d Voronoi cells has to be extended by further paths. This was eg. efficiently carried out by [O'Dúnlaing et al.] in the case of a line segment moved translational and rotational in polygonal obstacles in the plane.

The problem with retraction is that region Voronoi diagrams are complicated to maintain in higher dimensional space and for complex regions. It is here where rasterization helps to simplify. The solution proposed is based on visible surface calculation. Let be given functions $f_i : I\!R^2 \rightarrow I\!R$ drawn over the x-y-plane in a x-y-z-coordinate system. We suppose that the range of the functions is bounded from below by some constant. If we look at these functions in direction parallel to the z-axis, from "below", the visible points define a function f which is

$$f(\mathbf{x}) = \min_{i=1,\dots,n} f_i(\mathbf{x}).$$

This means that the minimum of a set of functions, also called their *lower envelope*, can be obtained by visible surface calculation.

We can make use of this fact in the calculation of Voronoi diagrams. Let be M_i, $i = 1, \dots, n$, convex regions, and

$$d_i(\mathbf{x}) := \min\{d(\mathbf{x}, \mathbf{m}) \mid \mathbf{m} \in M_i\}.$$

Here $d(.,.)$ denotes the euclidean distance function. Then, for a given point $\mathbf{x}$, the index i^* of an M_i closest to $\mathbf{x}$ satisfies

$$d_{i^*}(\mathbf{x}) = \min_{i=1,\dots,n} d_i(\mathbf{x}).$$

Fig. 9 shows the result when applying the z-buffer-algorithm to the distance functions $d_i(\mathbf{x}) = d(\mathbf{x}, \mathbf{m}_i) - r_i$ for disks of radius r_i centered at $\mathbf{m}_i$. Figure 10 shows the region Voronoi diagram for oval-shaped line segments which was obtained the same way.

Because of the lack of d-dimensional hardware z-buffers for $d > 2$, the calculation of Voronoi diagrams in this manner in higher dimensional spaces has to be reduced to the 2-d case. This is achieved by sweeping the d-space in equi-distant steps by a 2d-plane. At each location of the plane, a suitable 2-d Voronoi diagram is calculated. Putting the slices together gives a d-dimensional rasterized Voronoi diagram. For instance, a 3-d PVD in x_1-x_2-x_3-space of points $(m_{1,i}, m_{2,i}, m_{3,i})$ can be obtained from slices with planes $x_3 = x_3^*$ and distance functions

$$d_i(x_1, x_2, x_3) = \sqrt{(x_1 - m_{1,i})^2 + (x_2 - m_{2,i})^2 + (x_3^* - m_{3,i})^2}.$$

With these observations, rasterized retraction can be supported by calculating the Voronoi diagram using the z-buffer algorithm. From the resulting d-dimensional voxel space the one-dimensional edges have to be extracted. This can be achieved by curve tracking algorithms of image processing or a marching cubes adaptation for curves instead of surfaces [Lorensen, Cline, 1987]. The algorithm should work in a sweeping fashion hand-in-hand with the z-buffer sweep. This avoids storing the whole voxel space. The network of curves can be stored as voxel chains eg. as chain code. If the curves are known to be straight-line, a connection list of the vertices of the network is sufficient. This is possible for PVDs or Voronoi diagrams of spheres with equal radius. In this case it is known, cf. [Edelsbrunner], that the number of k-dimensional cells of a diagram in d-space is bounded by

$$O(n^{\min(d+1-k, \lceil d/2 \rceil)}), \ 0 \leq k \leq d.$$

This means that the network consists of $O(n^{\lceil d/2 \rceil})$ curve segments connecting $O(n^{\lceil d/2 \rceil})$ vertices.

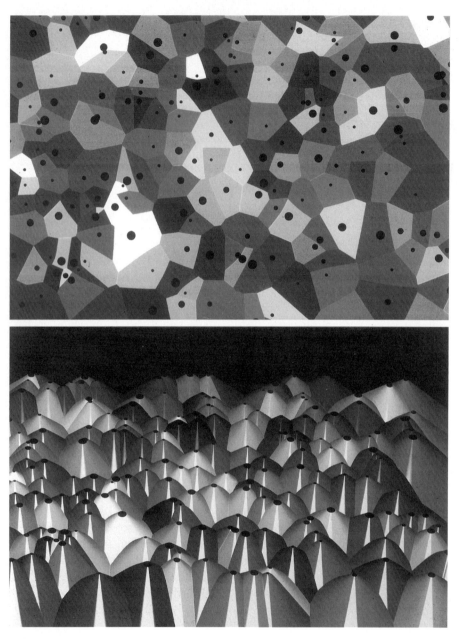

Figure 9: A Voronoi diagram for disks obtained by visible surface calculation.

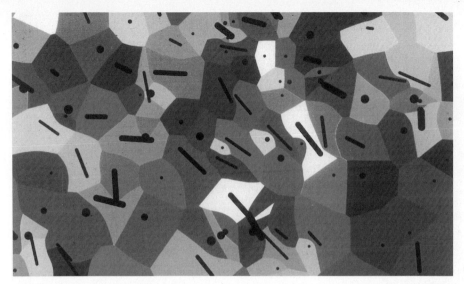

Figure 10: A Voronoi diagram for oval shaped line-segments obtained by rasterized visible surface calculation.

The problem remains how to perform the projection onto the network. This can be done by assigning a curve segment of the network to each of the d-dimensional cells induced by the Voronoi diagram. These cells in turn are assigned to that one of the obstacles for which it belongs to the environment of nearest neighbors. For an arbitrary point $\mathbf{p}$ in d-space, the nearest neighbor obstacle can be found by one-dimensional z-buffering along a straight line with the distance functions of the Voronoi diagram. This partitions the line into intervals. The interval that contains $\mathbf{p}$ identifies the nearest obstacle of $\mathbf{p}$. Since the environment of nearest neighbors has not to be connected for extended obstacles, some more analysis of the obstacles defining the environment might become necessary.

2.3 Path Planning by C-space Partitioning

The idea of path-planning by C-space partitioning is to construct the path in two steps. First, a path of full-dimensional cells induced by the region Voronoi diagram of C-space is determined between start and target configuration, if any does exist. Then, within each of these cells, a path segment is determined so that the chain of all these segments makes up a simple path from start to goal. The steps are as follows:

1. Calculate the neighborhood graph of the full-dimensional cells induced by the region Voronoi diagram of C-space.

2. Find the cells of start and target point (point location).

3. Find a path between the start and target cell in the neighborhood graph.

4. Find a path in the cell path.

The vertices of the *neighborhood graph* represent the full-dimensional cells. Two cells are connected by an edge iff they are neighbors in the partition induced by the Voronoi diagram. The neighborhood graph can be calculated by sweeping the voxel volume row by row in order to check the neighboring colors. This can be achieved by including the checking into the sweep required for Voronoi diagram construction in higher dimensions.

Steps 1 and 2 carry over from rasterized retraction. Step 3 can be solved by methods from graph theory, eg. depth-first-search. The only crucial point is finding a path in the cell path. For this purpose points connecting the segments have to be identified which lie on the common boundary of two neighboring cells. Then the entry and exit point of each cell have to be connected by a path completely in the cell. This might cause troubles for highly non-convex cells, but is not too difficult for cells induced by point Voronoi diagrams or Voronoi diagrams of spherical obstacles, in particular if they have equal radii.

Concerning efficiency, the advantage is that the neighborhood graph should have small size. In particular for PVD, if its number of vertices is $O(n)$, the number of edges is $O(n^2)$ according to the general estimations mentioned above. Again, this approach does not require storage space for the complete rasterized C-space.

Path planning by C-space partitioning seems to be the most practical approach among those presented here. It should be further investigated for (hyper-)spheres as C-space obstacles. In this case, all steps are simplified considerably, although the number of spheres might become considerably higher than for obstacles modeled by more flexible geometric items.

2.4 The General Case

In general, a C-space is given by a system of inequalities

$$\mathbf{f}(\mathbf{x}) \geq \mathbf{0}, \; \mathbf{f} : I\!\!R^d \to I\!\!R^n.$$

In oder to find out whether there is a path connecting two given points $\mathbf{x}_1$ and $\mathbf{x}_2$ in the space of solutions, one idea could be to calculate the "visible surfaces" for the scene of component functions $f_i(\mathbf{x})$ of $\mathbf{f}$. This might also induce some cell decomposition of reasonable complexity which can be used for path planning. The main question is which functions $\mathbf{f}$ are suitable to get solutions at all, and how the efficiency depends on properties of these functions.

3 Free Placement

The problem of *free placement* can be stated as follows.

Input. A scene S, an object O.

Output. For a given location of O, does O intersect S?

This problem can be solved by visible surface calculation through the faces of O, and supposing that the obstacles of S are given by boundary surfaces colored red inside and blue outside. If the faces are flat, the plane of a face is used as back clipping plane. If the resulting picture does not show any background color or does have red portions, a collision of O with the obstacles is detected.

Other applications of visible surface calculation are distance measuring by depth cueing or reading the z-values from the z-buffer, or identifying the obstacles relevant in the environment of O in its current location by using a different color for each obstacle. The knowledge of the environment may speed up calculations which can be restricted to just these obstacles, thus avoiding inspection of the whole scene.

4   Conclusion

The conclusion of these investigations is that rasterization might be similar useful in motion planning as it is in computer graphics. The basic operations seem to be quite similar in both fields, although motion planning often requires them in more than two dimensions. This, however, is limited in practice by the space requirements which can be diminished by applying the lower dimensional operations in a sweeping fashion.

References

H. Edelsbrunner (1987) *Algorithms in Combinatorial Geometry*, Springer-Verlag

B. Geiger (1993) *Construction and Utilization of Organ Models from the View of Assistance in Diagnostics and Surgery*, PhD-thesis, Ecole des Mines de Paris, France

J. Lengyel, M. Reichert, B.R. Donald, D.P. Greenberg (1990) *Real-time Robot Motion Planning Using Rasterized Computer Graphics Hardware*, Computer Graphics 24(4), 327-336

W.E. Lorensen, H.E. Cline (1987) *Marching Cubes: A High Resolution 3D Surface Construction Algorithm*, Computer Graphics 21(3) 163–169

L. Lozano-Perez (1983) *Spatial Planning: A Configuration Space Approach*, IEEE Transactions on Computers C-32, 108–120

C. Ó'Dúnlaing, C.K. Yap (1987) *A Retraction Method for Planning the Motion of a Disk*, in: J. T Schwartz, M. Sharir, J. Hopcroft, ed., Planning, Geometry, and Complexity of Robot Motion Planning, Ablex Publishing Corp., Norwood, NJ, 187–192

C. Ó'Dúnlaing, M. Sharir, C.K. Yap (1987) *Retraction: A New Approach to Motion Planning*, in: J. T Schwartz, M. Sharir, J. Hopcroft, ed., Planning, Geometry, and Complexity of Robot Motion Planning, Ablex Publishing Corp., Norwood, NJ, 193–213

CSG Based Collision Detection

W. Purgathofer and M. Zeiller
Technical University of Vienna, Institute of Computer Graphics,
Karlsplatz 13/186, 1040 Vienna, Austria

Abstract

This paper describes a complete method to detect collision among CSG modeled objects within a computer animation system. Since objects that are modeled with the constructive solid geometry paradigm can have very complex shapes, especially when they consist of curved primitives, collision detection is performed in three stages. Bounding volumes in each node of the CSG tree are used to determine whether a collision is likely to occur between each pair of objects. If overlapping bounds are discovered, spatial subdivision is used to reduce the complexity of the CSG objects for further analysis. In those voxels, which cover parts of both objects, a redundancy test is performed for each primitive to determine whether the objects interpenetrate. Curved primitives are adaptively approximated by circumscribed and inscribed polyhedrons.

1   Introduction

In computer animation we want to model various changes of objects over time. The major concern is to model the movement of these objects. Several techniques exist, which describe an object's motion [PUEY88]. If the motion shall appear very realistic, we have to simulate it due to physical laws, which is well known as dynamic simulation [THAL91]. An external force that is acting on a body will cause it to move. The equations of motion have to be set up and the state (i.e., position and orientation) of the body is derived for each time step. In a realistic simulation the moving bodies are not allowed to interpenetrate other bodies. They cannot move around freely, but have to obey certain constraints. We have to detect whether two bodies collide or are in contact and to respond to the collision or maintain the contact.

Collision detection can be performed in two major ways [BARA93]. The continuum methods view the problem of determining a collision between two instants of time t_0 and t_1 as a single, continuous function of time. They solve the problem of determining the time and location when two bodies come into contact in the given time interval. The methods presented in [CANN86] and [DUFF92] belong to this group. The usability of continuum methods is limited since they presuppose the motion path of the bodies, but this it what the dynamic simulation tries to find. Therefore, discrete methods that analyze a series of instants of time $t_0 < t_0 + \Delta t_1 < t_0 + \Delta t_2 < \ldots < t_0 + \Delta t_n < t_1$ are more popular. For each time step $t_0 + \Delta t_i$ these methods are given the state of the bodies and determine whether they interpenetrate or are in contact. They are based on a geometric analysis, since two bodies A and B collide if their surfaces intersect, that is, their intersection is not empty ($A \cap B \neq \emptyset$, null-object detection NOD). Examples for this kind of method are [MOOR88] and [HAHN88]. The efficiency of discrete methods can be highly increased by taking similarities between the current and previous time steps into account. Coherence-based methods are described, e.g., in [BARA90] and [LIN92].

Most of the existing algorithms for collision detection work on rigid bodies of polyhedral shape that are described with a boundary representation. The majority of them is based on finding vertices inside the other body or edges that intersect the other body. However, in this paper we want to deal with bodies modeled with constructive solid geometry. Tilove [TILO84] presents a collision detection algorithm for CSG objects using null-object detection. He reduces the CSG representation to the null set by determining redundancy of primitives. Cameron [CAME89] detects collisions among CSG objects using three stages. First he creates a set of bounding volumes called S-bounds around the nodes of the CSG tree. In the next stage he splits the problem into simpler subproblems using spatial subdivision. Finally he generates a set of sufficient points that are classified regarding to the objects being tested. While these algorithms are restricted to CSG objects constructed from polyhedral primitives, Duff's algorithm [DUFF92], which uses interval arithmetic, deals with primitives described by implicit functions.

After a collision or contact has been detected, the involved bodies are not allowed to interpenetrate. Again, there are two basic ways to do collision response [BARA93]. The constraint-based or analytical methods compute constraint forces that exactly cancel external accelerations that would result in an interpenetration. If the bodies are colliding, their velocity has to change discontinuously at the moment of impact, which is achieved by impulsive forces. Collision response based on impulsive collision forces is presented in [MOOR88], [HAHN88], and [BARA89]. Bodies that are in resting contact are prevented from interpenetration by repulsive contact forces that push them apart [BARA90]. The second method for collision response is called penalty method. It places a spring at each contact point between two colliding or contacting bodies. If there is an interpenetration, a restoring (penalty) force, that increases as the amount of interpenetration increases, acts to push them apart. Although penalty methods, as they are presented in [MOOR88] and [TERZ87], are much simpler than constraint-based methods, they cannot eliminate interpenetration completely and cause numerical problems.

2 Outline of the Method

In a dynamic simulation the moving bodies have to be prevented from interpenetration using collision detection and response. The moving bodies and the entire scene can be modeled in various ways. Constructive solid geometry is a flexible and powerful way of representing objects, especially if primitives are not restricted to be polyhedrons, but may consist of curved surfaces, as well. Throughout the rest of the paper we refer to CSG objects as objects constructed by the regularized set operations union (A∪B), intersection (A∩B), and difference (A–B), which are represented by a binary tree structure. Without restricting generality, primitives are presumed to be either natural quadrics (sphere, cylinder, cone) or regular convex polyhedra (Platonic solids: tetrahedron, cube, octahedron, dodecahedron, icosahedron).

The dynamic simulation provides the state of the moving CSG objects for consecutive time steps. At each of these time steps we apply the collision detection algorithm, which is described in the rest of this paper. The basic algorithm is a discrete method, i.e., it does not exploit the knowledge of previous time steps. If a collision has been detected and the time and location of the first contact have been determined, one of the well-known methods for collision response has to be applied, but this is beyond the scope of this paper.

Detecting a collision among two CSG objects can be performed in two ways. The CSG objects can either be converted to a boundary representation which is then used for the collision detection, or the collision detection is performed directly on the CSG representation. In the first case, we would have to do a complicated conversion task for the entire objects. This conversion becomes even more complicated if primitives have curved surfaces, e.g., quadrics. Using a BREP approximation is impracticable for such objects, since an accurate approximation would require a tremendous amount of polygons. In the second case, we have to apply the collision detection to the CSG representation which is much more complicated to do than for a BREP. However, we can restrict the detailed analysis of the objects' surfaces only to those small regions, where a collision is likely to occur. The method we propose in this paper is based on the second approach.

A scene for computer animation consists of static (i.e., not moving) and dynamic (i.e., moving) objects. We have to analyze each pair of dynamic objects and each pair of one static and one dynamic object. Our collision detection algorithm consists of three stages, which is similar to [CAME89]. We want to eliminate as many objects, respectively, at least parts of them, as possible from further consideration by fast tests and perform an exact analysis only for those objects and regions where a collision is likely to take place.

In the first stage, bounding volumes are used to reject those pairs of objects where even the bounding volumes do not overlap. Since bounding volumes of the entire objects are only a very coarse approximation of an object's shape, bounding volumes in each node of the CSG tree are considered in this stage, too. S-bounds

[CAME91] provide an efficient means to handle this problem for the intersection test of two CSG objects. If the resulting bounding volume is empty, the objects cannot intersect and they do not collide. Otherwise, they may collide and we have to continue with stage two.

The bounding volume of the S-bounds test restricts the region of interest where a collision may take place. Spatial subdivision is used in the second stage to reduce the complexity of the CSG objects inside this volume for further analysis. The bounding volume is adaptively decomposed into voxels until we get to a configuration where we can decide whether there is an intersection, or there is no intersection, or we reach a certain spatial resolution.

If the second stage did not end up with a definite decision and resulted in some voxels, that cover parts of both objects, a third stage, giving an exact (within tolerances) solution has to be performed. The voxels may be partially covered by single primitives or by CSG structures. Due to the two preprocessing stages these CSG structures are (hopefully) very small and cover only a fraction of the CSG objects we started with. To determine whether they interpenetrate inside the voxel, a redundancy test based on Tilove's work [TILO84] is used. Curved objects have to be approximated adaptively with an outer and an inner bounding polyhedron. If the redundancy test of the outer bounds gives a different result than the test of the inner bounds, then the approximation has to be refined and the test is repeated. Testing continues until we get equal results (i.e., collision or no collision) or we reach the required accuracy.

In chapter 3 we will give an overview of S-bounds and how they are useful for collision detection. Chapter 4 reduces the complexity of the remaining CSG tree using spatial subdivision. In chapter 5 we will describe how to do the redundancy test for polyhedral and curved primitives. Section 6 covers the calculation of the collision time, and the computational cost of this method will be analyzed in section 7. Chapter 8 takes a look at future work.

3 Bounds

We do not want to perform complicated and time consuming null-object detection tests on the entire objects. A collision will only affect a small part of an object's surface and in most cases no collision will occur. It is preferable to limit the CSG representation of the objects under investigation only to those regions of space where a collision is likely to take place when the detailed NOD test is performed.

A very efficient means of accelerating computations on arbitrary kinds of objects are bounding volumes. They enclose the objects and have much simpler shapes. Therefore, an approximate solution to a given problem can be obtained much faster. In CSG modeling a hierarchy of bounding volumes can be established, that is, in each node there is a bounding volume that encloses the corresponding subtree. In this first stage, we are using S-bounds [CAME89] [CAME91] that have proved to be very efficient bounds for null-object detection. S-bounds are a set of bounding volumes in each node of the CSG representation. The upward rule computes the bounding volume of an intermediate node by combining the bounding volumes of its subtrees according to the set operation. The downward rule prunes the bounding volume of a subtree due to the bounding volume of its preceding node. Starting with the bounding volumes enclosing the leaf nodes the upward theorem is applied to the whole CSG tree in a bottom-up way and then the downward theorem is applied in a top-down way. This can be done several times, until it reaches a stable configuration.

At startup time the S-bounds algorithm is run on each CSG object to refine its bounds. We are using bounding spheres and axis-aligned bounding boxes, because spheres are independent of rotation, but axis-aligned boxes give tighter bounds. Then for each time step the dynamic simulation runs and computes a new state of the dynamic objects. The bounding volumes that enclose the entire objects are updated and used as a first estimate, whether they may intersect. For many configurations this test will be sufficient. Otherwise, if two bounding volumes overlap, the S-bounds algorithm is applied to the respective pair of CSG objects.

Two CSG objects collide if their intersection is not the null set. We create a new temporary CSG object, that is the intersection of these two objects. The S-bounds algorithm is applied to the new combined CSG tree [CAME89]. The reduction of the bounding volumes will be significant, because in collision detection the original objects are apart from each other in most cases. If this intersection object is null-bounded (Fig. 1 left), then the original objects do not collide and we can stop testing these two objects. Otherwise, the S-bounds overlap and they are likely to intersect (Fig. 1 right). Therefore, we have to continue and take a closer look at the objects themselves. In this second case we can still gain from the bounds test. We end up with a bounding volume in the root node that is not empty, but hopefully very small. A potential intersection can only take place inside this region, and everything outside can be ignored in the further NOD test. Those subtrees of the intersection tree, that have empty bounds, have no influence on the intersection and can be removed from the CSG tree.

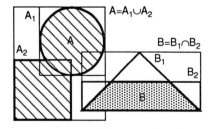 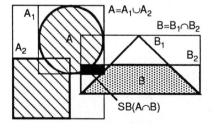

Fig. 1. Empty S-bounds (left) and non-empty S-bounds (right) in 2D

The S-bounds algorithm is performed with bounding spheres first, because they can be updated more easily and provide a very quick first test. If the bounding sphere of the root node is empty, we can stop immediately and report that there is no collision. Otherwise, the intersection tree is simplified by removing the null-bounded subtrees. Then the axis-aligned bounding boxes of the leaf nodes in the remaining tree are updated and the S-bounds algorithm is applied for the axis-aligned bounding boxes. If we end up with empty bounds, we can stop, too. Otherwise, the intersection tree is pruned and we continue with stage two.

4 Spatial Subdivision

In the first stage, a region of space where a collision is likely to occur and a reduced CSG tree for this region have been generated. However, the CSG tree may still be very complex, which would result in expensive NOD tests. To speed up the computation, spatial subdivision is performed in the second stage. The NOD problem is spatially split into a number of subproblems. Improvements arise from the fact that at the same time the size of the CSG tree for each subproblem is being reduced. A popular strategy for spatial subdivision is based on divide-and-conquer. For a given region and a CSG tree it decides dynamically whether to conquer the problem (i.e., easy decision or direct NOD) or to perform another subdivision. Two major problems arise in this stage: One task is to decide whether the region shall be further subdivided or not. The other task is to perform the subdivision. Subdividing a region is not a problem at all, but due to this subdivision those parts of the CSG tree, that lie inside these subregions, have to be determined. Thus, the CSG trees will get smaller when the region gets smaller and the NOD problem can be dealt with more easily. Fig. 2 shows a 2D example of two CSG objects and their representations in the intersection tree. After performing one subdivision in Fig. 3, the CSG trees of the upper subregions are reduced to the null set. The lower subregions are not empty, but their associated CSG trees have been simplified, too.

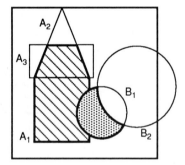 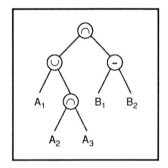

Fig. 2. Two intersecting objects A and B (2D) and their CSG representation

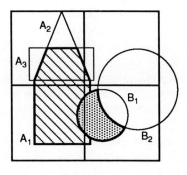 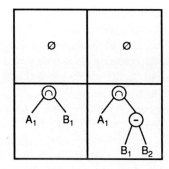

Fig. 3. One subdivision of the bounding region and its CSG representation

The axis-aligned bounding box associated with the root node of the CSG tree is the region of space we are interested in. The easiest way to subdivide an axis-aligned cube is to decompose it into eight octants of equal size. Then we have to determine which parts of the CSG objects are inside these boxes. This problem is similar to the top down approach for the octree creation of a CSG object [ELBE88]. We are interested to know whether the box is completely inside (*full*), partially inside (*partial*), or outside (*empty*) according to the CSG tree. To classify the CSG tree, we start at the root node of the CSG tree and traverse it recursively in postorder. Table 1 shows the decision table for the combination of the classification. If a leaf node is reached, the box has to be classified according to the primitive. Therefore, this method heavily relies on efficient algorithms that decide whether the box is completely inside, partially inside or outside a primitive.

Table 1. Decision table for the combination of classifications

classification left subtree	classification right subtree	union left $\cup$ right	intersection left $\cap$ right	difference left - right
empty	*empty*	*empty*	*empty*	*empty*
empty	*full*	*full*	*empty*	*empty*
empty	*partial*	*partial*	*empty*	*empty*
full	*empty*	*full*	*empty*	*full*
full	*full*	*full*	*full*	*empty*
full	*partial*	*full*	*partial*	*partial*
partial	*empty*	*partial*	*empty*	*partial*
partial	*full*	*full*	*partial*	*empty*
partial	*partial*	*partial*	*partial*	*partial*

If the root node is classified as *empty*, we do not have to consider this box any further, since the objects cannot intersect in this box. If it is classified as *full*, we can stop, too, because we have discovered a region of space that is covered by both objects. Thus, they intersect and a collision is found. The classification *partial* of the root node requires additional investigations. If one subtree of the root node is classified *full* and the other one *partial*, some region of space inside this box is covered by both objects and they intersect. If both objects partially cover the box, we have to decide whether to tackle the NOD problem directly or to subdivide the box again. Before doing this, the CSG tree can be simplified. Some of the subtrees may be classified *empty*, that is, they are completely outside this box, and can be removed from the CSG tree.

Before we subdivide a box into subboxes, we have to decide whether we should do so or to tackle the NOD problem directly. Since we do not want to subdivide forever, a minimum size of the box has to be fixed in the subdivision algorithm. If this minimal resolution is reached, we continue with stage three, no matter how complex the CSG tree still is. The decision, whether to subdivide or not, obviously depends on the complexity, i.e., the number of primitives, of the CSG tree. If the tree consists of only two primitives, i.e., one of each object, another subdivision usually does not pay for and we continue with the next stage. Otherwise, as long as the CSG tree has a certain complexity, e.g., more than N primitives, where N is a small number, the box is subdivided again.

5 Removal of Redundant Primitives

In the previous stages the regions of interest and the complexities of the CSG trees within these regions have been reduced considerably. The complexity of the NOD problem has decreased, but the basic question still has to be solved: Given a region of space and a CSG tree, does this tree represent the null set? We use a method based on Tilove's work [TILO84] where he tests primitives for redundancy. A primitive is redundant, if it can be removed from the CSG representation of the object, but the object stays the same. Tilove can deal only with primitives that are rectangular blocks. The extension to polyhedral primitives is straightforward, but most CSG objects are also constructed from curved primitives. To test curved primitives for redundancy they are adaptively approximated by an inner and an outer bounding polyhedron. Tilove's redundancy test is applied to the inner and the outer bounds. If they give different results, the approximation has to be refined and the test is repeated. Testing continues until the redundancy of a primitive can be decided or the required precision has been reached.

The spatial subdivision resulted in a number of boxes with associated CSG trees. We have to test all boxes for NOD, but we can stop immediately after the first intersection is detected. Boxes with CSG trees constructed from few primitives will be tested before boxes with more primitives. The next two subsections will show that it is preferable to test CSG trees constructed from polyhedra before testing CSG trees including curved primitives.

5.1 Polyhedral Primitives

Null-object detection for CSG trees that consist entirely of polyhedral primitives can be done using Tilove's method of redundancy testing [TILO84]. If a CSG object S is represented by a CSG tree T with primitives P_1, P_2, ..., P_n, then $S(P_i \leftarrow W)$ denotes the set represented by T where P_i has been replaced by W. A primitive P_i is called to be $\emptyset$-redundant if $S=S(P_i \leftarrow \emptyset)$. Tilove states that if every positive primitive in a CSG representation of S is $\emptyset$-redundant, then S is null. The sign of a primitive is a measure of the number of times it has been subtracted. Tilove determines $\emptyset$-redundancy with the test "Is $S \cap P_i = \emptyset$?". He solves this problem by classifying a sufficient set X of candidates with the property that $S \cap P_i$ is null, if each candidate x in X is completely outside $S \cap P_i$. A sufficient set of candidates are the straight line segments that are obtained when all faces of the block primitives are intersected in pairs. If no subset of any edge of X is contained in the boundary of S, then S has no edges. Thus, it has no faces and has to be null.

Tilove uses this method only for primitives that are rectangular blocks. There is no restriction to blocks and we apply the same technique to arbitrary convex polyhedral primitives (actually Platonic solids). Ray tracing is being used to classify an edge of X against $S \cap P_i$ and to determine whether it is completely outside. The spatial subdivision has reduced the CSG tree to those primitives that intersect the box. However, parts of their volumes may be outside the box. The primitives have to be clipped at the box and only those bounding faces inside the box must be considered in the redundancy test.

A CSG tree may also consist only of two primitives. In this case both objects that are tested for collision inside the given box are represented by a single primitive. There is no need for the redundancy test, and collision detection can be performed directly. We use a standard collision detection algorithm for polyhedral objects based on Moore and Wilhelm's method [MOOR88].

5.2 Quadric Primitives

Curved primitives, e.g., quadrics, cause much more trouble than polyhedral primitives. Tilove's redundancy test cannot be applied to them, because a set of edges that can be tested for being inside or outside the intersection object cannot be derived. To be able to apply the redundancy test we have to generate a sufficient set of candidates, that cover the boundaries of the primitives, by intersecting their faces. The intersection curves of quadrics and other types of curved primitives are extremely difficult to compute [MILL88] and these (very complex) curves would have to be classified against the intersection object.

To test objects with curved primitives for redundancy, they are approximated by polyhedra. However, the accuracy of the result depends on the quality of the approximation. A coarse approximation is very easy to test, but gives inexact answers with high tolerances. On the other hand a fine approximation provides results of high accuracy, but is very costly. Since we require accurate results, we use an adaptive refinement technique similar to the boundary evaluation method of Beacon et al., that uses inner and outer sets [BEAC89]. The curved primitives are circumscribed by an enclosing outer bounding polyhedron (OBP) and are inscribed by an inner bounding polyhedron (IBP). An outer bounding polyhedron for the entire CSG tree can be created by replacing the positive primitives with their OBPs and the negative primitives with their IBPs. Consequently we get an inner bounding polyhedron of the CSG tree by replacing the positive primitives with their IBPs and the negative primitives with their OBPs. This leads to an interval, inside which the exact boundaries of the object lie. Then Tilove's redundancy test is applied to the CSG tree twice, one time to its OBP and the other time to the IBP. If the tests give different results, no decision can be made. The approximation has to be refined and the test is repeated. Testing continues until a definite decision can be made that the approximated objects intersect or not intersect, or the required accuracy has been reached. If we get down to the required spatial precision, the objects are assumed to intersect.

Let us consider the following example: In a given region two objects A and B shall be tested for interference, thus, the redundancy test is applied to S=A∩B. Let $\overline{S}$ denote the OBP of S and $\underline{S}$ the IBP of S. If $\overline{S} = \overline{A} \cap \overline{B}$ is empty, A and B definitely do not collide, and we can stop. Otherwise we have to test $\underline{S}=\underline{A}\cap\underline{B}$. If $\underline{S}$ is not empty, A and B definitely collide, and we can stop, too. If $\underline{S}$ is empty, but $\overline{S}$ is not, we cannot make a correct decision, yet. The OBPs and the IBPs in $\overline{S}$ and $\underline{S}$ are replaced by a better approximation and the process is repeated. In figure 4 $\overline{S} = \overline{A} \cap \overline{B}$ is not empty, whereas $\underline{S}=\underline{A}\cap\underline{B}$ is empty, and another pass is necessary.

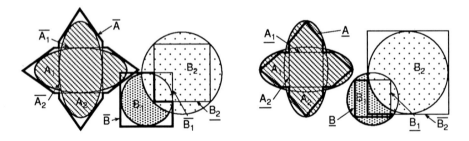

Fig. 4. Outer and inner bounding polyhedron

To create and OBP and an IBP of an object we need an OBP and an IBP of each primitive. The IBP and the OBP of polyhedral primitives are the polyhedra themselves. For curved primitives we need polyhedra that give a very tight approximation. In this paper we restrict the curved primitives to natural quadrics (sphere, cylinder, cone), but arbitrary shapes can be used as long as an OBP and IBP can be created and refined. The initial approximation for a sphere is an icosahedron, whose equilateral triangular faces are decomposed into four equilateral triangles in each iteration. A cylinder is initially approximated by a hexagonal prism and a cone is approximated by a hexagonal pyramid. In each refinement step each face is split into two halves. In case that the primitives have been nonuniformly scaled (e.g., sphere changes to ellipsoid), the bounding polyhedra can be generated before scaling or the approximation tries to cope with the nonuniform curvature.

In each step of refinement the length of the edges is (nearly) bisected. However, the thickness of the interval between the outer and the inner bounding polyhedron is reduced to one quarter. In R steps of refinement we gain a precision of $1/2^{2R}$ (e.g., 10 steps for a precision of 10^{-6}). In each step the number of polygons increases, but the number of polygons that have to be considered in the redundancy test stays nearly the same throughout the refinement, because the relevant region of interest shrinks with the same order of magnitude. If we have to refine, only those polygons of the OBP that intersect and their related polygons of the IBP have to be refined and considered in the next step. The region of interest (ROI) shrinks with each iteration to a half and the number of polygons in it and the computational cost of each step stays nearly constant (Fig. 5).

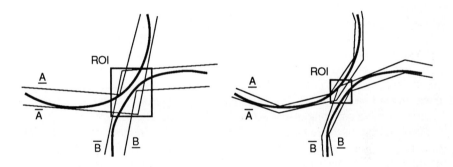

Fig. 5. Refinement of the bounding polyhedra

6 Collision Time and Point

The NOD algorithm described above, determines whether two objects intersect at a given time or not. If there is no intersection at time t_0, but there is an intersection at the next time step $t_0+\Delta t$, then a collision has occurred in the time interval $[t_0,t_0+\Delta t]$. To be able to respond to the collision correctly, we have to determine the collision time and the collision point, i.e., the time and location where they come into contact first. We compute the collision time with binary search. The simulation is run to compute the state of system at time $t_0+\Delta t/2$ and the NOD algorithm is applied again. If there is an intersection at time $t_0+\Delta t/2$, the collision has to occur before it in the interval $[t_0,t_0+\Delta t/2]$, otherwise, it occurs after it in the interval $[t_0+\Delta t/2,t_0+\Delta t]$. This process is repeated until we are satisfied with the precision of the collision time. After I iterations we gain an increase in precision of $1/2^I$. After determining the collision time, the collision point has to be found for that instant of time. We do not consider multiple collisions and assume that there is only one collision point. If there is a single interpenetrating vertex, it is taken as the collision point, otherwise, the point of greatest interpenetration is chosen.

7   Computational Cost and Numerical Stability

The bounds test has to be applied to each pair of dynamic objects and to static-dynamic pairs, as well. For N_s static and N_d dynamic objects the computational cost is $O(N_s \cdot N_d + N_d^2)$. The S-bounds test depends on the number of primitives N_1 in the CSG tree and has a worst-case cost of $O(N_1^2)$. If the spatial subdivision is performed, the bounding volume is subdivided at worst O(ld subdivision resolution) times. Starting with N_2 primitives in the CSG tree, at worst $O(N_2)$ primitives have to be analyzed in each step to localize them in the box. Thus, the computational cost of stage two is $O(N_2 \cdot$ld subdivision resolution). Tilove's redundancy test has a worst-case cost of $O(N_3^4)$ for N_3 primitives in the CSG tree. If it contains curved primitives, several iterations are performed with a refined approximation and we get a worst-case cost of $O(N_3^4 \cdot$ld spatial precision) for stage three. In the normal case N_3 is a very small. The collision time is computed using binary search whose computational cost is O(ld temporal precision).

The precision of the redundancy test is limited by the numerical stability of the calculation of the candidate edges. To create a sufficient set of edges the polygons of the primitives have to be intersected. When we approach to a contact the orientation of polygons will be nearly the same, which may cause numerical problems if the precision of the depth of interpenetration shall be very high.

8   Future Work

The proposed method for detecting collisions among objects modeled by constructive solid geometry is currently under implementation. Therefore, we cannot give timings of running simulations, yet. This method, as it has been presented, belongs to the discrete methods for collision detection. Since the computational cost may become quite remarkable in certain configurations, especially when two curved objects are nearly in contact, we have to think about optimization. One obvious source of optimization is coherence [GRÖL92] which is inherent in the method, but not exploited, yet, to improve the computation times.

The computational cost may get very high in a situation where two CSG objects collide with curved surfaces that have equal or very similar curvature. In this case the number of polygons of the polyhedral approximation will increase during the refinement of the approximation, but the area of interest will not shrink. Therefore, we would have to deal with an ever increasing number of polygons in the redundancy test, resulting in a tremendous computational cost. A separate solution to this situation has to be found to prevent the algorithm from endless calculations.

9   Conclusion

We have described an algorithm to detect collisions among objects that have been modeled with constructive solid geometry. In contrary to most other algorithms, the objects can be constructed from polyhedral and quadric primitives, too. To speed up the computation and to avoid expensive calculations for each time step, it consists of three stages. The first stage uses bounding volumes and the second stage uses spatial subdivision to reduce the complexity of the collision detection problem and to split it into a number of simpler subproblems, that can be treated more easily. However, the initial problem still has to be solved, which is done with testing the primitives for redundancy. The redundancy test can be applied to curved primitives, as well, since we approximate their shape by outer and inner bounding polyhedra. Due to an adaptive refinement of the approximation, the computational complexity of this test is kept low. This approach can be applied to all types of curved primitives, since it should be possible to create the approximation very easily. Using a new kind of primitive for modeling only requires to provide the generation of the outer and inner bounding polyhedra. This method provides results of variable precision depending on the requirements of the user. Inaccurate results can be achieved very fast, whereas precise results require several iterations at a higher cost.

Acknowledgements

We would like to thank Heinrich Müller for very helpful discussions at the Dagstuhl Seminar and Florian Zwerina for his help on implementing this method. The equipment used in this project was supported in part by 'Fonds zur Förderung der wissenschaftlichen Forschung' grant number P09303-PHY. A preliminary version of this paper has appeared at VIDEA'93 [ZEIL93].

References

[BARA89]   Baraff, D., "Analytical Methods for Dynamic Simulation of Non-penetrating Rigid Bodies", *Computer Graphics*, Vol. 23, No. 3, pp. 223-232, July 1989.

[BARA90]   Baraff, D., "Curved Surfaces and Coherence for Non-penetrating Rigid Body Simulation", *Computer Graphics*, Vol. 24, No. 4, pp. 19-28, August 1990.

[BARA93]   Baraff, D., "Non-penetrating Rigid Body Simulation", *State of the Art Reports of EUROGRAPHICS '93*, Eurographics Technical Report Series, 1993.

[BEAC89]   Beacon, G., Dodsworth, J., Howe, S., Oliver, R., Saia, A., "Boundary Evaluation Using Inner and Outer Sets: The ISOS Method", *IEEE Computer Graphics & Applications*, Vol. 9, No. 2, pp. 39-51, March 1989.

[CAME89]   Cameron, S., "Efficient Intersection Tests for Objects Defined Constructively", *The International Journal of Robotics Research*, Vol. 8, No. 1, pp. 3-25, February 1989.

[CAME91]   Cameron, S., "Efficient Bounds in Constructive Solid Geometry", *IEEE Computer Graphics & Applications*, Vol. 11, No. 3, pp. 68-74, May 1991.

[CANN86]   Canny, J., "Collision Detection for Moving Polyhedra", *IEEE Transactions on Pattern Analysis and Machine Intelligence*, Vol. PAMI-8, No. 2, pp. 200-209, March 1986.

[DUFF92]   Duff, T., "Interval Arithmetic and Recursive Subdivision for Implicit Functions and Constructive Solid Geometry", *Computer Graphics*, Vol. 26, No. 2, pp. 131-138, July 1992.

[ELBE88]   Elber, G., Shpitalni, M., "Octree creation via C.S.G definition", *The Visual Computer*, Vol. 4, No. 2, pp. 53-64, July 1988.

[GRÖL92]   Gröller, E., *Coherence in Computer Graphics*, PhD thesis, Technical University of Vienna, September 1992.

[HAHN88]   Hahn, J., "Realistic Animation of Rigid Bodies", *Computer Graphics*, Vol. 22, No. 4, pp. 299-308, August 1988.

[LIN92]   Lin, M., Canny, J., "Efficient Collision Detection for Animation", Proceedings of *Third Eurographics Workshop on Animation and Simulation*, Eurographics Technical Report Series, 1992.

[MILL88]   Miller, J., "Analysis of Quadric-Surface-Based Solid Models", *IEEE Computer Graphics & Applications*, Vol. 8, No. 1, pp. 28-42, January 1988.

[MOOR88]   Moore, M., Wilhelms, J. "Collision Detection and Response for Computer Animation", *Computer Graphics*, Vol. 22, No. 4, pp. 289-298, August 1988.

[PUEY88]   Pueyo, X., Tost, D., "A Survey of Computer Animation", *Computer Graphics Forum*, Vol. 7, No. 4, pp. 281-300, 1988.

[TERZ87]   Terzopoulos, D., Platt, J., Barr, A., Fleischer, K., "Elastically Deformable Models", *Computer Graphics*, Vol. 21, No. 4, pp. 205-214, July 1987.

[THAL91]   Thalmann, D., "Dynamic Simulation as a Tool for Three-dimensional Animation", in: Magnenat-Thalmann, N., Thalmann, D. (Eds.), *New Trends in Animation and Simulation,* John Wiley&Sons, pp. 257-272, 1991.

[TILO84]   Tilove, R., "A Null-Object Detection Algorithm for Constructive Solid Geometry", *Communications of the ACM*, Vol 27, No. 7, pp. 684-694, 1984.

[ZEIL93]   Zeiller, M., "Collision Detection for Objects Modelled by CSG", in: Connor, J., Hernandez, S., Murthy, T., Power, H. (Eds.), *Visualization and Intelligent Design in Engineering and Architecture*, Computational Mechanics Publications and Elsevier Science Publishers, pp. 165-180, 1993.

Interactive Graphics Design with Situated Agents

Ipke Wachsmuth and Yong Cao
Faculty of Technology, University of Bielefeld,
P.O. Box 100131, 33501 Bielefeld, Germany

1 Introduction

Along with sophisticated techniques for natural visualization and rapidly increasing power of modern graphics workstations, high-quality 3D graphics is becoming most attractive for design and simulation. One area in which this new media proves especially useful is architecture and interior design. For example, the visualization of an office room or a building prior to its physical realization could help a designer to obtain realistic impressions of a construction while it is evolving and give free way to imagination at the same time. It is one of the aims that, eventually, a designer is able to explore, and interact with, a manipulable environment without wasting physical matter and with the ability to readily change the immaterial model.

In this paper, a scenario for one of the projects in a new research program on "Artificial Intelligence and Computer Graphics" at the University of Bielefeld is described. In the VIENA project ("Virtual Environments and Agents") we want to provide a way of intelligent communication with a technical system for designing and generating 3D computer graphics[1]. To do so we apply new AI methods and techniques that build on ideas of situated communication and agents. We think of agents as mediating systems which cooperate with a user by exploiting internal scene information not readily available to the user. For instance, specialized agents can take on particular jobs with respect to geometry or material manipulation. To master communication with the user (designer), the mediating agents are informed about the actual scene as it is seen from the perspective of the user. By moving the camera it is possible to place the designer's eye in different perspectives. This way, the designer is situated in the developing scene and can issue commands from his or her current perspective.

In the following section, we focus on current efforts attempting to bridge the gap between high-quality visualization and interactive systems. We argue that interaction modalities include language and symbols as means of communication. In Section 3, we point out how situated communication could help in interactive graphics design. An important issue is that the system has to know about the spatial structure as it is perceived and experienced by the human user. In Section 4, we sketch various

[1]Research in the VIENA Project is partly supported by the Ministry of Science and Research of the federal state North-Rhine-Westphalia under grant no. IVA3-107 007 93. The authors are indebted to Norbert Siekmann, Britta Lenzmann, Majid Amanzadeh, Tanja Jörding, Stefan Fischer Rivera, and Karsten Otto for assisting during the research.

notions of agents that are currently found in literature, and we explain further the idea of intelligent mediation by way of situated agents. In Section 5, we give more details about our scenario and include a brief overview of a multi-agent system that we develop for the mediation of verbal instructions. The current state of our work is also described in this section. We conclude by arguing that artificial intelligence techniques can provide a communication link between humans and multimedia and also merge into more immersive environments.

2 Interactive Graphics Design

Not far ago, the output of conventional graphics systems was exclusively thought for viewing by a human user, that is, there was little possibility to interact with the displayed images. A major goal of current efforts is to bridge the gap between high-quality visualization systems which present output to a passive user, and interactive systems which are able to accept and display user interventions as soon as they are issued. In the ideal case, the user is immersed in a scene and is able to interact with objects in the scene. Examples have been given (e.g., Brooks 1987; Krüger 1993) how such a setting can be used for a three-dimensional pre-exploration of building construction-plans and interior design.

Accurate and natural visualization is important for obtaining a realistic impression of an evolving design. To give an idea, Figure 1 shows a synthetic scene of our lab interior which we use for exploring object arrangement, materials, and illumination. On the other hand, interactivity is an important asset to support a creative process in graphics design. Among most urgent research questions for virtual environments, an enhancement of software techniques for modeling has been called for (Bishop *et al.* 1992). In this context, modeling refers to the data structures which are used to record the scene information for a synthetic environment. These data structures describe the shape of the objects, their parts and physical properties, and how they interact with other objects in the environment and with the user.

While progress has still to be made before natural visualization can be used other than with largely precomputed models, the issue of modeling has its own difficulties and challenges. In manipulating a model, a designer needs to communicate with a technical device and may face crucial obstacles in the ease how the model is arranged and changed. A comfortable human-computer interface can keep the designer free from technical considerations such as planning of geometric detail. The user should be able to move through the model and change it interactively. At least part of physics should be in effect, for instance, it should not be possible for objects to pass through one another.

Some researchers have begun to use the data glove for rearranging objects in a scene (Böhm *et al.* 1992). To a human, it seems more natural to grasp a chair, lift it from the ground, and put it down at a new position, than to calculate an exact target position for changing the geometric model. The advantages of such a direct object handling – at least as it pertains to spatial manipulation – need not be mentioned. But changing the material (e.g., the color) or the size of an object would most likely involve a mental detour, for example, a "space menu" might have to be used.

We think that so-far available means of interaction, e.g., the data glove, are but one way to manipulate the arrangement of a scene. An alternative we explore in the VIENA project is to use verbally communicated changes which are put in effect by a mediating system. Interaction modalities would be further enhanced if designers could use *language* and *symbols* as a means of communication. Thus, we want to instruct the system to carry out changes where gestural manipulation is impossible or unnatural. Eventually, voice input and gestures could be used as parallel input modalities.

Fig. 1. A manipulable 3D object scene

3 Situated Communication

When using verbal interaction in geometry modeling, we need to be aware of the fact that the way we refer to details in a scene is "situated." For instance, it may depend on the objects themselves where we would speak of "front" and "back," e.g., a chair and a desk impose local reference structures on space, and they may have opposite "front" parts (Levelt 1986; *cf.* Figure 2). We may use still different notions of "front" and "back" – and also of "left" and "right" – when making reference to our current aspect of view. Thus, the system has to know about the spatial structure as it is perceived and experienced by the human user.

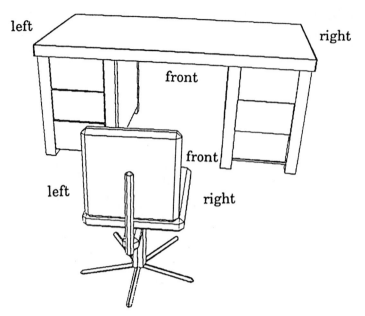

Fig. 2. Different use of particles 'left', 'front' and 'right' in a scene with a chair and a desk (after Levelt 1986)

To give another example, the three instructions, "move the table here, more to the front, more to the wall" incorporate different frames of spatial reference. In the first case, reference refers to the speaker's position while it is anchored externally in the second and the third case. The metrical structure does not only depend on geometry but also, for example, on how far one could reach from a position. Thus the system – as the human – has first to find out which frame of reference is relevant, secondly, in which direction the table is to be moved, and thirdly, how far. It should not be possible to move an object further than permitted by a physical boundary. When the table is moved, the things on it should move with it (Fig. 3).

When a deictic reference is involved ("here"), the point of anchoring a reference frame depends on the current position of the speaker which could be identified with the camera position in a virtual environment (Fig. 4). In Fig. 4, 5, and 6 we show an observer of the scene to indicate the position of the camera. The current position of the observer (camera) can help to resolve ambiguity in instructions; e.g., "put the chair in front of the table" can be interpreted in different ways depending on the speaker's position (Fig. 5). Finally, the environment is modified by the objects present in that an object can impose its own reference scheme. For example, the phrase "in front of" is most likely interpreted in different ways – by a human, and should be so by the system – in the scenes shown in Fig. 5 and 6.

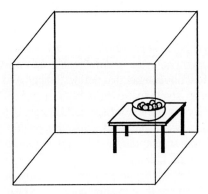 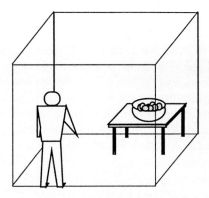

Fig. 3. "Move the table to the front!"
(What happens to the bowl?)

Fig. 4. "Move the table here!" (Deictic
reference includes speaker's position)

We want to exploit findings from cognitive research to deal with these topics. For instance, object schemata have been proposed (Lang 1989) that describe how space is modified by the objects present. The human visual-perceptive system gives rise to spatial relations between object and the observer's body (Bryant 1991) which could be mapped onto an implicit camera. Different frames of reference were identified: (1) the egocentric frame, defined by the three body axes head/foot, front/back, and left/right; (2) the allocentric frame, defined by orthogonal axes independent of the observer. Such axes can be anchored in a prominent landmark in the environment or be oriented according to global directions (Cao 1993). In gravity, head/foot is identified with top/down when the observer is in upright position. Axes are experienced differently in other environments, e.g., in zero gravity (Friederici 1989).

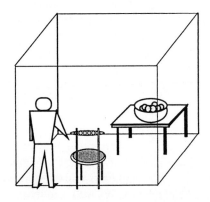 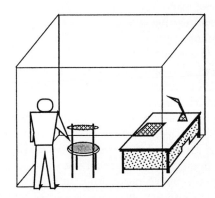

Fig. 5. "Put the chair in front of the table!"
(Modification of space by speaker's position)

Fig. 6. "Put the chair in front of the desk!"
(Modification of space by objects present)

4 Agents

One theme in the mentioned research agenda (Bishop *et al.* 1992) is the development of knowledge-based agents for human-computer interfaces. An agent is an entity consisting of a structural definition, a set of functional units that defines its behavior repertoire, and some means for selecting and sequencing (possibly concurrent) behaviors (Zeltzer 1991). In our approach, we use a number of specialized agents to conceptualize and realize a system interfacing between verbal user instructions and a technical system for modeling/rendering. Before we explain how we go about this, we briefly sketch agent notions found in the current literature.

Ideas of a general intelligent agent that uses knowledge to perform actions in the service of goals have been researched in AI for more than twenty years (*cf.* Newell 1981). A novel perspective was taken by Minsky (1986) in explaining intelligence as a combination of many simple processes he refers to as agents. Recent attempts to develop more complex knowledge-based systems have revealed shortcomings of centralized, single-agent architectures and have acted as a springboard for research in Distributed AI (Adler *et al.* 1992).

Various models and notions of agents are currently found in diverse literature in the fields of autonomous and distributed systems (Meinkoehn and Knoll 1993), language-action systems (Chapman 1991), and graphics animation (Badler *et al.* 1991). Of interest, in our context, is work on "interface agents" (Laurel 1990; Maes and Kozierok 1993) which typically use knowledge about tasks, habits, preferences of their users to perform actions on their behalf. Such an idea has been adopted in visions of future user interfaces, for instance, in the Japanese Friend21 project and in the Newton project of Apple (*cf.* Marcus 1993).

On the other hand, more recent work in Distributed AI incorporates approaches for "cooperating agents" that work together in achieving an overall task. Multi-agent systems as discussed in (Steiner *et al.* 1990) emphasize the aspect of task-related cooperation of independent (autonomous) systems. Each agent is ascribed a basic functionality (it can solve certain problems), a cooperative head (for participating in a cooperation with other agents), and communication abilities (by way of accessing communication channels to other agents).

In particular, the idea of "situated agents" which can gain and exploit information from an actual situation is of interest to us. A situated agent integrates aspects of perception, action, and communication in one system to succeed in a situation without having a complete model of it (Brooks 1991). The term "situatedness" refers to the ability of an intelligent system to exploit the actual situation, to the extent possible, as a source of information in perceiving and manipulating its environment and communicating with cooperating partners.[2]

In our work, we conceive a situated agent as an "intelligent mediator." Such an agent – which may consist of several subagents – communicates and cooperates with a human user in an overlapping perceptual situation. The key idea is to have an

---

[2]Situated communication is a focus theme in a newly established special research unit at the University of Bielefeld (SFB 360, "Situated Artificial Communicators").

agent inspect the internal description of a scene that the user can experience by eye inspection, so both of them – agent and user – can communicate about scene details from their "point of view." But whereas the user is likely to have a qualitative grasp of the scene, the agent has knowledge of exact object locations, colorings, etc. Qualitative communications of the user to change scene details will have to be evaluated by the agent(s) so as to produce appropriate quantitative changes in the scene description. The altered scene description is then visualized for the user. We refer to this overall process – which will be explained in more detail below – as "intelligent mediation."

5 Agent-mediated user interaction in VIENA

In an example application of interior design, the overall goal of the VIENA Project is to enable and establish an intelligent communication with a technical device for the interactive design and exploration of 3D computer graphics. Our specific scenario is as follows: In a modeling session, the designer keeps track of the evolving design by viewing it in a 3D display setting. The designer can change the model by communicating with the system via simple verbal instructions (e.g., "move the table more to the front"). The system offers a view of a resulting scene where "more" is interpreted on the basis of a default value. The offer can be changed in further interaction ("still more", "not that far"). In other words, computing the semantics of an instruction is a situated activity which leads to a scene modification, and the user can negotiate the semantics of an instruction.

To realize the mediation of verbal instructions, we have constructed a multi-agent system. As an 'agency' this system communicates with the human user (designer) to receive and process verbal instructions. Internally, agents cooperate with each other to realize the user's instructions with respect to the current situation. We conceive agents as systems with restricted ability they bring to bear with respect to a given instruction. Some agents carry out spatial inferences to meet the expectations of the human user. In doing so, agents exploit the current situation to the maximum extent possible. By using information about the most previous manipulations, possible ambiguity in an instruction can often be resolved. Other agents know how to find out current locations and materials of objects, still others about how to change a color or an illumination ("darker!"), etc. The more competent, by agent mediation, the system becomes, the more successful the designer's instructions can be interpreted and executed.

Overall System Description

In this subsection we give a brief overview of the VIENA system. Our current working environment includes a Silicon Graphics Indigo ELAN R4000 for the main project demonstrator. This machine supports the real-time hardware shading we make use of for fast scene visualization. Currently, we use SOFTIMAGE for scene modeling and rendering. Besides this, several Sun SPARC stations are available for algorithm and model development. These are also the site for some of the agents, as we make use of distributed processing.

We have specified a client-server architecture were agents are autonomous processes which can send and receive messages by interprocess communication. For experimental implementation, we use two – exchangeable – realizations: (a) communication files in the Unix Network File System; (b) a low-level but fast realization with communication via sockets. We are also exploring higher-level protocols based on Remote Procedure Call for an improved realization of the specified communication system.

Our system acts as an interface between a human user and a 3D graphics modeler/ renderer (*cf.* Figure 7). The user communicates changes to the system by way of verbal instructions. A Parser agent translates a user instruction to a structured representation which outputs to the mediating agents. Parser asks back if an incomplete instruction cannot be resolved by the agents themselves (or if it cannot be parsed). The user observes changes from the Viewing graphical output medium.

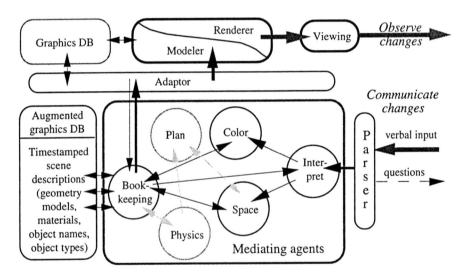

Fig. 7. Evolving architecture of the VIENA system: A multi-agent system mediates qualitative verbal instructions by translating them to quantitative commands that are used to update the visualization scene model (further explanation in text).

The core system is designed to be portable, hence a special adaptor unit converts data back and forth between the mediating agents and the loosely coupled graphics system. The adaptor also establishes a 'pipeline' to the modeler/renderer unit so that modified scene data can be visualized instantaneously. The graphics database is mirrored in the mediating system in an augmented graphics database which is local to a Bookkeeping agent. All data about the scene can only be modified via the Book-keeping agent. Besides the current scene description, the augmented database holds information about previous scenes to be exploited in situated communication.

A major part of our work has concentrated on the technical environment in which mediating agents can come to bear. We have experimental implementations for an Adaptor unit (specific to the SOFTIMAGE modeler/renderer), a Parser unit, and an augmented graphics database (*cf.* Fig. 7). Based on this evolving working environment, we have begun to specify and to implement agents for intelligent mediating. We have worked on two types of changes so far, spatial and material, which are dealt with by the "Space" and the "Color" agent.

Adaptor

The Adaptor must translate data from SOFTIMAGE's database to an augmented database and filter modified data to the renderer. In our experimental implementation we manipulate 3D scene objects by way of channels in the SOFTIMAGE (version 2.6.2) motion environment. At present, there are 1000 channels available where each channel is mapped exactly onto one pre-defined feature. In this way, about 80 objects can be controlled. The solution with SOFTIMAGE's channel driver interface is limited in that we must prepare for each object which is to be controlled interactively. For this reason, we have also started to use the custom script language provided with the SOFTIMAGE actor environment. Custom scripts provide another means of interfacing user-defined functions with SOFTIMAGE. Using the Developer Kit, all types of scene data can be read and modified by way of appropriate script commands.

Augmented database/Bookkeeper

The modeler/renderer has its own data structures in a graphics database which holds information necessary for visualization. These data structures need to be augmented to be suitable for intelligent mediation. For instance, 'non-visualizable' (type) information is added that enables the system to distinguish between movable and non-movable scene objects, or to make reference to intrinsic perceptive features of scene objects. Also, previous features of a changed scene model are kept for evaluating elliptic discourse ("a little more"). To support such situated communication, data structures in the augmented database accomodate the scene history where each scene is tagged with a timestamp. Only the Bookkeeping agent, acting as a "gate keeper," is authorized to access and modify the augmented database (*cf.* Figure 7). When piping a new scene for visualization, the augmented graphics database is updated accordingly. When a session is completed and quit, the current scene description is transferred to the SOFTIMAGE graphics database while the augmented database is abandoned.

Parser

While the Adaptor unit constitutes an interface between the agent system and the visualization, the parser unit interfaces between verbal input and the mediating agent system. In our setting we think it adequate that user input is kept to the minimum significant information. Thus we are not trying to process very complex sentential structures. However, the system should be able to process discourse that negotiates the semantics of instructions. That is, if the effect of an instruction does not satisfy the user's expectations, corrective statements need to be analyzed based on previous discourse. Our parser (PARSY) translates simple qualitative English instructions to structured (deep-level) representations which output to an Interpret agent. The structured representation PARSY constructs for an instruction as "move the table to the right") contains an operator ("move"), an objectname ("table"), a degree (" ") as well as a location ("right") or color specification. PARSY is also able to resolve simple ellipses such as "a little less". In Figure 8, a sample discourse and generated parser outputs are shown.

```
saturn%parsy
PARSY> move the table to the right
       move(obj=table, deg=, loc=right)
PARSY> a little less
       modify(obj=table, deg=little, loc=negativ)
PARSY> make the chair red
       make(obj=chair, deg=, col=red)
PARSY> a little more
       modify(obj=chair, deg=little, col=positiv)
PARSY> move the chair
       You must enter a direction.
PARSY> left
       move(obj=chair, deg=, loc=left)
PARSY>
```

Fig. 8. Input and internal output (bold face) of the parser PARSY

Within a session discourse, an elliptic phrase ("a little less") will be represented as a modification of the previous instruction. (A modify-command will make agents compare the most current scene model and the previous one by way of time-stamped entries in the augmented graphics database; see below.) When analyzing an incomplete instruction, PARSY may prompt the user for further input (*cf.* Figure 8). Again, consecutive input is processed in discourse.

Interpret agent

The structured representation of a verbal instruction is further elaborated by an Interpret agent which transmits commands to specialized agents for evaluating semantics. If an instruction refers to a previous one (e.g., "a little less" following "move the table to the right"), the system must exploit the session history to compute the semantics. To this end, the Interpret agent cooperates with the Bookkeeping agent to access the augmented database so the situated communication can successfully arrive at offering a new resulting scene. At present, the Interpret agent serves as a router which decides to which following agent (Space or Color) an instruction is issued. We take into account that certain instructions can be posted to several agents, e.g., "show the chair better" could be taken on by both the Color and the Space agent and result in an enhancement of the color of the chair, as well as in a move of the camera to change the aspect from which the scene is viewed.

Space agent

The Space agent has the following responsibilities: (1) to identify mentioned objects and (2) to determine where and how an object will be moved – in relation to other objects and avoiding collisions – in order to satisfy a user input. In the simple cases we have considered so far, only the target scene description is transferred for visualization. If a more complex scene modification is to take place, e.g., rearranging a collection of objects, a Plan agent – not yet realized – could become active and cooperate with other agents to generate a series of images.

The Space agent takes structured outputs from Parser, resembling qualitative instructions, and processes them to quantitative, absolute geometry data changes (i.e., translations in approriate coordinates). The system is able to take into account all situational data of a current scene, including previous discourse. Thus, ambiguity in instructions can be greatly reduced. If a system response does not meet the user's expectations, a follow-up instruction can build on the previous response.

To process a representation like **move(obj=table, deg=, loc=right)**, the Bookkeeping agent determines first which object named "table" is addressed by the instruction, and then reads the geometry data of this object to the Space agent. If more than one object is named "table", the "table" object with the most current time stamp is selected, or further input is requested. The Space agent finds out which location is "right" in the current situation, how far "right" can range, and which moderate degree of a "right" move is offered in response to the command. More precisely, the space agent
- decides which is the current reference frame
- takes account of objects in the target area to avoid collisions
- calculates an according translation vector

The translation vector also depends on the size of the object to be moved (that is, a table undergoes a larger move that a bowl). The Adaptor transfers the change of "table's" geometry data to the renderer, and the Bookkeeper updates the augmented database accordingly. To deal with a "modify" instruction, Bookkeeper accesses according entries in the augmented database and finds out the last change. A new change is inferred based on the last recorded change and the current change command.

Further work

Other agents will incrementally enhance the system's ability for mediating verbal instructions. We have started to work on a Color agent which acts in a similar fashion as the Space agent: a qualitative instruction is processed to quantitative material data changes (e.g., changings of rgb-values of objects or lights). We also consider conceptualizing subagents of an agent to take on special tasks. For instance, we work on a subagent for "Space" to determine which objects are *currently* on an object to be moved so they move with it (e.g., a bowl on a table). The general idea is that each agent is just "smart" enough to meet its special responsibility. By this, modular system development is supported.

6 Summary and Outlook

In this paper we have described how interaction modalities in the design and exploration of 3D computer graphics can be enhanced by "intelligent" (symbolic) communication. In the VIENA project, we use an example application of interior design to explore how verbally communicated changes of the scene can be put in effect by a mediating system. Our conceptualization of the mediating system involves a number of specialized subsystems – agents – which cooperate with the designer by exploiting internal scene descriptions.

An important part in this mediation is that agents transfer qualitative descriptions of scene changes to quantitative internal commands which can be processed by the graphics system. We also provide ways to deal with elliptic discourse (i.e., communications which refer back to previous ones) to make verbal interaction more natural. Finally, "situated" communication makes it possible for the user to issue commands from changing perspectives and by incorporating egocentric reference frames (like "left/right").

Besides using agent ideas as helpful metaphors for human-computer-interaction, we have also found them useful for conceiving the architecture of the interface software in a modular way, and independent of a particular programming environment. That is, special-purpose machinery can be included in the designer's workplace as necessary.

Interactivity is an important asset to support a creative process in graphics design. The so-far available means of interaction, e.g., the data glove, are but one way to manipulate the arrangement of a scene. Interaction modalities are further enhanced when designers can use language and symbolic qualities as input. On the other hand, our work on intelligent mediation is not restricted to solely verbal interaction; it seems also relevant for direct (gestural) manipulation. For instance, when a table is moved by grasping it with a data glove, the things on it could move with it by agent mediation as indicated above.

To conclude, we think that, in general, techniques from artificial intelligence can provide a more comfortable communication link between humans and multimedia. Eventually, we see the use of voice input and gestures as parallel input modalities. While we do not have equipment to exploit the usefulness of our work in a more immersive environment (e.g., with head-mounted display or a boom), we think it can be incorporated in such a setting at a later time.

References

Adler, M., Durfee, E., Huhns, M., Punch, W., and Simoudis, E. (1992). AAAI workshop on cooperation among heterogeneous intelligent agents. *AI magazine 13*(2), 39-42.

Badler, N.I., Webber, B.L., Kalita, J., and Esakov, J. (1991). Animations from Instructions. In N.I. Badler, B.A. Barsky and D. Zeltzer (eds.): *Making Them Move - Mechanics, Control, and Animation of Articulated Figures* (pp. 51-93). San Mateo (Cal.): Morgan Kaufmann.

Bishop, G., Bricken, W., Brooks, F., Brown, M., Burbeck, C., Durlach, N., Ellis, S., Fuchs, H., Green, M., Lackner, J., McNeill, M., Moshell, M., Pausch, R., Robinett, W., Srinivasan, M., Sutherland, I., Urban, D., and Wenzel, E. (1992). Research Directions in Virtual Environments: Report of an NSF Invitational Workshop (March 23-24, 1992, University of North Carolina at Chapel Hill). *Computer Graphics 26*(3), 153-177.

Böhm, K., Hübner, W. and Väänänen, K. (1992). GIVEN: Gesture driven interactions in virtual environments: A toolkit approach to 3D interactions. *Proc. Conf. Interface to Real and Virtual Worlds* (Montpellier, France, March 1992).

Brooks, F. (1987). Walkthrough – A Dynamic Graphics System for Simulating Virtual Buildings. *Proc. of ACM Workshop on 3D Graphics* (Chapel Hill, Oct. 1987), 9-21.

Brooks, R.A. (1991). Intelligence without reason. *Proceedings IJCAI-91*, 569-595.

Bryant, D.J. (1991). *Perceptual Characteristics of Mental Spatial Models* (Dissertation). Stanford University: Dept. of Psychology.

Cao, Y. (1993). *Zur Darstellung und Verarbeitung von Wissen über Himmelsrichtungen – Geometrische und Kognitionswissenschaftliche Aspekte* (Dissertation, University of Hamburg/Dept. of Computer Science). Sankt Augustin: Infix (DISKI-33).

Chapman, D. (1991). *Vision, Instruction, and Action.* Cambridge (MA): MIT Press.

Friederici, A.D. (1989). Raumreferenz unter extremen perzeptuellen Bedingungen: Perzeption, Repräsentation und sprachliche Abbildung. In Ch. Habel, M. Herweg and K. Rehkämper (eds.): *Raumkonzepte in Verstehensprozessen.* Tübingen: Niemeyer.

Krüger, W. (1993). Virtual Reality – Anwendungen in Wissenschaft, Technik und Medizin. *it – Sonderheft "Multi Media",* April 1993.

Lang, E. (1989). Objektschemata und räumliche Konfiguration. In Ch. Habel, M. Herweg and K. Rehkämper (Hrsg.): *Raumkonzepte in Verstehensprozessen* (pp. 150-173). Tübingen: Niemeyer.

Laurel, B. (1990). Interface agents: Metaphors with character. In B. Laurel (ed.) (1990): *The art of human-computer interface design.* Addison-Wesley.

Levelt, W. (1986). Zur sprachlichen Abbildung des Raumes: Deiktische und intrinsische Perspektive. In H.-G. Bosshardt (Hrsg.): *Perspektiven auf Sprache* (S. 187-211). Berlin: DeGruyter.

Maes, P. and Kozierok, R. (1993). Learning interface agents. Proceedings of the Eleventh National Conference on Artificial Intelligence (AAAI-93) (pp. 459-465). Menlo Park: AAAI Press/The MIT Press.

Marcus, A. (1993). Future directions in advanced user interface design. In Thalmann, N.M. and Thalmann, D. (eds.): *Communicating with virtual worlds* (pp. 2-13). New York: Springer-Verlag.

Meinkoehn, J. and Knoll, A. (1993). Recent results in organization and performance evaluation for large sensor networks. *Int. Conf. on Intelligent Autonomous Systems (IAS-3),* Pittsburgh.

Minsky, M.L. (1986). *The society of mind.* New York: Simon and Schuster, Inc.

Steiner, D., Mahling, D., and Haugeneder, H. (1990). Human Computer Cooperative Work. In M. Huhns (ed.). *Proc. of the 10th International Workshop on Distributed Artificial Intelligence.* MCC Technical Report No. ACT-AI-355-90.

Newell, A. (1981). The knowledge level (Presidential address, AAAI-80). *AI magazine 2*(2), 1-20.

Zeltzer, D. (1991). Task-level graphical simulation: Abstraction, representation, and control. In N.I. Badler, B.A. Barsky, and D. Zeltzer (eds.): *Making Them Move - Mechanics, Control, and Animation of Articulated Figures* (pp.3-33). San Mateo (Cal.): Morgan Kaufmann.

Assembly Planning Using Symbolic Spatial Relationships

R. Gutsche, F. Röhrdanz and F. M. Wahl
Institute for Robotics and Computer Control, Technical University of Braunschweig
Hamburger Str. 267, D-38114 Braunschweig, Germany

Abstract

After a short overview about different assembly planning techniques, our assembly planning system working with symbolic spatial relationships is presented. The spatial relations are used to define an assembly graph and to deduce automatically the homogeneous transformations between the parts of the assembly from symbolic information. The local depart space efficiently computed by symbolic relations delivers the basis for an estimation of a global translational depart vector. In addition, we have developed a concept of arbitrary assembly hierarchies which is integrated into the well-known cut-set method of the assembly graph and into the AND/OR-graph representation.

1   Introduction

Assembly planning and the subsequent execution of the generated plans by robots will be one of the key technologies of a modern and flexible manufacturing process. The choice of an assembly sequence can drastically affect the efficiency of the assembly process. For example, one sequence may require less fixturing, less changing of tools, and include simpler and more reliable operations than other. Therefore early consideration of assembly sequences is important for productivity, quality control, flexibility, and market responsiveness. During the last years several techniques dealing with mechanical assembly planning were published. An overview can be found in [Mello91a].

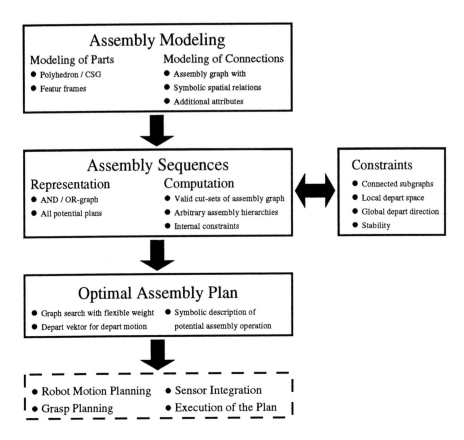

Figure 1: Concept of our assembly planning system

Assembly planning is a computational complex task because many constraints have to be taken into account, e.g. *stability* of the created subassemblies, *geometric feasibility* and *mechanical feasibility* of the assembly process of the concerned subassemblies (see [Mello89] for more details). In this paper we only take into account constraints which are caused by the assembly itself. These constraints are called *internal constraints*. Examples for internal constraints are: the existence of a collision free path for an assembly operation, the stability of an assembly, the accessibility of fasteners etc. In addition to internal constraints a valid assembly sequence has to satisfy constraints which also depend on the devices available to execute the assembly. These *external constraints* are the shape of the robot workspace, the maximal payload, the kind of gripper and so on.

Assume, no internal or external forces are present; the reverse of a valid disassembly sequence yields a valid assembly sequence. Therefore valid assembly sequences can be found by a backward approach. In this case the problem of generating assembly sequences is transformed into the problem of generating disassembly sequences. This transformation leads to a decomposition approach in which the problem of disassembling an assembly is decomposed into distinct subproblems each being the disassembly of the created subassemblies.

This assembly by disassembly approach is used in our assembly planning system. Some ideas of our system are similar to the system introduced in [Mello89]. But in addition, we use a symbolic description of the assembly to automatically compute the numerical values of the homogeneous transformations between the parts. Consequently it isn't necessary to specify manually homogeneous transformations between components.

After a brief explanation of the assembly planning problem in section 2, known assembly planning techniques are outlined in section 3. Figure 1 illustrates the architecture of our assembly planning system. First of all, the complete assembly consisting of the single parts and the connections between them is modeled. One key method for this step are symbolic spatial relationships, explained in section 4. This symbolic description is used by our cycle finder to automatically compute the homogeneous transformations between the different parts. In section 5 the internal representation of an assembly in our planning system is explained. It consists of the assembly graph augmented by the definition of physical contacts. In addition the optional declaration of subassembly hierarchies and stability is described.

After the modeling of the assembly, all potential assembly sequences are computed (figure 1). The generation of valid cut-sets inside the assembly graph and the computation of the corresponding AND/OR-graph are discussed in section 6. For this purpose, additional constraints are taken into account. Finally, the optimal assembly plan is computed, using a graph search with a flexible weight function (section 6.2).

The resulting output consisting of a symbolic and numerical description of the necessary operations can be used for further planning steps. These additional steps, which are not treated in this paper, take into account e.g. robot motion planning and grasp planning (figure 1). Finally, we indicate further research directions.

2 The Assembly Planning Problem

Figure 2 shows an arbitrary arrangement of the single components of one of our test assemblies. The corresponding exploded view of the assembled part is sketched in figure 3. The key problem in assembly planning is the following: Find a sequence of valid assembly/disassembly operations to transfer the initial state (e.g. figure 2) to the goal state which is the completed assembly.

If a first assembly operation corresponds to the insertion of Pin2 into the hole of Side2 (figure 3), the whole assembly can't be completed because the insertion of Bolt2 will be blocked by Pin2. A valid assembly sequence specifies

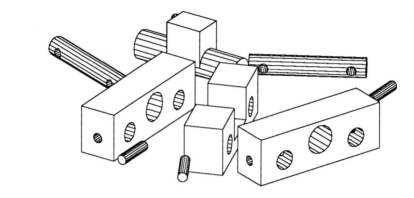

Figure 2: Components of test assembly

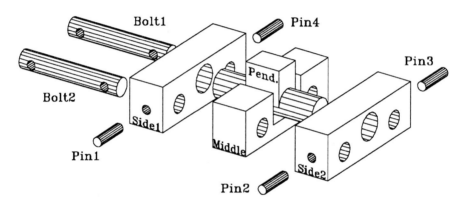

Figure 3: Exploded view of test assembly

the order of the necessary mating tasks which yield the completely assembled product.

To reduce the computational cost, most of the assembly planning systems including our own planner make use of sequential and monotone planning only. A plan is *sequential* if it can be executed by one active device at any time instant, such as a one-handed robot. Consequently, at any instant only one set of parts (those held by the robot) will be in motion and parts within this set will remain in fixed positions relative to each other. Thus, each operation moves a set of parts as a unit from one position to another. A plan is *monotone* if no operation ever separates any pair of parts or part sets which were already in their goal position relative to each other and every operation leaves all moved parts in their goal positions relative to at least one unmoved part [Mello91b].

One main problem in assembly planning is the computation of a collision free path to join two subassemblies[1]. First of all, the two subassemblies have to be *local free*, i.e. there exists an incremental motion which separates the concerned physical contacts. If the subassemblies are local free, a *global free* depart motion has to exist which separates the two subassemblies completely from each other. In general, arbitrary depart motions can be taken into account, but in the actual version of our assembly planning system described here, we determine translational depart motions only.

If two subassemblies are both local and global free, additional constraints of the manufacturing process mentioned above can be taken into account.

3   Known Assembly Planning Techniques

The automatic generation of assembly plans can be divided into two different categories. One way is to design a system with user interaction to gain knowledge about an assembly from a production engineer. On the other hand a system without user interaction can be built. In this case a precise representation of the assembly is necessary to automatically generate all valid assembly sequences.

In this section these two different techniques are outlined on the basis of three planning systems which are known from literature. All presented methods assume, that the parts to be assembled are rigid.

3.1   Question/Answer Systems

In Bourjault's system [Bourjault87] an assembly is described by a graph (*liaison diagram*). The nodes of this graph represent parts of the assembly and the edges between these nodes correspond to certain user defined relations. These relations, called *liaisons*, generally correspond to physical contacts between parts. Figure 4 shows the sectional drawing of an assembly example which is adopted from Bourjault. It is a plastic "throw-away" ball-point pen consisting of six parts[2]. The liaison diagram for the assembly is shown in figure 5.

Starting from the disassembled state Bourjault's system generates yes/no-questions. The questions are of two general forms (the symbol "L_i" is read "the liaison numbered i"):

Q1) Is it true that L_i cannot be done after L_j and L_k have been done?

Q2) Is it true that L_i cannot be done if L_j and L_k are still undone?

---

[1]For the rest of the paper a subassembly will be a single component or an assembly consisting of several parts.

[2]For the planning process the ink is assumed to be a rigid body and it is shown in approximate shape when it is injected into the tube.

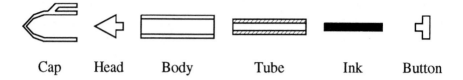

Figure 4: Sectional drawing of the ball-point pen assembly

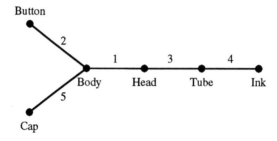

Figure 5: Liaison diagram of the ball-point pen assembly

To minimize the number of questions, rules like the superset and subset rules are applied which make heavy use of previously answered questions to deduce answers to other questions. The system records the answers and generates an implicit representation of all valid liaison sequences by precedence rules characterized as forbidden states. The assembly sequences are presented as branches of an inverted tree with the initial disassembled state (no liaison established) at the top rank.

Using Bourjault's method numerous questions have to be answered by the system user. Individual questions can be difficult to answer. The number of questions (Q) depends on the topology of the assembly and on the number of liaisons (l). In [Fazio+87] the following bounds have been given:

$$l * 2^l > Q \geq 2 * (l^2 + l)$$

For simple assemblies with a small number of liaisons this approach has the advantage that it exploits the intuitive understanding of parts relations and feasibility of operations of a human expert answering the questions. Evaluating the answers avoids exhaustive and complex computations to determine all assembly sequences by geometric reasoning. But for complex assemblies it may be difficult to guarantee the correctness of the answers and to answer the number of questions which can increase exponentially.

Considering the simple ball-point pen assembly in figure 4 the user has to answer 64 questions; 12 liaison sequences are found.

De Fazio and Whitney have modified Bourjault's method to analyze assemblies with a greatly increased number of parts [Fazio+87]. The salient difference between the two methods is the form and the number of questions. Analogous to Bourjault's technique, the liaison diagram of the assembly is generated in the first step. The start state corresponds to the completely disassembled part. Instead of yes/no-questions they use questions which require geometric reasoning and anticipation by the user. For every liaison in the liaison diagram the user has to answer the following two questions:

Q1) What liaisons must be done prior to doing L_i?

Q2) What liaisons must be left to be done after doing L_i?

The answers have to be expressed in the form of a precedence relationship between liaisons or between logical combinations of liaisons, e.g. (the symbol "→" is read as "must precede"):

A1) $L_j \vee (L_k \wedge L_m) \rightarrow L_i$

A2) $L_i \rightarrow (L_j \wedge L_k)$

For the ball-point pen assembly ten questions are required. De Fazio and Whitney generate the corresponding assembly sequences directly from the answers by forward chaining through the relations, starting with liaisons which have no precedents. Instead of a tree representation for all valid plans they use a compact directed graph representation (*diamond diagram*) in which each assembly state is shown only once.

The directed graph for all assembly sequences of the ball-point pen assembly is shown in figure 6. The nodes correspond to the assembly states during the assembly process. At the 0th rank the initial, i.e. disassembled, state is represented and the goal state, i.e. the completely assembled product, corresponds to the 5th rank. Black cells indicate completed liaisons and an arc between states represents a physically possible assembly operation. Each sequence is a path which starts at the top and ends at the bottom of the diagram. Considering the liaison diagram in figure 5, only one liaison is established in each assembly step. Therefore the directed graph of all feasible assembly operations consists of 5 ranks.

Although only the half number of questions is necessary, the reduction of the number of questions is accompanied by an increase of difficulty to answer each question. The liaisons in the assembly representation are user defined and the user has to consider which and how many liaisons are to be added in the liaison diagram. A wrong or an incomplete liaison specification can lead to wrong assembly sequences. But the implicit representation of all assembly sequences by precedence relationships facilitates to impose external constraints if they can be expressed in logical or even tabular form.

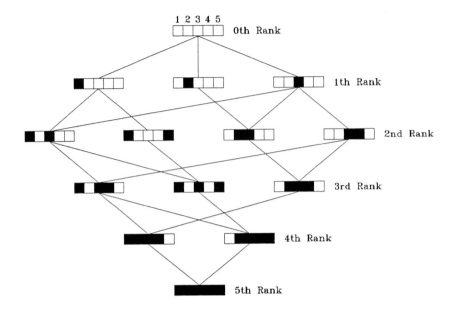

Figure 6: Directed graph for all valid assembly sequences of the ball-point pen assembly (cell numbering corresponds to arc labeling of figure 5)

3.2 The approach by Homem de Mello and Sanderson

Homem de Mello and Sanderson have developed an assembly planning system which generates assembly sequences without any user interaction. For the automatic generation of all assembly sequences a pure geometric description of the product is not sufficient. Therefore they use a relational model for the assembly representation which incorporates contact geometry and connection information at one level of representation and complete part geometry at a second level. The class of represented assemblies is restricted to assemblies with special types of contacts and attachments. A more detailed description of this relational model can be found in [Mello89].

The problem of generating assembly sequences is transformed into the problem of generating disassembly sequences. This decomposition approach assumes, that the reverse of a feasible assembly operation is a feasible disassembly operation. In this disassembly problem Homem de Mello and Sanderson take into account monotone and sequential planning only. Therefore each disassembly operation splits one assembly into two subassemblies, maintaining all contacts between the parts in either of the subassemblies. To determine valid disassembly sequences the relational model is transformed into the graph of connections wherein nodes represent the assembly components and edges correspond to pairs of parts which have at least one physical contact in the assembled state. In this graph each edge corresponds to a physical

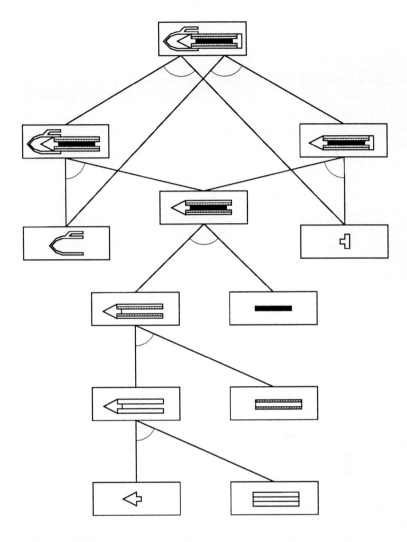

Figure 7: AND/OR-Graph representation of two valid assembly sequences for the ball-point pen assembly

contact and therefore it is different from the liaison diagram proposed by Bourjault.

The decompositions of an assembly are found by generating cut-sets of the assembly's graph of connections. A cut corresponds to a feasible disassembly operation if several constraints are satisfied. In [Mello89] a correct and complete algorithm is shown which takes the relational description of an assembly as input and returns all feasible decompositions of that assembly. In this procedure only internal constraints like the geometric feasibility, mechanical feasibility and stability of the subassemblies are taken into account; but no external constraints are considered which depend e.g. on the devices available to execute the assembly.

Homem de Mello and Sanderson choose an explicit representation of all valid assembly sequences, using an AND/OR-Graph. Each feasible decomposition corresponds to a hyperarc in the AND/OR-Graph. Each hyperarc connects the node corresponding to the assembly and the two nodes corresponding to the two subassemblies. Figure 7 shows an AND/OR-Graph for the ball-point pen assembly. For clearness only 2 of all 12 assembly sequences are depicted.

3.3   Motivation for our own assembly planning system

Bourjault's method has shown, that an interactive planning system requires answering a big number of questions. A reduction in question count is accompanied by an increase in the difficulty of answering the questions. This can lead to wrong answers and therefore to incorrect assembly sequences.

For these reasons we have developed a system with minimal user interaction. This approach requires a precise model of the assembly instead of a simple representation like the liaison diagram of Bourjault. We have chosen a similar two-level assembly representation like Homem de Mello and Sanderson (section 3.2). This precise description of the assembly requires a careful modeling of the product by the user which can be tedious and time consuming. Thus, in contrast to the approach by Homem de Mello and Sanderson, we are using symbolic spatial relationships.

In [Mello91b, chapter 6] an overview of possible implicit and explicit representations of assembly sequences can be found. The choice of an appropriate representation depends on the type of application. An AND/OR-Graph constitutes a compact representation of all feasible assembly sequences and time dependencies and independencies between assembly tasks can be represented. It provides a useful tool for the selection of the best assembly plan, recovery from execution errors, or opportunistic scheduling. For these reasons we have chosen an AND/OR-Graph for the representation of all assembly sequences in our planning system like Homem de Mello and Sanderson.

Before our assembly planning system will be described in detail we will introduce symbolic spatial relationships in the following. Symbolic spatial relationships are one key element for our assembly planning system.

4   Symbolic Spatial Relationships

The principle of symbolic spatial relationships bases on [Poppelstone79] and can be divided into the modeling of abstract assemblies and the generation of homogeneous transformations between the components using a cycle finder.

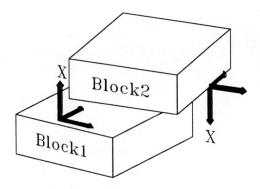

Figure 8: Against relation between 2 blocks

To improve the cycle finder published in [Poppelstone79], we have integrated some powerful new features (section 4.2).

4.1 Abstract modeling of assemblies

An abstract assembly consists of m bodiless parts. Each part O_i ($1 \leq i \leq m$) is defined by one object base frame OB_i and a number of n_i feature frames $OF_{i,j}$ ($1 \leq j \leq n_i$). Each $OF_{i,j}$ corresponds to one feature type ($f\_type(OF_{i,j}) \in \{face, shaft, hole, edge\}$) and is defined by a homogeneous transformation $^{OB_i}\mathbf{T}_{OF_{i,j}}$ relative to OB_i. These feature types are infinite, e.g. a *face* corresponds to a mathematical plane. Thus, the objects have no body and they are defined by a set of rigid, numerically given feature frames.

A set of symbolic spatial relations $R(OF_{i,j}, OF_{k,l})$, each defined between two features of different objects O_i and O_k ($i \neq k$), is used to model the abstract assembly. The type of these relations $r\_type(R(,))$ corresponds to one of $\{against, fits, coplanar, aligned, fix\}$ and describes the geometrical degrees of freedom between $OF_{i,j}$ and $OF_{k,l}$.

Thus, e.g. $R(OF_{i,j}, OF_{k,l}) = against$ means, that the y- and z-axes of the frames $OF_{i,j}$ and $OF_{k,l}$ lie in the same mathematical plane and the x-axes have opposite directions. Consequently three degrees of freedom – two translational and one rotational – remain between these two feature frames, if only this relation is taken into account. Figure 8 illustrates such an *against* relation between the top of Block1 and the bottom of Block2. Block2 can only be translated in the contact plane and/or rotated around the normal vector of the contact plane to keep the physical contact to Block1.

The only difference between *coplanar* and *against* is the different direction of the x-axis; they are pointing in the same direction. Relation *fits/aligned* means, that the x-axes of $OF_{i,j}$ and $OF_{k,l}$ lie on the same line and have the opposite/same direction. Thus one translational and one rotational degree of freedom remain along the common line. The relation *fix* corresponds to a

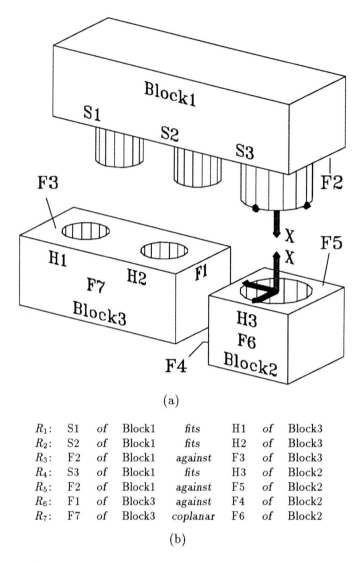

(a)

R_1:	S1	of	Block1	fits	H1	of	Block3
R_2:	S2	of	Block1	fits	H2	of	Block3
R_3:	F2	of	Block1	against	F3	of	Block3
R_4:	S3	of	Block1	fits	H3	of	Block2
R_5:	F2	of	Block1	against	F5	of	Block2
R_6:	F1	of	Block3	against	F4	of	Block2
R_7:	F7	of	Block3	coplanar	F6	of	Block2

(b)

Figure 9: (a) Test assembly; (b) Symbolic spatial relationships for the test assembly

rigid transformation with no degree of freedom between the two frames.

In figure 9a an example is shown consisting of 3 blocks with the following features: *shafts* of Block1: S1, S2, S3; *face* of Block1: F2; *hole* and *faces* of Block2: H3, F4, F5, F6 and *holes* and *faces* of Block3: H1, H2, F1, F3, F7. The feature coordinate systems are only shown for H3, F5 (identical with H3) and S3. The shapes of the bodies are only sketched to support the imagination of the abstract assembly. The relations defining the assembly

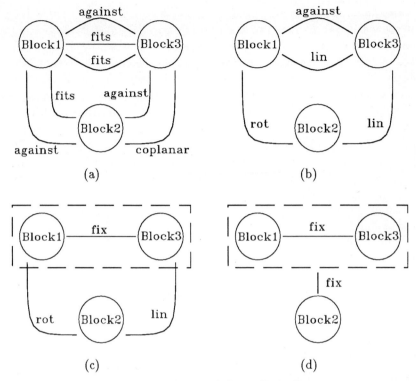

Figure 10: Steps of the cycle finder

are listed in figure 9b. These relations are also shown as graph in figure 10a.

4.2 The cycle finder

The key idea of the cycle finder [Poppelstone79] is the reduction of the degrees of freedom defined by symbolic relationships R by searching cycles consisting of two appropriate relationships $R(OF_{i,j}, OF_{k,l})$ and $R(OF_{i,n}, OF_{k,m})$ between the same objects (arbitrary features of these objects) and combining these relationships to a new one with equal or less degrees of freedom. The cycle finder runs until no further reduction can be made. In comparison to [Poppelstone79] we have integrated in our cycle finder important additional features to improve the reduction process (see below).

In figure 10 a sequence of reduction steps of our cycle finder is illustrated for the example shown in figure 9. In the first step the two *fits* relations between Block1 and Block3 (figure 10a) are reduced to a *lin* relation (figure 10b). The relation *lin* is not allowed as direct input and means a translational degree of freedom along one axis. In general a *fits-fits* pair between two feature frames of different objects can be reduced to *fits* (the two x-axes of the two *lin* relationships are colinear), to *lin* (the two x-axes are parallel, but not colinear) or to *fix* (the two x-axes aren't parallel). Based on the feature coordinate systems the correct case is automatically chosen by the system. In addition, the *coplanar-against* pair between Block2 and Block3 is substituted to *lin*.

During the next step from 10b to 10c the *lin-against* pair is reduced to *fix*. The cycle finder published in [Poppelstone79] would stop at this step, without finding any further simplification. For that reason we extended the approach by [Poppelstone79] by adding a special kind of union feature to our cycle finder. In our system all objects which have a *fix* relationship between each other at an arbitrary point of the reduction are united to a new *virtual object* (figure 10c). Subsequently the reduction process finds the *rot-against* pair and reduces it to *fix* (figure 10d). In this example the whole assembly is *fixed* and all homogeneous transformations are automatically generated from the symbolic spatial relationships.

If the cycle finder can't reduce the assembly to a *fix* one, two reasons are possible: the modeled assembly has some degrees of freedom in itself, like mechanisms; or there are cycles in the graph consisting of more then two nodes and two relationships and these cycles can't be reduced using the concept of virtual objects. To increase the efficiency of our cycle finder, relations are automatically included by a *transitive rule* if an assembly can't be reduced to *fix* using the above mentioned methods. The transitive rule inserts $R(OF_{i,j}, OF_{k,l})$ of type r, if two relationships $R(OF_{i,j'}, OF_{m,n})$ and $R(OF_{m,n'}, OF_{k,l'})$ of type r exist and these relationships have the same orientation.

Building a cycle finder working with arbitrary long cycles is very complicated because this corresponds to the inverse kinematic problem of arbitrary mechanisms, which is known to be very hard.

Figure 11 illustrates the limits of our cycle finder. The example assembly depicted in figure 11a consists of four parts. In reality, the components Shaft1, Shaft2 and Block are *fix* to each other and the component Cross has a rotational degree of freedom. Figure 11b shows an intermediate state of the graph used by the cycle finder to automatically compute the relative position between these parts. As no cycles of length 2 can be found and no virtual object can be included, our cycle finder automatically introduces a *rot*-relation by the transitive rule between Shaft1 and Shaft2 (dashed edge in figure 11b). In this special example, no additional cycle of length 2 can be found, using the transitivity rule. Thus, the cycle finder stops. It can't determine, that Shaft1, Shaft2 and the Block are *fix* to each other because cycles consisting of more than two nodes won't be reduced by our system.

In the current version of our assembly planning system we assume, that the whole assembly is *fix*. If the implemented cycle finder can't reduce the input assembly to *fix*, the user is asked to make it *fix*. Then the system suggests a possible *fix* relation which can be accepted by the user or the user can

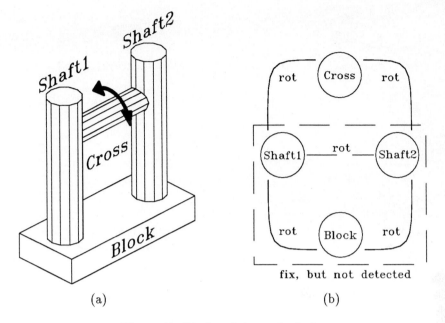

(a)   (b)

Figure 11: Limits of the cycle finder

specify a desired, appropriate fix relation, e.g. by an angle for a remaining
rot relationship. In our case *fix* means, that the position relative to some
other object is known. It doesn't include mechanical stability (section 6).
One further advantage of our system is the automatic consistency check,
which reports an error during the reduction, if a set of relationships is given,
which can't be fulfilled in reality. In the example shown in figure 9, the
relation R_7 isn't necessary to generate a *fix* assembly, but it is consistent
with the other relations.

4.3   Transforming World States

Besides the transformation from symbolic to numerical data, the actual state
of the world can be manipulated in our modeling system, using the *move*-
instruction. Actually this feature isn't necessary for our assembly planning
system. But in future, the *move*-instruction can be used to integrate the
operations really executed by a robot into the internal world model. This
actual model can be very usefull e.g. for error recovery.

A *move*-instruction is used to change the current state of the world to a new
one. There is no generation of real moves and therefore no path planning,
but objects which shall be moved get new symbolic descriptions. Hierarchies
of *ties* or *subassemblies* can be defined to generate new rigid objects by other
objects or to generate sets of objects with internal degrees of freedom as a
union.

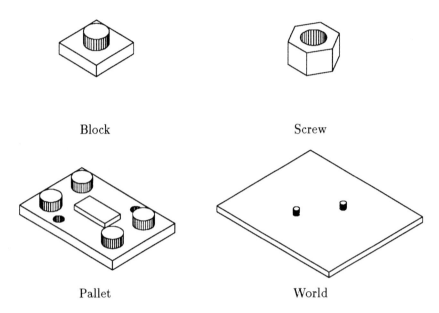

Figure 12: Components of the example world

To illustrate the transformation form one world state to an other a simple example is given. First of all, four different objects are defined namely a Pallet, which can carry four Screws, one Block to pile up the Screws, the Screws, and the World consisting of a base with two bolts to fix the Pallet. Figure 12 shows the components of this example world. In addition, the user can specify a subassembly named Tower consisting of the block with four piled-up screws. This subassembly and the pallet can be placed into the world like it is shown in figure 13a. The statements to define this world state are listed in figure 13b. The *.CYCLE*-instruction calls the cycle finder which determines the relative positions of the parts based on the symbolic world description. After the *.BREAK*-instruction the system changes into an interactive mode. In this mode the user can input commands to get information about the actual homogeneous transformations, relations between the parts etc..

If the current computed state should be changed, the *.MOVE*-instruction has to be applied. The new state of a world corresponding to the specifications stated in figure 14b (statements in the task file) is shown in figure 14a. After the subassembly definition is broken up (*.BREAK_SUBASM*-instruction) the piled screws are moved onto the pallet (*.MOVE*-instructions). The new positions and orientations of the four screws are described by new spatial symbolic relations and the cycle finder is called to determine the corresponding homogeneous transformations of the moved parts.

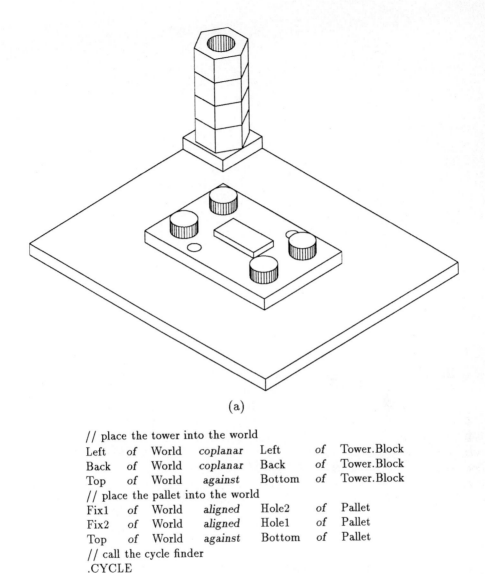

(a)

```
// place the tower into the world
Left    of  World  coplanar  Left    of  Tower.Block
Back    of  World  coplanar  Back    of  Tower.Block
Top     of  World  against   Bottom  of  Tower.Block
// place the pallet into the world
Fix1    of  World  aligned   Hole2   of  Pallet
Fix2    of  World  aligned   Hole1   of  Pallet
Top     of  World  against   Bottom  of  Pallet
// call the cycle finder
.CYCLE
// jump into the interactive mode
.BREAK
```

(b)

Figure 13: (a) Actual state of the robot's world; (b) Statements in the task
file to define this state

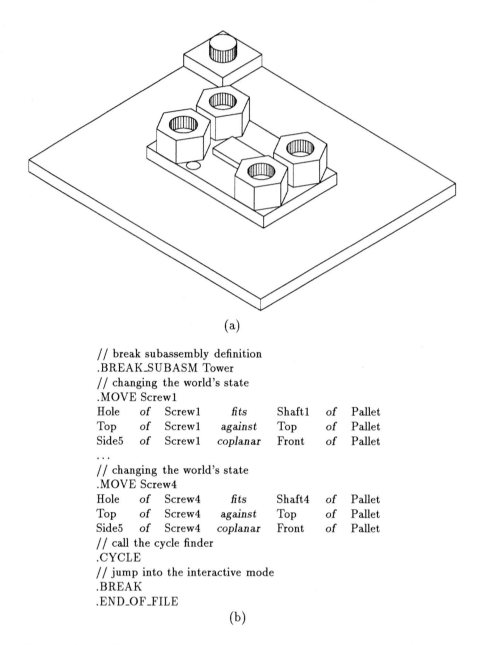

(a)

```
// break subassembly definition
.BREAK_SUBASM Tower
// changing the world's state
.MOVE Screw1
Hole    of  Screw1   fits       Shaft1  of  Pallet
Top     of  Screw1   against    Top     of  Pallet
Side5   of  Screw1   coplanar   Front   of  Pallet
. . .
// changing the world's state
.MOVE Screw4
Hole    of  Screw4   fits       Shaft4  of  Pallet
Top     of  Screw4   against    Top     of  Pallet
Side5   of  Screw4   coplanar   Front   of  Pallet
// call the cycle finder
.CYCLE
// jump into the interactive mode
.BREAK
.END_OF_FILE
```

(b)

Figure 14: (a) New state of the example world; (b) Statements in the task file to define the new state

5 Modeling for Assembly Planning

Our assembly planning system handles rigid parts, modeled at two levels. At an abstract level parts are represented as bodiless objects consisting of a set of mathematical frames (section 4.1). At the other level the parts are geometrically represented as polyhedrons and optionally as CSGs. Often some faces of a polyhedron correspond to infinite feature frames and vice versa. However, this is not necessary, e.g. a feature frame of type *face* which is used to position a part in a certain distance to an other has no correspondence to a real face. Another example would be a real face which is only important to represent the surface of the object and not the position. Thus, this real face would not be represented by a feature frame.

The whole assembly consisting of a combination of these components is defined by an assembly graph which roughly corresponds to a relation graph (section 4.1) with additional obligatory and optional attributes. These additional attributes are described in the following sections.

5.1 Obligatory attributes of the model

Each relation $R(OF_{i,j}, OF_{k,l})$ has to be augmented by one of two contact types $(c\_type(R(,)) \in \{$**R_CONTACT**,**V_CONTACT**$\})$. **R_CONTACT** has the following meaning: there is a finite, real contact between these two parts in the real assembly, restricting the local depart direction and the mechanical degrees of freedom in the goal position. In the example of figure 9 the c_type of R_1 up to R_6 is **R_CONTACT**. R_7 is a **V_CONTACT** because the relation between the corresponding features has only virtual character and doesn't restrict the local depart space.

A simple stability type $s\_type(\textbf{R\_CONTACT} R(,)) \in \{$**STUCK**,**MOBILE**$\}$ has to be declared to each physical contact. **STUCK** is used for contacts being mechanically fixed after established, e.g. glueing of two faces, **MOBILE** for contacts with at least one mechanical degree of freedom.

All contacts between Bolt2, Side1 and Middle, which can be used to model the assembly sketched in figure 3 are shown in the following list. The additional contacts between the other parts can be deduced easily.

R_CONTACT	Back	of Side1	*against*	Front	of Middle	**MOBILE**
V_CONTACT	Right	of Side1	*coplanar*	Right	of Middle	
V_CONTACT	Top	of Side1	*coplanar*	Top	of Middle	
R_CONTACT	Hole3	of Side1	*fits*	Shaft	of Bolt2	**MOBILE**
V_CONTACT	Front	of Side1	*coplanar*	Front	of Bolt2	
R_CONTACT	Hole2	of Middle	*fits*	Shaft	of Bolt2	**MOBILE**

In figure 15 all **R_CONTACT**s are represented in a graph, using the following substitutions:

place_on for **R_CONTACT** ... *against/coplanar* ...
insert   for **R_CONTACT** ... *fits/aligned* ...

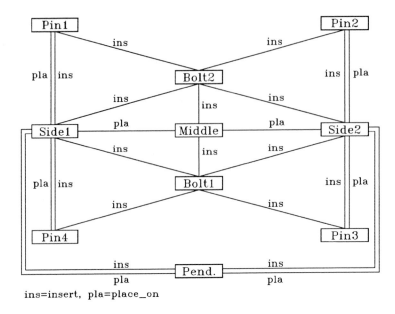

ins=insert, pla=place_on

Figure 15: Assembly graph of the test assembly shown in figure 3

5.2 Optional attributes of the model

One possibility to speed up and to guide the generation of valid assembly sequences (section 6) is to define an arbitrary hierarchy of assemblies inside an assembly graph. We distinguish between assemblies with and without base part (section 6). The example in figure 16 illustrates the following formal definition:

$$\begin{aligned}
\text{assbly} &= \text{assbly\_with\_base} \vee \text{assbly\_no\_base}; \\
\text{assbly\_no\_base} &= \{\text{single\_part} \cup \text{assbly} \}^{+}; \\
\text{assbly\_with\_base} &= \text{base} \cup \{\text{single\_part} \cup \text{assbly} \}^{*}; \\
\text{base} &= \text{assbly}
\end{aligned}$$

The definition of Block12 (name of assbly) as assembly without base part consisting of Block1 and Block2 and the definition of assembly Block123 with base part Block12 and the component Block3 is possible as:

GROUP Block12 Block1, Block2 **END**
GROUP Block123 **BASE** Block12 Block3 **END**

In addition to the assembly hierarchy, the stable attributes **TOTAL** (stable in any orientation), **INSTABLE** (stable in no orientation) or **PARTIAL** (neither **TOTAL** nor **INSTABLE**) can be optionally declared for *arbitrary* groups of parts, e.g. (figure 9):

STABLE TOTAL Block1, Block2, Block3 **END**

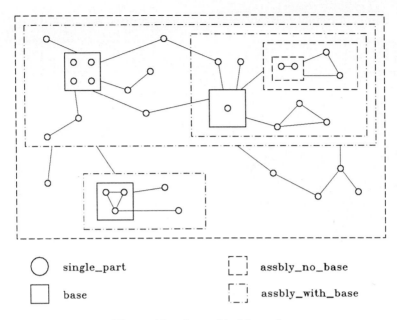

○ single_part	[⌐_] assbly_no_base
□ base	[⌐_] assbly_with_base

Figure 16: Assembly hierarchy

6 Generation of Assembly Sequences

The generation of valid assembly sequences bases on the well-known disassembly technique into two subassemblies combined with a cut-set method of the assembly graph, similar to [Mello89, chapter 7]. Our cut-set method uses the assembly-subgraph defined by the object nodes and the **R_CONTACT** edges (figure 15).

Figure 17 shows a part of an arbitrary assembly graph. Each node P_i symbolize a single part or a subassembly. Each connection between two nodes corresponds to a real contact (**R_CONTACT**) between the appropriate components. At the actual hierarchy level each P_i is treated as a single component, regardless whether P_i is a single part or a subassembly in reality. If P_i corresponds to a subassembly, it will be decomposed into single parts at a deeper hierarchy level. A valid cut (see below) inside the actual part of the assembly graph, corresponds to a hyperarc in the AND/OR-graph (figure 17). Each hyperarc corresponds to a potential assembly operation.

To avoid blind recursion of the cut-set generation, a guided recursive search of connected subgraphs has been implemented which automatically generates the hyperarcs of the AND/OR-graph which is used to store all possible assembly sequences. The key ideas of the guided search are:

- A valid cut-set of an assembly *ass* into two connected subgraphs (s_1, s_2) with $s_1 \cap s_2 = \emptyset$ and $s_1 \cup s_2 = ass$ is modified by adding one $e \in s_2$ to

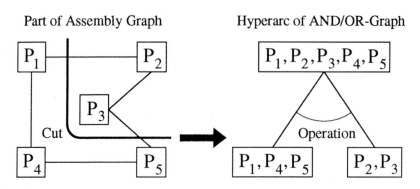

Figure 17: Valid cut in the assembly graph and the resulting hyperarc in the AND/OR-graph

s_1 ($s_1 = s_1 \cup \{e\}$, $s_2 = s_2 - \{e\}$), if the two new subgraphs s_i remain connected and additional constraints are satisfied (see below). Then the *calculate_cut* procedure is started with (s_1, s_2), $(\emptyset, s_1)$ and $(\emptyset, s_2)$. The last two calls are only executed, if these cuts aren't already known! At the very beginning *calculate_cut* is started with $(\emptyset, assembly)$.

- Each pair (a, b) is only computed by *calculate_cut*, if the number of nodes in a is less or equal than the number of nodes in b

Declaring an optional hierarchy of assemblies (section 5.2), the *calculate_cut* procedure and consequently the structure of the AND/OR-graph is influenced. As sketched in figure 16, the *calculate_cut* procedure sees only the top level of the subassembly hierarchy inside the actual assembly. Thus, at this decomposition level each subassembly is treated as a single part and is managed as complete union. If *calculate_cut* is called with $(\emptyset, assbly)$ the top level of the assembly hierarchy is splitted and the next level of the hierarchy is seen and so on. At each disassembly level, called with $(\emptyset, assbly)$, we distinguish three types of assemblies (figure 18 and section 5.2):

- **single part** = *single_part*:
  End of recursion because single parts can't be decomposed further.

- **assembly without base part** = *assbly_no_base*:
  Inside this assembly all assemblies (*single_part* or *assbly*) are treated equally. Consequently all cut combinations are computed.

- **assembly with base part** = *assbly_with_base*:
  Inside this assembly the specially marked base part (= *base*) is the start part for the assembly process of this level and all other assemblies (*single_part* or *assbly*) are iteratively added to this *virtual base*. The *virtual base* is permanently updated and corresponds to the union of the *base* with all parts already iteratively added.

The generation of a special cut of *ass* into (s_1, s_2) will be only blocked,

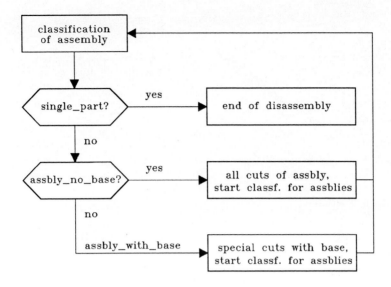

Figure 18: Disassembling using hierarchies of subassemblies

if the resulting graphs aren't connected (see above) or constraints are violated. In our current implementation the existence of a depart motion is the only constraint (section 6.1). The **INSTABLE**-attribute could be used additionally, but the stability of groups influence the weight of the nodes of the AND/OR-graph and consequently the optimal assembly sequence. We think, it is more consistent to focus the influence of stability only on the search of the optimal assembly sequence. In addition, if the only assembly path goes through an **INSTABLE** node in the graph, additional tools or fixtures can be used to make the node stable.

6.1 Depart motions

Computing the shape of the local depart space between s_1 and s_2 for only translational movements, the **R_CONTACT** edges with the automatically generated transformations are used.

The system determines the concerned physical contacts which should be separated or established respectively. For many types of contacts there exist only very few feasible motions between the parts. For example, a pin in a hole (*fits*-relation) can translate along and rotate around the axis of the hole. Whenever a subassembly has such a constraining contact, the analysis of the local depart motion can be done by checking the compatibility of the most restrictive contact with all other contacts. In the case of the pin in the hole, the analysis consists in checking whether a translation of the pin along its axis is not blocked by any other contacts between the pin and the other

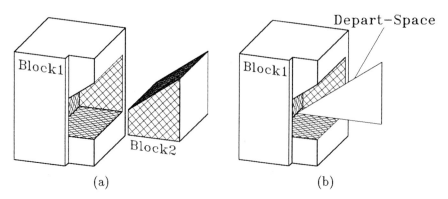

Figure 19: Example for the depart space of type *sector of a plane*

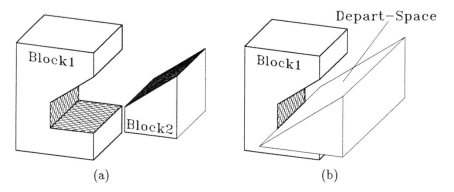

Figure 20: Example for the depart space of type *infinite wedge*

subassembly. This local analysis is more difficult when the subassembly to be disassembled is constrained by planar contacts only (*against*-relations). Each planar contact leaves an infinite number of unconstrained directions along which a translation is possible. These directions lie in and above the contact plane and define the *depart space* of the contact. For a planar contact the corresponding depart space is of type *halfspace*.

Similar to [Mello89] we use the following types of local depart spaces: *no depart space, half line, line, halfplane, sector of a plane, plane, halfspace, infinite wedge, polyhedral cone, space.*

In figure 19 an example for the depart space of type *sector of a plane* is shown. The contact faces (**R_CONTACT**) are hatched in figure 19a. Any vector, starting in the sharp corner of the depart space of figure 19b and lying in the sketched depart space, is a valid local depart vector for this example. However, only the direction of this vector is important and not its absolute position. Consequently the depart space of 19b can be translated to any other position. In figures 20 and 21 the depart spaces of type *infinite wedge* and *polyhedral cone* are sketched. In figure 20b each valid depart vector has

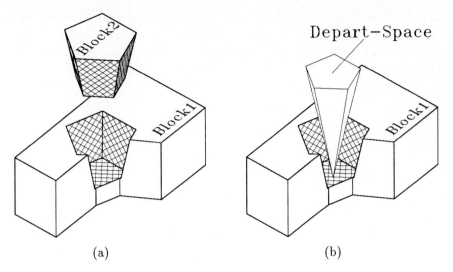

Figure 21: Example for the depart space of type *polyhedral cone*

to start in the middle of the line defined by the acute angle of the wedge. The endpoint of the local depart vector has to lie inside the volume defined by the wedge. For the depart space of type *polyhedral cone* all valid depart vectors start in the tip of the cone (figure 21b) and lie completely in the volume defined by the cone.

In order to decide whether a set of planar contacts does not completely constrain one subassembly, the corresponding depart spaces are iteratively intersected. If the resulting depart space is of type *no depart space* then no local depart motion is possible and the separation into s_1 and s_2 is invalid. Otherwise the shape and the position of the depart space is mathematically known. The following interface was designed to use the space information:

- Test a given vector, whether it lies inside the depart space.

- Compute an *optimal* depart vector. Optimal in our case means, that all **R_CONTACT** connections are removed simultaneously, e.g. for the polyhedral cone the sum of all vectors defining the cone.

- Calculate a valid angular range of depart vectors (depart vectors are defined in sphere coordinates) lying in a given plane. This function only can calculate a result if one of the following condition is fulfilled: (a) the depart space lies in a plane corresponding to the given plane or (b) the depart space has a volume and the given plane intersects the volume.

Our system tries to estimate a global depart motion which corresponds to a valid local one. First the *optimal* (see above) local depart vector is tested. For that purpose the swept volume generated by the translational movement of the polyhedral description of s_1 along the depart vector is computed and intersected with the polyhedral model of s_2. If no intersection occurs, the depart vector is valid as global depart motion. Having an intersection, several valid local depart vectors lying in planes bounding the depart space (if these plane exists) are tested in a similar way, e.g. for each boundary plane of a *polyhedral cone* the boundary vectors and the middle vector of the sector of this plane are taken as potential global depart vectors. If no global depart vector can be computed, the user is asked for a valid one, which is automatically tested by the system.

6.2 Optimal assembly sequences

Using the cut-set method with the mentioned constraints, an AND/OR-graph is generated, representing all possible assembly sequences. The best one is selected, minimizing the costs from the initial to the goal nodes. For that purpose costs are assigned to the nodes and to the hyperarcs:

- Node weights include:
  - Stability: One group of parts is only **TOTAL** stable, if all of the **R_CONTACT**s are **STUCK**. If one contact is **MOBILE**, the group is **PARTIAL** stable. All automatically generated stable attributes can be overwritten by an explicit declaration (section 5.2). **INSTABLE** nodes are avoided.

- Hyperarc weights include:
  - Shape of the local depart space: The costs are increased with the narrowness of the local depart space, e.g. *halfline* costs more than *line*, *line* costs more than *sector of a plane* and so on.
  - Ratio between the number of parts in the left ($\#s_1$) and right ($\#s_2$) branch of the hyperarc: in mode (a) the estimated maximal parallelism is supported ($cost = (max(\#s_1, \#s_2))/(min(\#s_1, \#s_2)))$, in mode (b) little groups are added to large groups ($cost = (min(\#s_1, \#s_2))/(max(\#s_1, \#s_2)))$.
  - Costs of the two nodes (s_1, s_2) assembled by the hyperarc.

The search is very flexible because our system can start with arbitrary initial and goal nodes, e.g. to restart in case of error recovery (groups of parts are already assembled) or to assemble only subassemblies.

6.3 An assembly planning example

To illustrate the operation of our planning system the disassembly of our test assembly shown in figure 3 is described.

If the user doesn't specify an hierarchy, all possible cuts in the assembly graph (figure 15) are taken into account. The system automatically analyses that the Pendulum and the four Pins have a rotational degree of freedom in the assembled state. Possible *fix-relations* are suggested which can be

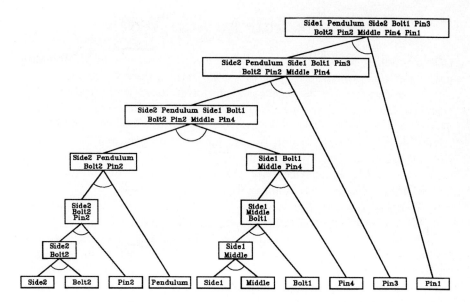

Figure 22: AND/OR-graph of the optimal assembly sequence for the test assembly of figure 3

accepted by the user or the user can define desired fix-relations. This interactive part can be avoided if appropriate fix-relations for the concerned components are explicitly specified in the task file of the planning system. The AND/OR-graph of the optimal assembly sequence is shown in figure 22. If the user doesn't influence the calculation of the node and hyperarc weights then maximal parallelism is supported. After the removal of Pin1 and Pin3 the rest of the assembly is splitted into two subassemblies consisting of the same number of parts. Subsequently these subassemblies can be disassembled by two different robots.

If first all of the four pins should be separated from the assembly, the user has to specify an appropriate hierarchy. For instance he can define an assembly without a base part consisting of the Pendulum, Middle, Side1, Side2 and the two Bolts. This corresponds to the following specification:

GROUP Main Pendulum Middle Side1 Side2 Bolt1 Bolt2 **END**

Due to this hierarchy only all possible cuts in the assembly graph of this group are considered and accordingly the computation time is reduced. Thus the specification of an assembly hierarchy can drastically influence the computational burden of our system. However, the user should be careful in defining such hierarchies. If, e.g., the four Pins, Middle, Side1 and Side2 are combined, no possible assembly sequence can be found. The system tries to separate the remaining parts (Bolt1, Bolt2, Pendulum) from the specified group but no collision free removal is possible.

7 Conclusions and Future Work

In this paper, we have introduced our assembly planning system which makes use of the comfort and efficiency of spatial relationships to model the assembly, to generate the homogeneous transformations automatically and to calculate the local depart spaces. Our approach integrates a new concept of arbitrary assembly hierarchies into the well-known cut-set method and AND/OR-graph representation. In addition we have developed a hypothesis test method to generate translational global depart motions from the local depart space. Our system has been designed as an experimental system to test additional components of assembly planning.

In the future, we will improve the generation of the global depart motions, using a path planning approach. In addition we plan to automatically find a hierarchy of assemblies and a better stability concept. In general we will try to minimize the interactive part. One long-term goal is the execution of the calculated paths by a robot and we hope, that the concept of spatial relationships can help to automatically generate complex sensor guidance information from the given symbolic spatial relationships.

References

[Bourjault87]   A. Bourjault: Methodology of assembly automation: A new approach. In *Abstracts of 2nd Conference on Robotics and Factories of the Future*, 1987.

[Mello91a]   Luiz S. Homen de Mello and Sukhan Lee, (editors). *Computer-Aided Mechanical Assembly Planning*. Kluwer Academic Publishers, 1991.

[Mello91b]   Luiz S. Homen de Mello and Arthur C. Sanderson: Representation of mechanical assembly sequences. *IEEE Transactions on Robotics and Automation*, 7(2):211–227, 1991.

[Fazio+87]   Thomas L. De Fazio and Daniel E. Whitney: Simplified generation of all mechanical assembly sequences. *IEEE Journal of Robotics and Automation*, 3(6):640–658, 1987.

[Mello89]   Luiz S. Homen de Mello: *Task Sequence Planning for Robot Assembly*. PhD thesis, The Robotics Institute, Carnegie Mellon University, 1989.

[Poppelstone79]   R. J. Poppelstone: Specifying manipulation in terms of spatial relationships. Technical Report 117, Department of Artificial Intelligence, University of Edinburgh, 1979.

From CAD Models to Assembly Planning

R. Caracciolo[1], E. Ceresole[1], T. De Martino[2] and F. Giannini[2]
[1]Dipartimento di Innovazione Meccanica e Gestionale - Università di Padova ,
via Venezia,1, 35131 Padova, Italy
[2]Istituto per la Matematica Applicata- C.N.R.
via De Marini, 6, 16149 Genova, Italy

1. Introduction

The use of robots for assembly tasks has not had the expected diffusion. As a matter of fact, assembling robots are today used only in specific environments like for example electronic board assembly or car mass-production. The main reason of this limited use is the robots high cost and the only apparent flexibility. Complete flexibility requires either evolution of the off-line programming systems which is still complex and machine dependent, and the realisation of efficient and reliable task level planning systems, directly related to both design and programming phases.

The use of a flexible robots could be a great advantage especially for small and medium companies having a rather little production volume of a great variety of different items. Robots can be used instead of dedicated-machines only if robot programming can be easily performed. The factory layout should have specific characteristics as well: it should be composed by some flexible cells where robots could work.

Return on investment is strictly linked to robot productivity. High productivity can be reached if the robot is not used during programming phases, which can be multiple and necessary when products are modified in order to satisfy the market requirements.

This goal can be achieved only if the assembly plan is designed together with the product itself and updated when the product is modified.

CAD systems are currently used in companies for supporting design activity. Thus, the automatic definition of assembly plans should start from the CAD models of the components.

The geometric information about the assembly together with the information about the workingcell and the robot, allow to automatically obtain a task level program for assembly where not only the order of manipulation of the components but also the operations to be performed are specified. The set of operations should include optimised handling operations, choice of tool, re-orientation of components, subassemblies identification. Knowledge about the available tools, the robot, the feeders and the physical cell is needed in order to obtain a complete operation definition. Moreover, the information about the workingcell is also necessary for the path planning phase.

Previous researches have been done in order to define and to classify assembly plans. According to these classifications, three distinct representation are given [1]:

- *state sequence*, representing assembling plans as sequence of operations. This is the representation adopted in our work.
- *partial assembly tree*, the assembly plan is seen as a recursive decomposition into subset; AND/OR tree is an example.
- *subassembly tree*, representing assembly plans as operation sequence inserting parts or subassembly into a fixture.

Moreover some restrictions [2], like sequentiality, monotonicity, coherence and history independence, are introduced to limit the class of the considered sequence.

The main goal of all these researchers is the definition of representations able to easily describe all the possible assembling sequences like for instance the representation proposed by Homen de Mello and Sanderson [3] based on an AND/OR graph. The attention is more focused on the simplicity and completeness of the represented information rather than on its quality. For instance, the graph representation is allowed by the hypothesis of history independence, that implies the planning of only mating operations.

Homen de Mello and Sanderson compare five different representations with the AND/OR graph to demonstrate its compactness [4]. The same authors in another paper [5] discuss the plan evaluation problem and propose a cost based method, in which costs are associate to the arcs of the AND/OR representation. Since the AND/OR graph contains all the subassemblies, this cost representation enables the choice of the subassembly to be used.

De Fazio and Whitney [6] focus on the knowledge base acquisition, in particular the automatic acquisition of geometric interference constraints is considered. These constraints are needed for creating the AND/OR graph proposed in [3], all the other non geometric constraints, such as stability and coherence, are included in the cost function.

This paper describes a new approach to assembly planning, starting from the components CAD models and from the geometric and kinematic models of the cell elements. The functional analysis of the component models is performed by a form feature recogniser which analyses the boundary representation of each object and generates a feature-based representation. The correspondence between features belonging to different components is obtained analysing the adjacency and is stored in a relational representation of the whole assembly, called liaison graph.

The proposed planner finds a set of optimal sequences using artificial intelligence techniques, without identifying all the possible sequences. This is possible by considering constraints and costs associated to each operation during the assembly sequence generation.

The planner is history dependent, i.e. it keeps track of the planning history. This means that a state is identified by the operations sequence and not only by the components that are assembled in that state. This planning typology, that implies a tree representation schema instead of a graph structure, is made possible by means of the above optimisation criteria which performs the on-line sequence evaluation. In this way it is also possible to plan the non-mating operations, i.e. tool change and subassembly positioning.

The planner solves the non-linearity given by sub-assemblies, through a module which determines possible sub-assemblies on the basis of stability and manipulation characteristics.

2. The System Architecture

The presented system is addressed to automatically cover the gap between the design phase and the assembly plan generation.

Traditional CAD systems store the object representations in terms of low level entities, that is the boundary elements (i.e. faces, edges and vertices) [7] or of the constituting volumes (i.e. blocks, cylinders,...) [8]. On the other side, assembly planners work on higher level information, so they cannot refer to these structures. The required data include adjacencies between components, assembly directions, mating operations referred either to a component or to a pair of components or to the whole assembly.

Form features are the key elements for associating this information to the geometric model of the object, because they are semantic data which allow the association of specific meaning and functional behaviour to the shape. In our work, we define a feature as a set of faces corresponding to a concavity or a convexity of the object that can fit with another component part.

In our system a correspondence between tools and features has been defined.

Thus, in order to specify which assembly and locking operations must be performed and how, two levels of geometric model interpretation have been defined (see fig. 1):

- component features identification, (*feature recogniser*).
- identification of the adjacency between components in the assembly, (*adjacency identifier*).

This two levels of identification can be easily related to the operation definition and tool choice. In fact, tools are classified according to:

- the operations they can perform;
- predefined manipulation features of the object.

In other words, a tool can be thought as composed by two parts and a two level classification: the operation to be performed determines the gripper and the identified feature detects a specific finger.

Thus, the proposed *planner* interprets contact regions between components in terms of mating operations. The considered operations, that can be associated to specific contacts and features are the following: free, uncertain and clamped coupling, normal mating operation (simple contact), screwing using parallel gripper and screwing of unified parts. Features in the components are also used to specify the operation and the locking method.

For example, a screwing operation may be deduced by the presence of a contact region between two components constituted by a threaded hole in one component and a complementary threaded protrusion on the other component. The tool associated to the operation is the screwdriver (first classification level). The type of the screwdriver end-effector is determined by the dimension and the shape of the hole (second classification level).

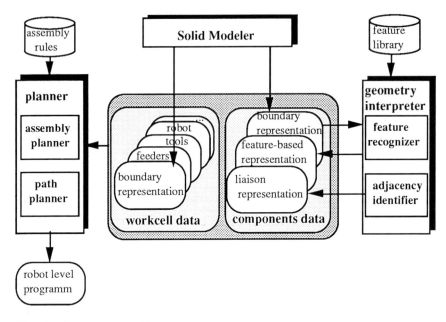

Fig. 1. The system architecture

Starting from this correspondence between adjacencies and operations, allowed by the geometric interpreter, it is possible to carry out a task level plan. Thus, it is possible to determine the component handling order and all the procedures referred to such manipulation.

Moreover, the assembly planner is integrated with a *path-planner*. Thus, the generated sequence is translated into a set of commands and paths (*robot level program*). This is possible thanks to the special operation definition.

Finally, the developed assembly plan is visualised by a robot simulator in order to check its correctness.

3 Component Data

The data concerning the assembly components are stored in different CAD models: a boundary representation and a feature-based model are considered for each component while a liaison representation is defined for the assembled object.

By using a traditional 3D boundary based modelling system, each component is modelled and positioned with respect to the whole assembly in a given reference frame.

The B-rep we have adopted is the Face Adjacency Hypergraph (FAH), defined in [9]. The choice of this model, where the faces are considered as primary entities and the edges and the vertices as secondary ones, is not restrictive since it is possible to derive it from every complete and evaluated object representation. However, this information is not enough for our task.

In a boundary model, the geometry and the topology of the parts are completely described. What is left out, is the information linked to the specific application, which can be obtained only considering a feature-based model.

Moreover, the set of the FAH models represent the boundary description of the assembled object but the information about the contact parts between adjacent components are contained only implicitly. The correspondence between features belonging to different components should be obtained as well.

All this information necessary for the planning phase is extracted by the geometric interpreter, see figure 1.

The Feature Recogniser analyses the B-rep of each component and builds a feature-based model in which the assembly features affecting the part are represented.

The recognition process is performed in two steps, at first all the shape features are identified on the basis of geometric reasoning, then the shape features are interpreted as assembly features, according to specific requirements expressed in the feature library. A more detailed description of the system follows is in paragraph 5.

The feature-based model used for representing each component is the Shape Feature Object Graph (SFOG), defined in [10], which is a hierarchical graph, where root nodes correspond to the main shape volume and all the other nodes represent volumetric features. Each graph component is described by the corresponding boundary FAH model.

The hierarchical relationships between father and child components are expressed through the contact faces. The hierarchy is useful for the assembly sequence identification while the volumetric feature representation gives information about the parts of the object which can be accessible by the tool.

Another important characteristic of this model is its dynamic structure. An *expansion* and *abstraction* operators have been defined in order to modify the graph according to the application requirements. The expansion operator derives new volume features from existing ones, while the abstraction operator compacts the graph by grouping set of components.

In figure 2, a resonator and its SFOG representation are depicted. From the assembly point of view the resonator is characterised by some external and internal features. In (b) all the feature volumes composing the component are represented, both those which interest the external side and those which regard the internal part. This model is the result of the first step of the recognition process. Requiring a more detailed analysis of the internal part, an abstraction operation is performed by grouping all the features belonging to the resonator external part and the hexagonal pocket and the two through holes are classified by using the feature library. The final interpreted SFOG model is represented in figure 2(c).

The information about the hexagonal pocket can be useful in the planning phase, for example, for choosing the key for the component manipulation while the information about the two holes can be used for defining the type and the direction of the assembly operation which interests the parts. Moreover, the main shape, which represents the external part of the resonator, can be analysed for handling purpose.

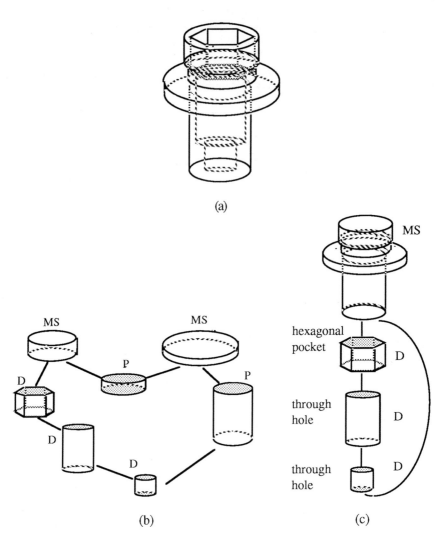

(a)

(b)   (c)

Fig. 2: (a) A resonator, its SFOG description (b) and the interpretation of the internal features (c)

The SFOG representations of the components are then considered all together by the Adjacency Identifier in order to obtain the liaison graph, which is the global representation of the whole assembly where also the contacts between adjacent components are represented.

Formally, our *liaison graph* is a connected graph, $G = (N, A, T)$ where N is a set of nodes and A is the set of the connecting arcs, such that for each node n in N there exists an element in the assembly, and each arc in A connecting two nodes, corresponds to a contact region between the two corresponding assembly components. Since contacts between two components can interest generic facesets or particular features, an attribute t in T is associated to each arc. The attribute specifies the type of relation exiting between two adjacent components: a face set face set relation, a feature feature relation and hybrid situations.

In figure 3, an example of an assembly is depicted, in which three types of contacts are shown: faceset-faceset between the cover and the basis, feature-feature between the screw and the basis, while between the screw and the cover the contact region is divided in two parts with two different types, feature feature for the contact between the hole and the screw protrusion and faceset faceset in the other parts.

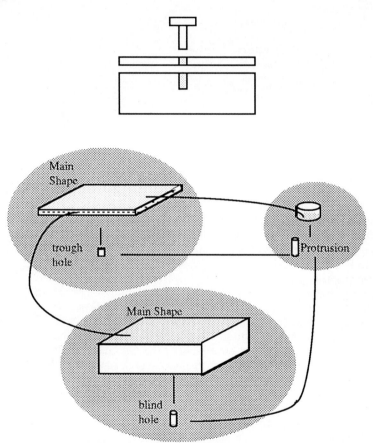

Fig. 3: An example of liaison representation

Thus, the complete organisation of the component data of our system results in picture 4.

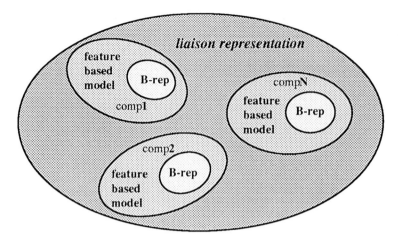

Fig. 4: Data components organisation

4. Workingcell Data

Since the assembly plan strongly depends on the working cell, it is necessary to have its complete description. Thus, both the boundary representation and the information about the behaviour of the working cell are stored. In fact, the cell elements may have different functional behaviour: some of them (pallets, feeders) have a fixed position, some others, like for example the robot arms, can move in order to perform the assembly operation. Due to this kind of behaviour, a tree structure is created in order to store time dependent configurations. The nodes store local reference frames associated to the cell elements and the arcs represent time dependent relationships between them. According to the tree structure, each child system is connected with its father system, thus a movement of the father coordinate system implies the movement of the associated children, see fig. 5. All the reference frames are represented as 4x4 rototranslation matrices.

This representation fits our needs since the kinematic model of open chain spatial mechanisms, as robots, can be represented by means of a set of rototranslation matrices relating together the local reference frame of each robot link.

The cell description in terms of reference frames allows an easy integration of the assembly planner with the path planner. Trajectories may be described as sets of reference frames, representing the discrete positions of the robot end-effector. Thus, the output of the assembly planner may be directly used by the path planner.

The path planning problem requires the inverse kinematic model, mapping the planned trajectories in the joint space. In fact, collision-free trajectories are obtained by defining collision regions in the joint space [11]. Collision checks are performed for both robot and payload in the Cartesian space using boundary models.

In this paper we do not describe the system for the identification of grasping conditions, we only show that the proposed representation is suitable for the integration of handling analysis in the assembly planning system. By describing the cell through reference frames one can define a grasp operation in terms of a matrix relating the tool with the manipulated object.

Fixtures and tools are characterised by functional attributes. Fixtures are classified according to their locking typology based on the component geometry. Form features in the object are required to ensure mating stability.

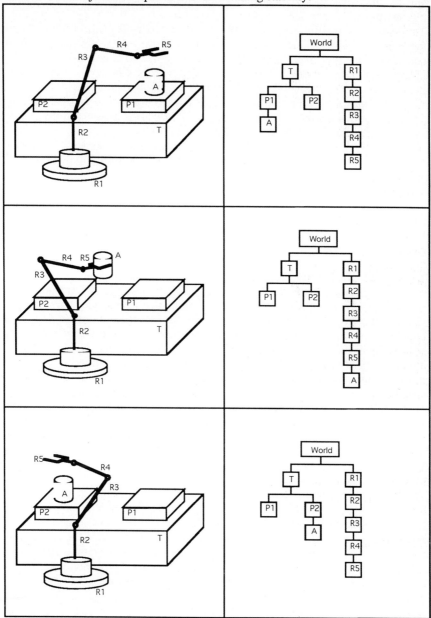

Fig. 5 Cell tree during an operation execution

5. The Geometry Interpreter

The CAD representation of the assembly is analysed by the Feature Recogniser which considers each component in order to obtain its shape feature based model and by the Adjacencies Identifier which extracts information on the contact regions and builds the liaison graph.

The feature recognition process is performed in two steps [12]. In the first step, the system recognises the depressions and the protrusions of a component by considering the type of the adjacency between faces. The system takes advantage of the method devised by Kypriano [13], who was the first one to use a feature grammar in which the building elements were concave and convex edges.

A *depression* is a set of faces which are adjacent through concave edges, while the set of faces adjacent through convex edges are classified as *protrusions* or *main shape* if they correspond to the main part.

In our system the set of faces belonging to the feature is completed in order to obtain the corresponding volume features, which are then used to determine the accessible volumes for tool manipulation.

The extracted features are then organised in a hierarchical graph structure, called Shape Feature Object Graph (SFOG) where the root nodes correspond to the main shape while all the other nodes correspond to the features of the object [10].

Links between components are expressed by means of the faces added during the completing phase and the faces to which the features are attached to the rest of the object.

The arcs are labelled depending on the boundary elements which have been added in order to create the feature volume. These labels are useful in the second module of the feature recogniser. In fact, at this point the system looks for features having special meaning for assembly purposes. Examples are threaded through or blind holes, which are usually associated to screwing operations, or pocket and holes which can fit with other components and can have only one access direction, etc. These classification can be done by using a feature library, where information about unified components, standard features and associated technological attributes are stored.

This library can be easily updated and extended with user-defined features by using a *teaching by example* technique: the user defines a simple object in which the feature template is present. Then, applying the feature recogniser, the SFOG representation of the feature example is obtained and is included into the library. The feature instances can be recognised by using a graph matching technique between the object and the feature SFOG representations.

The example in figure 6 shows the recognition of an hexagonal pocket in the resonator of figure 2. In the two windows on the left side, a simple object characterised by an hexagonal pocket, which is the feature example, and its SFOG representation are depicted. On the right side of the big window, the resonator is represented. A first graph matching on the two SFOG representations identifies a subset of candidate feature components, and a second graph matching on the boundary representations of these components allow the pocket classification.

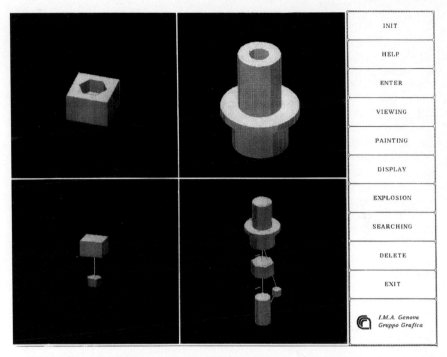

Figure 6: The recognition of an hexagonal pocket.

The Adjacencies Identifier analyses each pair of adjacent components in order to build the assembly liaison graph.

The contact regions between components in the assembly are determined by using a pre-processor of non-regularised Boolean operators. In current CAD systems only regularised operators are implemented which are used to preserve regularity and semi-analyticity. The regularised operations creates closed and dimensionally homogeneous sets, considering the closure of the interior of each set. Thus, regularization not only removes dandling edges and faces or isolated vertices, but also parts of the solid surface that are not expressed as entities belonging to the boundary of the object. Since contact regions usually correspond to portion of the object boundary, whose closure in E^3 is empty, regularised Boolean operators are not sufficient for their identification [14].

The Adjacencies Identifier recognises the contact regions by using non-regularised Boolean operators [15]. The implemented algorithms are composed by the following steps [16]:

- identification of the intersection points and edges;
- reconstruction of the contact regions.

When the contact parts have been identified, the system analyses the SFOG models of the components in order to check if feature association is possible. If the contact boundary entities do not belong to any recognised feature then the relationship between two components has type faceset faceset. If the contact parts is realised through a couple of features, the relationship between the two components has type feature feature. All the other cases are hybrid. The results of the analysis are then stored in the liaison graph.

6. The Assembly Planner

The planner structure depends on the definition given for the sequence to be obtained. In the simplest case, the assembly sequence is a manipulation order, while, in more complex cases, is an ordered sequence of operations. However, the type of the generated sequence depends on the quantity and the type of the available data.

The definition of a sequence in terms of operation needs a big amount of data and a compact representation schema.

An efficient representation schema has been defined by Homem De Mello and Sanderson [3] It is based on AND/OR graphs which allow to represent also non linear assembly plans, where sub-assemblies are defined.

This structure, defined in order to have all the possible assembly sequences, represents states which are sets of components or subassemblies and do not depend on the order of the assembly operations. In this structure the defined operations are expressed as relations between couples of components and/or sub-assemblies. Different operations such as component re-orientation and tool change are not considered in the final sequence.

The developed assembly planner takes into account also this kind of operations. In fact, two different groups of operations are considered:
- operations which express relations between pairs of components, called *mating operations*;
- operation which interest a single component, for example re-orientation of a component and tool change, which we refer as *non mating operations*.

Peculiar characteristics of the proposed approach are forward generation of assembly plans and history dependence.

Forward assembly planning is introduced to easily verify stability of partial assemblies and in general to minimise the number of extra-geometric constraint evaluations.

History dependence allows the introduction of the non-mating operation in the assembly sequence. A tree structure is then needed to correctly represent history dependence, containing information about operation order.

Since assembly trees imply expensive data structures to describe all possible plans, even using compact representations as AND/OR trees, in the proposed planner the complete tree computation is avoided. This is performed by using an AI technique for the dynamic node expansion.

Starting from the root (representing all disassembled components) a best first search algorithm generates step by step best promising node, by evaluating the cost function associated to each one [17].

This search method needs a complete description of the assembly state to calculate the global cost of the node without backtracking.

On the other hand, the dynamic tree generation does not requires a compact representation of all plans because only few subtrees are really created and stored. Thus, in our work a plan is a state sequence. Each state S is an ordered sequence composed of parts already assembled, active fixtures and used tools.

Given an assembly P made up by n parts $P = \{p_1...p_n\}$ and a workingcell $W = T \cup F$, where $T = \{t_1...t_k\}$ is the available tool set and $F = \{f_1...f_l\}$ is the available fixtures set, an assembly state S is defined as $S = \{s_1...s_m\}$ where s_i

$\in \{\{p_i\} \cup \{f_i\} \cup \{t_i\}\}$. Reorienting operations correspond to the fixturing operations: activating a fixture implies to consider a reorienting matrix.

The optimal assembly sequence is found exploring the tree dynamically created during the solution process. In this tree, each arc connecting two nodes represents the elementary operation which performs the state transition with an elementary cost.

Every node represents an assembly sequence, which consists of parts, fixturing, tool and global cost. A global cost of a node is the sum of the elementary costs associated to the arcs composing the path from the root to the node.

Elementary costs are calculated by using special sets of rules which evaluate the following properties:
• priority given to geometric interference;
• stability of components and subassemblies [18];
• contact coherence condition;
• need for a non mating operation;
• non mating operations optimisation;
• base cost related to the operation type;
• kinematic constraints imposed by the robot structure.

Before the tree generation process, two sets of rules identify respectively: all the possible subassemblies and all the mating operations between adjacent parts.

Moreover, the first set, among all the possible subassemblies identifies the stable subassembly to ensure manipulability. The identified subassembly is considered as a single macro-component inheriting form features, attributes and costs from the component parts.

Using this cost the planner decides if the subassembly has to be assembled.

The second set of rules has been defined for the identification of the mating operations. The adjacency between pairs of components and the form features which interest the contact parts are analysed.

In some cases, as described in the second paragraph, the presence of particular mating features gives directly the type of operation to be performed.

In general, simultaneous presence of features determines the constraints and consequently the degree of freedom.

Conclusions

An integrated approach is presented to connect design and assembly planning phases of a mechanical product. It differs from the existing approaches because non only simple contacts through faces have been considered, but this information has been structured in a higher level representation. In fact the information about contacts between parts has been improved with the specification of the involved form features. Form features are the fundamental entities enabling an high level geometric and functional representation. Thus, features belonging to different parts are connected in a relational model of the whole assembly.

In this way, a correspondence between operations and contact types (i.e. adjacency and form feature) has been defined.

Thus, the rules for the operation determination start from the analysis of the adjacencies between parts.

Moreover, the described planner is history dependent and performs a forward generation of the assembly plan. In this way, it is possible to avoid the creation of all the possible assembly plans. Thus, by evaluating each operation cost, only optimal assembly plans are returned.

The geometric interpreter has been implemented by three communicating modules, using C language and Motif tool kit for the interface. While the assembly planner has been developed inside the KBMS (Knowledge Base Management System) from AICorp.

6 Acknowledgement

This work was supported by a grant of Italian National Council of Research, in the Progetto Finalizzato Robotica. The authors would like to thank professor Aldo Rossi and professor Bianca Falcidieno for the useful discussions.

References

1. J.D. Wolter, A Combinatorial Analysis of Enumerative Data Structures for Assembly Planning, Proc. of the 1991 IEEE Inter. Conf. on Robotics and Automation, pp. 611-617, Sacramento, California, April 1991
2. J.D. Wolter, On the Automatic Generation of Assembly Plans, Proc. of the IEEE Inter. Conf. on Robotics and Automation, pp. 62-68, April 1989
3. L.S. Homen De Mello, A.C. Sanderson, And/Or Graph Representation of Assembly Plans, IEEE Trans. Robotics and Automation vol.6 no.2, pp. 188-198, April 1990
4. L.S. Homen De Mello, A.C. Sanderson, Representation of Mechanical Assembly Sequences, IEEE Trans. Robotics and Automation vol.7 no.2, pp. 211-227, April 1991
5. L.S. Homen De Mello, A.C. Sanderson, Two Criteria for the Selection of Assembly Plans: Maximising the Flexibility of Sequencing the Assembly Task and Minimising the Assembly Time Through Parallel Execution of Assembly Task, IEEE Trans. Robotics and Automation vol.7 no.5, pp. 626-633, October 1991
6. T.L. De Fazio, D.E. Whitney, Simplified Generation of All Mechanical Assembly Sequences, IEEE Journal of Robotics and Automation vol.RA-3, no.6, pp. 640-658, December 1987
7. M. Mantyla, An Introduction to Solid Modelling, Computer Science Press, Maryland 1988
8. A.G. Requicha, Representation of Rigid Solids: theory, methods and system, ACM Compt. Surv. 12, 4 1980
9. S. Ansaldi, L. De Floriani, B. Falcidieno, Geometric Modelling of Solid Objects using a Face Adjacency Graph Representation, (SIGGRAPH '85), Computer Graphics 19, no. 3, 1985
10. R. Caracciolo, M. Giovagnoni, C. Roncaglia, A. Rossi, A Collision Avoidance Technique for Automatic Programming of Assembly Robots, Proc. of the 8th International Conference on CAD/CAM, Robotics and Factories of the Future CARs & FOF 92, Metz, France, August 17-19, 1992

12. T. De Martino, B. Falcidieno, F. Giannini, Feature-based Model Transformations between different Application Contexts, Proc of CAPE, 1991 Bordeaux 10-12 Sept. 1991

13. L. K. Kyprianou, Shape Classification in Computer-Aided-Design, PhD Dissertation, Computer Laboratory, University of Cambridge, England, July 1980

14. F. Arbab, Set Models and Boolean Operations for Solids and Assemblies, IEEE Computer Graphics & Applications, November 1990

15. P. Collareta, Modellazione geometrica di assemblati: definizione e manipolazione di grafi relazionali per la rappresentazione di contatti eventualmente non manifold, Tesi Scienze dell'informazione 1993, Genova, Italy

16. P. Gugliermero, Operatori Booleani non regolarizzati per Modellatori Boundary Tradizionali, Tesi Scienze dell'informazione 1992, Genova, Italy

17. S. Lee, Y.G. Shin, Assembly Planning Based on Geometric Reasoning, Computer and Graphics, vol. 14, no. 2, 1990, pp. 237-250

18. R. Caracciolo, E. Ceresole, Forward Assembly Planning Based on Stability, Internal Report DIMEG, University of Padova, Italy, 1993

Feature Modelling for Assembly

Winfried van Holland, Willem F. Bronsvoort and Frederik W. Jansen

Faculty of Technical Mathematics and Informatics, Delft University of Technology
Julianalaan 132, 2628 BL Delft, The Netherlands

Abstract

A product modelling approach is presented that supports the assembly planning task with feature models. Mating and connection relations between components of an assembly can be specified by adding connection features to a product model with a design-by-features approach. In a second feature model, handling features can be specified. From the feature models, a decomposition of the assembly into sub-assemblies, and all possible assembly sequences can be derived. The features can also support grasp planning and motion planning. The design-by-features approach is embedded in an interactive design system that supports multiple feature views.

Key words: feature modelling, design by features, assembly planning

1 Introduction

There is a growing need in industry for flexible, automatic assembly systems to meet the challenges of short product life cycles, fast changing product mixes, and small batch sizes. Existing flexible assembly systems, however, show a low recon-figuration flexibility, due to difficulties in robot programming, tool design (grippers, part feeders), and error control. A truly flexible assembly system makes heavy demands on the planning and error-recovering capabilities of the program-ming and control system. Semi-automatic assembly planning using a (geometric) product model created by a CAD system is one way to improve the flexibility of planning.

Two approaches in planning on the basis of CAD models can be discerned: generic planning and goal-directed planning. The generic approach derives all information for assembly planning from the geometric model. This concerns information about how parts are connected, degrees of freedom of parts, possible interference of parts during assembly, how parts can be grasped, etc. A problem with this approach is that the geometric model describes the product on a too low level to answer these questions optimally. The alternative, goal-directed planning, applies more a top-down approach: the product is first described on a functional level, with information on the main design intentions, how the product is composed, how the parts are con-nected, and how they could or should be assembled. The geometric model is here only used to answer detailed questions that arise during planning.

An approach to goal-directed planning is to specify the properties of an assembly by use of features. Features attach functional connotations to geometric elements.

These connotations can then directly be interpreted by the assembly planning software, and need not be inferred from the geometry. In section 2, we will discuss some general concepts from assembly and assembly planning. In section 3, we will describe two classes of features for assembly: connection features, which describe the way components are linked, and handling features, which describe how parts can be grasped and fixed. With these two feature classes, two different feature models can be defined for a product. Each model represents a different aspect of, or 'view' on, the model. Within a concurrent engineering environment, these multiple views will have to be maintained simultaneously and be kept consistent. In section 4, we will describe an interactive design system that supports a design-by-feature approach and, in addition, supports multiple feature views. Conclusions and topics for further research are outlined in section 5.

2 Assembly and assembly planning

In this section, first some general concepts of flexible assembly will be shown by giving a short description of the DIAC (Delft Intelligent Assembly Cell) prototype, an assembly cell developed at Delft University of Technology. Then the functions in semi-automatic assembly planning will be described.

2.1 A flexible assembly cell

The DIAC prototype (Heemskerk 1990; Meijer and Jonker 1991; Boneschanscher 1993) is a flexible assembly cell consisting of three workstations: two assembly robots and one handling robot. The cell is connected to other systems in its environment with an Automatic Guided Vehicle (AGV) (see Fig. 1).

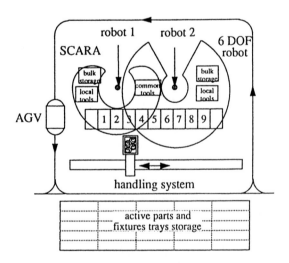

Fig. 1. DIAC assembly cell (Boneschanscher 1993).

To provide enough handling flexibility, product-specific parts are transported on trays of standard size. Actual assembly takes place on fixtures, which are also placed on trays. Trays can be routed through the cell by the handling workstation. Limited buffer space is provided both for part trays and fixture trays. Tools, such as grippers, are not assigned to a specific workstation, but can be interchanged via a common tool storage between the two assembly workstations.

The cell is aimed at assembling small batches of a wide range of products, which implies that it has to be very flexible in its use. This requires both advanced planning software, i.e. software for sequence planning, scheduling, grasp planning and motion planning, and advanced control software, i.e. software for controlling the equipment in the cell, which includes error-recovery. In this paper, we shall pay attention only to planning software, because here most benefits from the use of features are expected.

2.2 Assembly planning

Assembly planning for a flexible cell traditionally starts with a geometric description of the individual parts and their position and orientation in the assembled product. The result should be a schedule with all instructions for the robots and other devices in the cell. It consists of the following functions.

Decomposition into subassemblies

In most cases it is not useful to generate all possible sequences of how a product can be assembled from individual parts. For routing and scheduling it is most convenient to first assemble closely connected parts into subassemblies, before combining these subassemblies into a final product (Ko and Lee 1987). Subassemblies can be determined, either automatically or by hand, on the basis of a functional decomposition (e.g. electrical components versus hydraulic components), or on the basis of connectivity properties that describe the way parts interact and are connected to each other (welding, gluing, screwing, etc.). A useful data structure to represent the interrelations between parts is a relation graph, also called a connection, contact or liaison graph; see Fig. 2 (Libardi et al. 1988). Strongly interconnected parts are candidates for a subassembly. Additional clues are geometric stability and uniformity in assembly direction and connection type (Lee and Yi 1993), which can give rise to distinguishing part groups and clusters in the model (Boneschanscher 1993). Also whether a suitable base part, which can be fixed in an available fixture, is available for a subassembly is an important factor. The resulting decomposition can be represented by a hierarchical graph (see again Fig. 2).

Generation of assembly sequences

Given the decomposition into subassemblies, possible assembly sequences within each subassembly and for the whole assembly can be generated (Ko and Lee 1987; Homem de Mello and Sanderson 1991; Lee 1991; Wolter 1991; Waarts et al. 1992). To avoid too many possible sequences, parts can be grouped into clusters of components that do not have a preferred order. For instance, a set of screws attaching a lit to a base part can be handled without specifying the exact order. A further reduction in number of possible sequences can be realized by considering geometric feasibility. Most geometric configurations impose an order on the assembly of their parts. For instance, a part that is connected with a screw should be inserted prior to mounting the screw. These precedence relations can be established by letting the user impose a given ordering, or by using geometric feasibility tests, either applied locally or globally. Local geometric feasibility is concerned with the insertability of a part with respect to one or more other parts. The contact faces determine whether one or more assembly directions are feasible. Global geometric feasibility is concerned with the accessibility of a part into a subassembly, i.e. will there be a collision-free motion path to insert the part? Finally, also the stability of the subassembly is an important constraint, in particular if the subassembly has to be moved or turned up-side-down for a subsequent assembly operation. The resulting feasible assembly sequences can be efficiently represented in an AND/OR-graph, where AND-nodes represent the combination of two components, and OR-nodes represent alternative sequences for the same composed assembly (see Fig. 3).

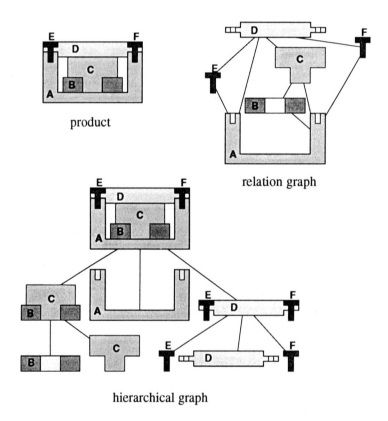

Fig. 2. Relation graph and hierarchical graph.

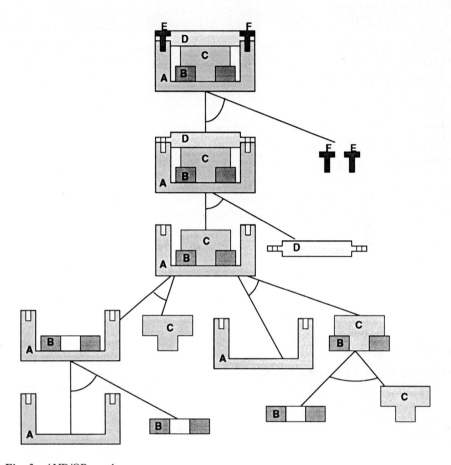

Fig. 3. AND/OR-graph.

Scheduling

Each of the alternative assembly sequences offers a planning alternative. However, each will have a different cost with respect to tool changes, transport, storage and fixture requirements, and will differ in flexibility with respect to error handling. The costs are estimated based on timing estimates for individual assembly motions, tool changes, etc. The scheduling task is to choose a path through the AND/OR-graph optimizing with respect to costs, available resources and flexibility. In most cases, it is not attractive to assemble only one product at a time, but will a number of products be scheduled as a batch to minimize the number of tool changes and transport activities. Batches in their turn can be decomposed into sections or cycles. The batch and section size will also be influenced by the available temporary storage in the cell. Dependent on the time constraints on the scheduling itself, different scheduling techniques may be used to find an optimal or an acceptable schedule (van Holland et al. 1992; Boneschanscher 1993).

Grasp planning

Another function is grasp planning: how can a part be grasped by a robot gripper, in such a way that it can be inserted into its position in the assembly? Aspects that are considered here include the finger size of the gripper, contact of the part with the part feeder and the assembly, and forbidden faces on the part. This function makes use of models of the robot gripper and of the part and the whole assembly. Van Bruggen et al. (1993) describe an approach for grasp planning that is based on geometric models for the parts and the whole assembly.

Motion planning

The last function is the generation of instructions for the devices in the assembly cell: the robots and the transport system. This includes, among other steps, gross motion planning, i.e. determining a collision-free approach path for a robot arm from a part feeder to the insertion point of a part, and fine motion planning, i.e. determining the insertion movement from the insertion point to the final point of a part (Lozano-Pérez and Wilson 1993).

2.3. Required information for assembly planning

Considering these different functions in assembly planning, most problems occur with the interrogation and interpretation of the product model for questions such as: what is a good assembly sequence for a product, how can a part be grasped with a gripper, and what is a suitable approach and insertion path to add a part to an assembly? It is difficult to derive answers to these questions from a geometric model only, because much information required for this, for example relations between parts, tolerances and symmetry axes, is not represented in the geometric model and cannot be easily computed from it either (Martens 1991).

We believe that using feature models, instead of geometric models, can be of great help in assembly process planning, and will illustrate this in section 3, where features specific for this purpose will be introduced.

3 Assembly features

To support the interrogation of a product model for assembly planning, it is convenient to define two classes of features: connection features and handling features. After a description of a general product model suitable for assembly, these types of features, and their use in assembly planning, will be discussed.

3.1 A product model for assembly

An assembled product consists of a hierarchy of components, where every component can possibly be further subdivided into other components. Components that cannot be further subdivided are called parts.

Traditionally, parts are described with a geometric model, e.g. a boundary representation or a CSG model. A more recent way of describing parts is with a feature model, in which, besides the geometry of the part, also the function or meaning of form elements or form features, such as holes and slots, can be stored (Pratt and Wilson 1985; Bronsvoort and Jansen 1993). A product model for a single part can then be split into three levels: part level, feature level and geometry level. An example of these three levels is shown in Fig. 4. The lowest level is the geometry level, where the model is described in terms of faces, edges and vertices. One level higher, functional information on some form elements is given by using features. On the part level, information concerning the complete part is stored, e.g. the local coordinate system for the position and orientation with respect to the other parts in the product, material, volume, centre of gravitation and symmetry faces or axes.

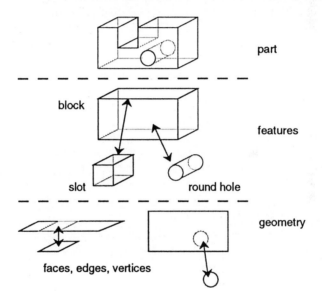

Fig. 4. Product model for a single part.

In a product model for assembly, besides information about the individual parts, also information about the relations between these parts in the assembled product has to be stored. These can be given in the form of a relation graph on part level, where several kinds of mating conditions can be distinguished, e.g. against, fit, and screw fit (Wesley et al. 1980, Homem de Mello and Sanderson 1991, Srikanth et al. 1991). For assembly planning as described in section 2.2, however, more information about the mating conditions between parts must be known. Therefore the mating geometric elements must be given in, or calculated from, the relation graph. Sometimes it is very hard to find the geometric elements that are responsible for the mating conditions, and also very difficult to give the precise conditions between the geometric elements.

Zussman et al. (1990) therefore describe a relation graph where the relations between parts are given on feature level. They called these relations assembly features. Mating geometric elements can be easier generated from these assembly features than from the part level relations, whereas fewer relations have to be given compared to the geometric level relations. We take a similar approach in our product model by using two types of assembly features connected to features occurring in the parts: connection and handling features.

3.2 Connection features

The idea of modelling with connection features is that some characteristics of connections can be directly connected to these features, for example final position (FP), insertion point (IP), insertion path (IPath), tolerances, contact faces, internal freedom of motion (IFM), and some geometrical refinements such as chamfers and rounds to ease the assembly operations. The FP is the position and orientation for the assembled part on the already assembled parts (called partial assembly PA) after the assembly operation has been finished. The IP is the position and orientation relative to the FP where there is no contact yet between the assembled part and the PA and where the insertion operation is started. The IPath gives a trajectory to get from the IP to the FP. Tolerances and contact faces between assembled part and PA give clues for calculation of the IFM.

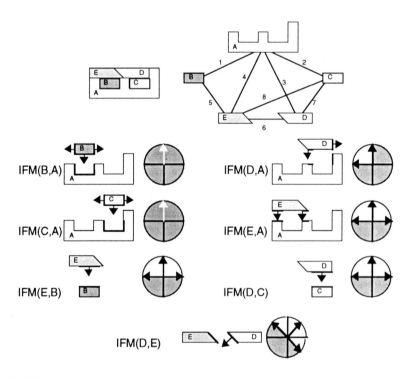

Fig. 5. IFMs between parts.

The IFM as defined by Lee and Yi (1993) is the set of motions that can separate two components along the three principal axes. We define the IFM not only along the principle axes, but in the whole 3D space, which can be done using halfspaces. Fig. 5 shows some examples of the IFMs between parts in 2D space. The white area in the circles give the allowed motions to separate the components. Combinations of two IFMs can be taken by intersecting both IFM spaces, as can be seen in Fig. 6.

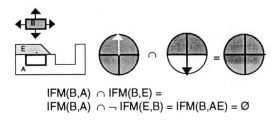

IFM(B,A) ∩ IFM(B,E) =
IFM(B,A) ∩ ¬ IFM(E,B) = IFM(B,AE) = Ø

Fig. 6. Combinations of IFMs.

We distinguish several types of connections, such as attachment, sliding, pen-hole, screw pen-hole, gluing and welding connections. The first two of this list can be further subdivided into (see also Fig. 7):

- attachment
  - plain attachment
  - wall attachment
  - corner attachment
- sliding
  - plain sliding
  - blind sliding
  - 2-way sliding
  - 2-way blind sliding.

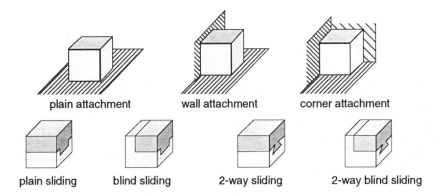

Fig. 7. Some connection features.

In Fig. 8, a connection feature with its characteristics is shown. Here the IP and FP are positioned exactly above each other. Chamfers are given as geometrical refine-ments to easily assemble both components. The IPath is one straight translation. The IFM shows that sliding may happen parallel to the yz-plane and in the positive z-direction.

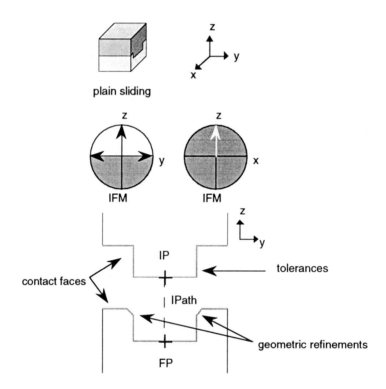

Fig. 8. A connection feature with its characteristics.

3.3 Handling features

To assemble a component, it is also important to know where and how a gripper can grasp the component. Some areas on the component cannot be grasped because these are error-sensitive for grasping or easy to damage, e.g. thread on a bolt. Contact faces between component and PA are areas that cannot be used for grasping either. These contact faces are, however, dependent on the PA, and so dependent on the chosen assembly sequence. Every part has a handling feature, which contains the error-sensitive or easy-to-damage faces, the gripper that can be used for grasp-ing, and the faces where the part can be grasped independently of any PA. Handling features are, besides to determine the grip faces, also used to determine which faces can be used to fix base parts in fixtures.

Connection and handling features do have a close link with each other: knowing the connection features between a part and a PA can also say something about the handling features, e.g. the grip faces are not primarily placed on the contact faces (this only done in special cases, e.g. a tiny pen in a large hole). Fig. 9 shows an example of a handling feature.

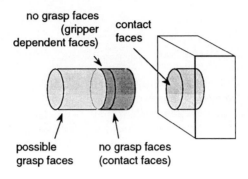

no grasp faces
(gripper
dependent faces)

contact
faces

possible
grasp faces

no grasp faces
(contact faces)

Fig. 9. Handling features.

3.3 Use of assembly features

We think that assembly features as defined above are useful in the assembly planning activities described in section 2.2. The concepts of connection and handling features, introduced above for parts, can be extended to components for this purpose.

In generating the possible hierarchy of an assembled product, the assembly features give more information about geometric stability and uniformity in assembly direction than only geometric information from a boundary representation or a CSG model.

In assembly sequence generation, also other aspects can be taken into account. Components with connections having no internal freedom of motion are most of the time used to hold other components in position, which has consequences for the assembly sequence. For example a screw must be assembled after the component that is connected by that screw.

Every connection feature can have a priority that gives the difficulty of the assembly operation. It is, for example, easier and faster to assemble three blocks from right to left, than to place first the two on the outside and thereafter the one in the middle. This information is captured in the assembly features, and can be used in generating a schedule.

The handling features in combination with the connection features give an appropriate set of faces that can be grasped. This gives faster grasp planning methods, because it is not necessary anymore to search the complete geometric model for grasp faces. The handling features give also the opportunity to take flexible grasp faces dependent on the PA that has already been assembled.

For some connection features, specific motion planning strategies can be given, with the advantage that the best strategies can be used.

Another advantage of using assembly features in the assembly planning functions is that redundancy in generated information is limited. The information generated in one function can be used by all other functions, because it is kept in the product model.

4 Design by features

For the designer and assembly planner to be able to specify and manipulate assembly features, a feature modelling system is required that supports a design-by-features approach (Pratt and Wilson 1985; Cunningham and Dixon 1988). Assigning (functional) meaning to form elements of an object is here not done by feature recognition after the creation of the geometric model, but during the design phase: the designer expresses his intentions directly with features.

In this section we discuss different feature representations and describe the facilities offered by GeoNode, an experimental feature modelling system developed at Delft University of Technology (van Emmerik 1990).

4.1 Representation of features

Features are parametrized procedural descriptions of form elements with a given functional connotation. Geometrically, features definitions can be based on the same representations as used in solid modelling: boundary models, CSG models, and halfspace models.

Boundary feature models represent features by an explicit set of faces, edges and vertices. Features are described either as an open volume (*surface feature*) or as a closed volume (*volume feature*). In both cases, non-manifold modelling can be used to represent reference faces, symmetry axes, virtual faces, etc. The main advantage of boundary feature models is that faces, edges and vertices can be directly indexed, because they are explicitly present in the model.

In a CSG feature model, features are represented by primitive solids that are combined with an object by use of set operators, mostly the difference operator. The main advantages of CSG feature models are the compact representation, the explicit dimensioning and positioning parameters, and the simple and intuitive way of defining them. A drawback is that individual faces and edges cannot be referenced.

Faux (1986) and van Emmerik (1990) combine the best of boundary and CSG feature models by using a halfspace representation. Just as primitives in a CSG representation, features can be represented as the intersection of a number of halfspaces. Features, however, do not necessarily have to form a closed volume, as for the primitives in a CSG representation. In Fig. 10, a slot is modelled as the intersection of three halfspaces.

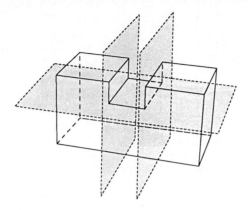

Fig. 10. Slot modelled with three halfspaces.

The halfspace feature model combines the advantages of a compact representation and the possibility of individual reference of the faces. A disadvantage is that the validity of an object is no longer guaranteed. This disadvantage can be overcome by using constraints, which can fix certain relations between halfspaces of a feature in such a way that the validity is guaranteed.

4.2 Feature specification

Besides facilities to geometrically represent features, a feature modelling system should offer facilities to support geometrical parametrization (variational geometry), topological parametrization (e.g. patterns), conditional geometry and constraints. These are best supported by a procedural language. A drawback of a procedural description is a less intuitive and interactive specification and editing mode. Preferably, one would have the opportunity of both procedural modelling and interactive graphical manipulation. This is realised in the GeoNode system.

Direct manipulation

Graphical manipulation with a mouse is supported in a graphics window showing the objects in wire frame representation. Objects can be instantiated from a predefined class of parametrized objects. Objects are positioned and oriented by a base coordinate system. One or more additional coordinate systems can be used to specify dimensions: the distances between the base and dimensioning coordinate systems determine the dimensions of the object. All base and dimensioning coordinate systems can be linked into one hierarchy, called the *geometric tree*. In this way geometric relations are specified in an intuitive and natural way.

In Fig. 11, b1 is the base coordinate system of the block, and the dimensions are determined by the dimensioning coordinate system d. For the cylinder, b2 is the base coordinate system, and d the dimensioning coordinate system.

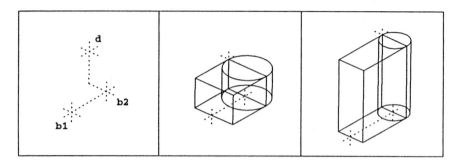

Fig. 11. Geometric tree with some coordinate systems and objects.

A coordinate system is always defined relative to an existing coordinate system, its parent coordinate system. The new coordinate system inherits the global position, scaling and orientation of the parent, after which these can be modified by a transformation relative to the parent. Manipulation of a coordinate system consists of dragging the origin or the end of one of the axes of the projection of the coordinate system; by dragging the origin, the coordinate system is moved, by dragging the end of an axis along that axis, scaling is performed, and by dragging the end of an axis parallel to one of the other axes, the coordinate system is rotated. In this way, position, dimensions and orientation of objects can be changed.

In Fig. 11, b1 is the parent coordinate system of b2, which in turn is the parent of d. Modification of the position of b1 moves the object, but does not change its shape, since b2 and d are defined relative to b1 and thus undergo the same displacement. Modification of b2 implies that the position of d relative to b1 also changes, and thus that the dimensions of the block change. Additionally the position of the cylinder also changes, because b2 is its base coordinate system, and this happens in such a way that the cylinder remains connected to the block in the same manner.

Procedural representation

Besides the graphical representation, a procedural representation of the model is maintained. The procedural representation consists of a number of modelling statements that describe the model; these statements are shown in another window (see Fig. 12). There are, for example, statements for creating coordinate systems, for arithmetical operations on and assignments to the x-, y- and z-components of a coordinate system, for connecting objects to coordinate systems, and for defining a number of objects with similar properties in a pattern.

Statements can be created both by graphical interaction on the geometric tree and by textual input via the keyboard. For example, for creating a new object, graphical interaction is fastest, but for exactly positioning an object, textual input is more suitable. The geometric tree and the procedural representation are automatically kept consistent: if something is modified in one representation, the corresponding change is introduced in the other representation.

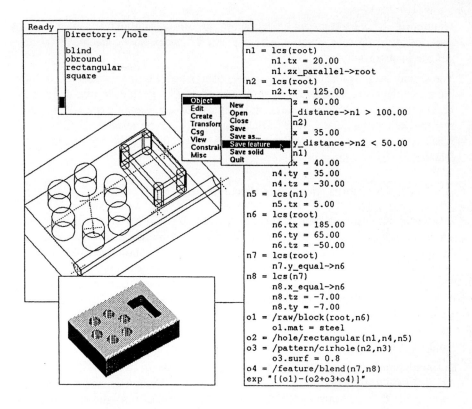

Fig. 12. User interface for feature modelling with GeoNode.

Constraints

Constraints in GeoNode fix relations between coordinate systems, and not directly between objects. Constraints directly between objects often require complex geometric computations to find a solution, which is not the case with constraints between coordinate systems. Therefore constraints are much easier to solve in the latter case, and interactive processing becomes possible. There are a number of standard constraints available in the system, such as distance and parallel constraints. Constraints can be graphically defined between coordinate systems in the geometric tree, and are graphically represented in the tree by special symbols. Constraints between objects can be added to the system by implementing a conversion routine that converts such a constraint into a set of constraints between coordinate systems. In this way, positioning constraints (e.g. an *against* constraint) have been implemented in the system.

Top-down design

A generic description of a feature can be created by constructing a shape from primitive objects or halfspaces, using constraints to guarantee the validity of the feature. Complex features can be defined by combining simple features. A class of generic features can be stored in a library, and instances can be created from these generic features.

The system very well supports a top-down design process of an assembly. Initially the parts can be represented by simple volumes. The geometric tree defines the general arrangement of these parts. At this point the arrangement can still be easily manipulated and adjusted. In a further stage parts can be refined and the mating relations can be specified with connection features. Finally the parameters of the features can be fine-tuned and optimized.

4.3 Multiple feature views and feature conversion

In general, for different applications, different classes of features will have to be used, and hence different feature models will result, although still describing the same object. For instance, in the assembly planning application described above, at least two different feature models will have to be maintained simultaneously: a connection feature model and a handling feature model. A complete design process will thus require multiple feature views, not only for specific applications such as design, part manufacturing, assembly planning, and stress analysis, but even for one application there will be different feature classes, and hence a need for different feature models.

In a concurrent engineering environment, one would like to have a CAD/CAM system that would support all different feature views simultaneously, and would maintain the consistency between the different feature models. It should be possible to impose new features on the model and the system should adapt the underlying geometric model as far as it does not invalidate other views. Further, it should be possible to propagate changes to parameters and constraints from one view to the other views. If a constraint in any view is violated, this should be reported, or the change should be prohibited by the system.

With a feature recognition approach, it is not possible to impose a specific feature directly onto the model. Instead, the geometric model will have to be changed before the feature can be recognized! If, for example, to avoid unnecessary tool changes, the same gripper would preferably be applied for more than one part, it would be desirable to impose the same feature on multiple parts. A feature recognition approach could only achieve this in an indirect way.

With a design-by-feature approach, the system is able to accommodate these requests directly. Feature conversion between views (i.e. the translation of a set of features into a different set of features) would in this sense be a matching process that would modify the underlying geometric model to accommodate the requests from the different feature views and that would maintain at the same time the consistency between the views. To implement such feature conversion, we are extending the GeoNode feature modelling system with facilities for multiple feature views.

5 Conclusions

So far, feature modelling has been mainly applied to process planning for manufacturing. It seems advantageous to use the feature concept also for assembly planning. By using features, the difficult bottom-up approach of recognizing mating conditions from the pure geometry is replaced by a more top-down, goal-directed specification.

By integrating the assembly feature approach in a multi-view feature modelling environment, a real simultaneous or concurrent engineering design process can be supported, opening opportunities for a real "design-for-assembly" approach.

References

Boneschanscher, N. (1993), Plan Generation for Flexible Assembly Systems. *PhD thesis*, Delft University of Technology, The Netherlands.

Bronsvoort, W.F. and Jansen, F.W. (1993), Feature Modelling and Conversion - Key Concepts to Concurrent Engineering. *Computers in Industry*, 21(1): 61-86.

van Bruggen, M., Baartman, J.P. and Bronsvoort, W.F. (1993), Grips on Parts. *Proceedings of the 1993 IEEE International Conference on Robotics and Automation, Volume 2*, 2-6 May, Atlanta, USA, IEEE Computer Society Press, Los Alamitos: 828-833.

Cunningham, J.J. and Dixon, J.R. (1988), Design with Features: the Origin of Features. *Proceedings of the 1988 Computers in Engineering Conference and Exhibition 1*, ASME: 237-243.

van Emmerik, M.J.G.M. (1990), Interactive Design of Parameterized 3D models by Direct Manipulation. *PhD thesis*, Delft University of Technology, Delft University Press, Delft, The Netherlands.

Faux, I.D. (1986), Reconciliation of Design and Manufacturing Requirements for Product Description Data using Functional Primitive Part Features. *CAM-I report R-86-ANC/-GM/PP-01.1*, CAM-I, Arlington.

Heemskerk, C.J.M.H. (1990), A Concept for Computer Aided Process Planning for Flexible Assembly. *PhD thesis*, Delft University of Technology, The Netherlands.

van Holland, W., Boneschanscher, N. and Bronsvoort, W.F. (1992), Task Assignment in a Flexible Assembly Cell Using AND/OR Graphs. *Proceedings 23rd International Symposium on Industrial Robots*, Basañez, L. (ed.), 6-9 October, Barcelona, Spain, Asociación Española de Robótica: 653-658 + 642.

Homem de Mello, L.S. and Sanderson, A.C. (1991), A Basic Algorithm for the Generation of Assembly Plans. *Computer-Aided Mechanical Assembly Planning*, Homem de Mello, L.S. and Lee, S. (eds.), Kluwer Academic Publishers, Dordrecht, The Netherlands: 163-190.

Ko, H. and Lee, K. (1987), Automatic Assembling Procedure Generation from Mating Conditions. *Computer-Aided Design*, 19(1): 3-10.

Lee, S. (1991), Backward Assembly Planning with DFA Analysis, *Computer-Aided Mechanical Assembly Planning*, Homem de Mello, L.S. and Lee, S. (eds.), Kluwer Academic Publishers, Dordrecht, The Netherlands: 341-381.

Lee, S. and Yi, C. (1993), Subassembly Stability and Reorientation. *Proceedings of the 1993 IEEE International Conference on Robotics and Automation, Volume 2*, 2-6 May, Atlanta, USA, IEEE Computer Society Press, Los Alamitos: 521-526.

Libardi, E.C. Jr., Dixon, J.R. and Simmons, M.K. (1988), Computer Environments for the Design of Mechanical Assemblies: A Research Review. *Engineering with Computers*, 3: 121-136.

Lozano-Pérez, T. and Wilson, R.H. (1993), Assembly Sequencing for Arbitrary Motions. *Proceedings of the 1993 IEEE International Conference on Robotics and Automation, Volume 2*, 2-6 May, Atlanta, USA, IEEE Computer Society Press, Los Alamitos: 527-532.

Martens, P. (1991), Cad/Cam for Assembly Planning. *PhD thesis*, Delft University of Technology, The Netherlands.

Meijer, B.R. and Jonker, P.P. (1991), The Architecture and Philosophy of the DIAC (Delft Intelligent Assembly Cell). *Proceedings of the 1991 IEEE International Conference on Robotics and Automation*, 7-12 April, Sacramento, USA, IEEE Computer Society Press, Los Alamitos: 2218-2223.

Pratt, M.J. and Wilson, P.R. (1985), Requirements for the Support of Form Features in a Solid Modeling System. *Report R-85-ASPP-01*, CAM-I, Arlington, Texas.

Srikanth, S., Turner, J. and Sanderson, A. (1991), Establishing Part Positioning in Assembly Modeling. *Product Modeling for Computer-Aided Design and Manufacturing*, Turner, J., Pegna, J. and Wozny, M. (eds.), Elsevier Science Publishers B.V. (North-Holland): 199-226.

Waarts, J.J., Boneschanscher, N. and Bronsvoort, W.F. (1992), A Semi-automatic Assembly Sequence Planner. *Proceedings of the 1992 IEEE International Conference on Robotics and Automation, Volume 3*, 12-14 May, Nice, France, IEEE Computer Society Press, Los Alamitos: 2431-2438.

Wesley, M.A., Lozano-Pérez, T., Lieberman, L.I., Lavin, M.A. and Grossman, D.D. (1980), A Geometrical Modeling System for Automated Mechanical Assembly. *IBM Journal of Research and Development*, 24(1): 64-74.

Wolter, J.D. (1991), On the Automatic Generation of Assembly Plans, *Computer-Aided Mechanical Assembly Planning*, Homem de Mello, L.S. and Lee, S. (eds.), Kluwer Academic Publishers, Dordrecht, The Netherlands: 263-288.

Zussman, E., Lenz, E. and Shpitalni, M. (1990), An Approach to the Automatic Assembly Planning Problem, *Annals of the CIRP*, 39(1): 33-37.

Triangular B-Splines

Hans-Peter Seidel

Universität Erlangen, IMMD IX, Graphische Datenverarbeitung,
Am Weichselgarten 9, 91058 Erlangen, Germany

1. INTRODUCTION.

Triangular B-splines are a new tool for the modeling of complex objects with non-rectangular topology. The new B-spline scheme is based on blending functions and control points and allows modeling piecewise polynomial surfaces of degree n that are C^{n-1}-continuous throughout [4, 15, 17]. An implementation of the new scheme at the University of Waterloo has succeeded in demonstrating the practical feasibility of the fundamental algorithms underlying the new scheme [6, 7].

One of the features that make triangular B-splines attractive for applications in graphics and robotics is their *low degree*: It is possible, e.g., to construct C^1-continuous surfaces with piecewise quadratics (total parametric degree $d = 2$) (in contrast to the more standard bi-quadratic tensor-product surfaces having total parametric degree $d = 4$).

Furthermore, it is possible to represent any piecewise polynomial surface (rectangular or non-rectangular topology) as a linear combination of triangular B-splines. Thus, triangular B-splines provide a *unified data format* for fairly arbitrary surface types.

Finally, triangular B-splines are ideally suited for *blending applications*. Using triangular B-splines, it becomes possible, e.g., to achieve smooth C^1-blends with piecewise quadratics. Again, this compares favourably with other approaches, where the parametric degree of the blending surfaces is typically exceedingly high.

Our presentation is organized as follows: Section 2 gives a brief introduction to triangular B-splines and outlines some of their main features. Section 3 discusses applications of triangular B-splines in solid modeling: Section 3.1 focuses on their low degree, Section 3.2 discusses representation conversion, and Section 3.3 applies triangular B-splines to the construction of smooth blends, and presents a solution to the polygonal hole problem. We finally finish off with some concluding remarks.

2. TRIANGULAR B-SPLINES

Let $T = \{\Delta(I) = [\mathbf{t}_{i_0}, \mathbf{t}_{i_1}, \mathbf{t}_{i_2}] \mid I = (i_0, i_1, i_2) \in \mathcal{I} \subseteq \mathbf{Z}_+^3\}$ be an arbitrary *triangulation* of the parameter plane $\mathbb{R}^2$, or of some bounded domain $D \subset \mathbb{R}^2$ (see Fig. 1), and suppose that a *sequence of knots* $\mathbf{t}_{i,0}, \ldots, \mathbf{t}_{i,n}$ is assigned to every vertex $\mathbf{t}_i$ in this triangulation in such a way that $\mathbf{t}_{i,0} = \mathbf{t}_i$, and such that any three knots form a proper triangle. Consider the sets

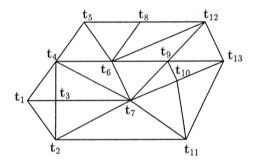

Figure 1: Triangulation of a bounded domain $D \subset \mathbb{R}^2$

$$V_\beta^I = \{\mathbf{t}_{i_0,0}, \ldots, \mathbf{t}_{i_0,\beta_0}, \ldots, \mathbf{t}_{i_2,0}, \ldots, \mathbf{t}_{i_2,\beta_2}\}. \tag{1}$$

and define the triangular spline $M_\beta^I(\mathbf{u}) = M(u|V_\beta^I)$ recursively as

$$M(u|\mathbf{v}_0, \mathbf{v}_1, \mathbf{v}_2) = \frac{\chi_{[\mathbf{v}_0, \mathbf{v}_1, \mathbf{v}_2]}(\mathbf{u})}{|d(\mathbf{v}_0, \mathbf{v}_1, \mathbf{v}_2)|}, \tag{2}$$

and

$$M(u|\mathbf{v}_0..\mathbf{v}_m) = \sum_{j=0}^{2} \lambda_j(\mathbf{u}) M(u|\mathbf{v}_0..\widehat{\mathbf{v}_{i_j}}..\mathbf{v}_m), \tag{3}$$

where

$$\chi_{[\mathbf{v}_0,\mathbf{v}_1,\mathbf{v}_2)}(\mathbf{u}) = \begin{cases} 1 & \text{if } \mathbf{u} \in [\mathbf{v}_0, \mathbf{v}_1, \mathbf{v}_2) \\ 0 & \text{otherwise} \end{cases} \tag{4}$$

is the characteristic function on the *half-open convex hull* $[\mathbf{v}_0, \mathbf{v}_1, \mathbf{v}_2)$ (see [15]),

$$d(\mathbf{v}_0, \mathbf{v}_1, \mathbf{v}_2) = \det \begin{pmatrix} 1 & 1 & 1 \\ \mathbf{v}_0 & \mathbf{v}_1 & \mathbf{v}_2 \end{pmatrix} \tag{5}$$

is twice the area of the triangle $\triangle(\mathbf{v}_0, \mathbf{v}_1, \mathbf{v}_2)$,

$$W_{i_0,i_1,i_2} = \{\mathbf{v}_{i_0}, \mathbf{v}_{i_1}, \mathbf{v}_{i_2}\} \subseteq \{\mathbf{v}_0, \ldots, \mathbf{v}_m\} \tag{6}$$

is any subset of affinely independent points, and $\lambda_j(\mathbf{u})$ are the barycentric coordinates of $\mathbf{u}$ w.r.t. v_{i_j}. Note that (3) is independent of the specific choice of W_{i_0,i_1,i_2} [11]. The following properties of the triangular B-splines $M_\beta^I(\mathbf{u})$ are immediate from their definition:

- Piecewise polynomial of degree $n = |\beta| = \beta_0 + \beta_1 + \beta_2$.

- Non-negativity: $M_\beta^I(\mathbf{u}) \geq 0$ for all $\mathbf{u} \in \mathbb{R}^2$.

- Local support on the closed convex hull $[V_\beta^I]$.

- C^{n-1}-continuity everywhere if the knots are in general position.

Furthermore, the triangular spline $M_\beta^I(\mathbf{u})$ can be computed by the recurrence (2), (3).

In order to make these splines useful for modeling applications, we first have to renormalize to ensure affine invariance. The *normalized B-splines* $N_\beta^I(\mathbf{u})$ are defined as

$$N_\beta^I(\mathbf{u}) = d(\mathbf{t}_{i_0,\beta_0}, \mathbf{t}_{i_1,\beta_1}, \mathbf{t}_{i_2,\beta_2}) M_\beta^I(\mathbf{u}). \tag{7}$$

These are the blending functions of the new triangular B-spline scheme. It can be shown that

$$\sum_{i \in \mathcal{I}} \sum_{|\beta|=n} N_\beta^I(\mathbf{u}) \equiv 1, \tag{8}$$

so the normalized B-splines form a partition of unity. We also note that specialization of the above approach to the curve case yields precisely the standard univariate B-spline functions $N_i^n(u)$.

An arbitrary triangular B-spline surface of degree n over a given triangulation T is then defined as

$$F(\mathbf{u}) = \sum_{I \in \mathcal{I}} \sum_{|\beta|=n} \mathbf{c}_{I,\beta} N_\beta^I(\mathbf{u}). \tag{9}$$

The points $\mathbf{c}_{I,\beta} \in \mathbb{R}^3$ are the *control points* that control the shape of the surface F.

Some of the main properties of the new scheme are summarized below:

Piecewise Polynomial: $F(\mathbf{u})$ is a piecewise polynomial of degree n.

Convex Hull Property: A B-spline surface lies in the convex hull of its control points.

Locality: Movement of the control point $\mathbf{c}_\beta^I$ only influences the region of the surface on the triangle $\triangle(I)$ and on those triangles surrounding it.

Smoothness A degree n B-spline surface is a piecewise polynomial of degree n over the sub-triangulation induced by its knot net that is C^{n-1}-continuous everywhere if its knots are in general position.

Affine Invariance: The relationship between the control points and the B-spline surface is invariant under affine coordinate transformations.

Although it is desirable in general to have surfaces that are as smooth as possible, it is necessary for practical applications to be able to model discontinuities like sharp edges or corners as well. It is easy to show that knot multiplicities along a line reduce the order of continuity along this line. For example, a degree 2 surface with knots in general position is C^1-continuous everywhere. Placing three knots on a line reduces the continuity to C^0 and placing four knots produces a discontinuity along the line. Thus, the underlying knot net provides additional degrees of freedom to control the shape of the surface. Figures 2 and 3 show the quadratic normalized B-spline blending functions over different knot configurations.

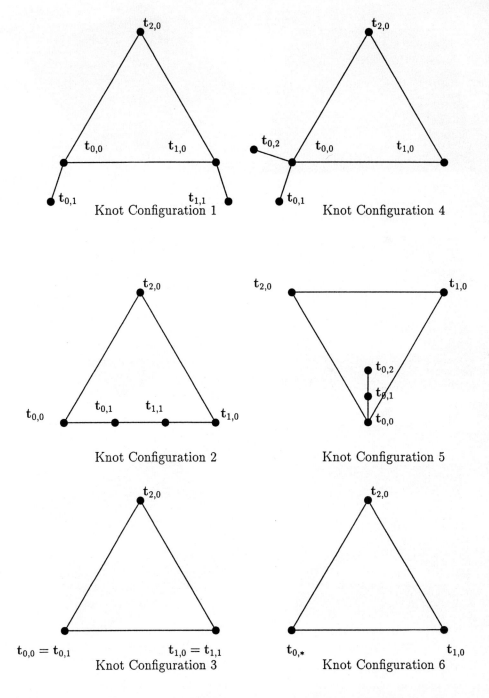

Figure 2: Six different knot configurations with different multiplicities for the quadratic normalized normalized B-splines $N_{110}^I(\mathbf{u})$ and $N_{200}^I(\mathbf{u})$.

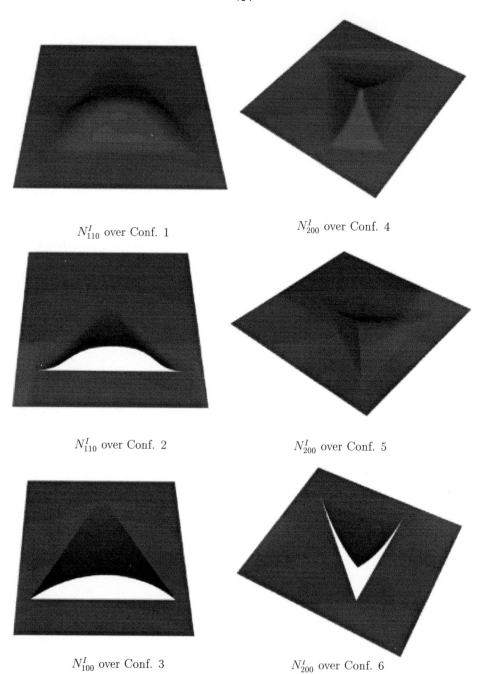

N_{110}^I over Conf. 1

N_{200}^I over Conf. 4

N_{110}^I over Conf. 2

N_{200}^I over Conf. 5

N_{100}^I over Conf. 3

N_{200}^I over Conf. 6

Figure 3: The quadratic normalized B-splines $N_{110}^I(\mathbf{u})$ and $N_{200}^I(\mathbf{u})$ over the six different knot configurations shown in the previous Figure.

3. Triangular B-Splines for Modeling in Graphics and Robotics

This section discusses the potential of triangular B-splines for modeling in graphics and robotics. Specifically, we focus on their low algebraic degree, on representation conversion, and on the construction of smooth blends.

3.1. Optimal smoothness and low degree

It is a fundamental goal in modeling to keep the complexity of the modeling primitives as low as possible. For parametric surfaces this translates into the requirement to use surfaces of low parametric degree: While it is possible, e.g., to compute exact intersections between piecewise quadratics, only approximate solutions are available for surfaces of higher degree.

A conflicting requirement stems from the need to construct surfaces that are also as smooth as possible. If tensor-product surfaces are used, e.g., we need bi-quadratic surfaces to achieve tangent plane continuity, and bi-cubic surfaces to achieve continuous curvature. Bi-quadratic surfaces are surfaces of total parametric degree $d = 4$, while bi-cubic surfaces have total parametric degree $d = 6$. Lower degree tensor-product surfaces will not yield the required order of continuity.

A different situation arises if triangular B-splines are being used. Section 2 shows that it is possible, e.g., to construct C^1-continuous surfaces with piecewise quadratics (total parametric degree $d = 2$) and C^2-continuous surfaces with piecewise cubics (total parametric degree $d = 3$). Thus triangular B-splines only require *half the degree* of tensor-product surfaces to achieve the *same order of continuity*.

3.2. Representation conversion

Another requirement in modeling is to be able to convert between different representations. In particular, one is interested in data formats that allow the representation of fairly arbitrary objects in a unified and coherent way. The following theorem [17] shows that triangular B-splines provide such a unified data format for any piecewise polynomial surface (rectangular or non-rectangular topology):

Theorem 3.1 *Any piecewise polynomial surface of degree n over a triangulation T can be represented as linear combination of triangular B-splines*

$$F(\mathbf{u}) = \sum_I \sum_{|\beta|=n} \mathbf{c}_{I,\beta} N_\beta^I(\mathbf{u}). \tag{10}$$

The coefficients $\mathbf{c}_{I,\beta}$ can be computed by evaluating the polar form (or blossom) [5, 13] of the spline on a sequence of knots.

Since any polygonal domain can be decomposed into triangles, the above theorem applies equally well to surfaces with triangular, rectangular, or arbitrary topology.

The benefits of Theorem 3.1 are further illustrated by Fig. 4 and Fig. 5. Fig. 4 shows a piecewise quadratic test surface with its Bézier control net (top) and triangular B-spline control net (bottom). While the movement of a single Bézier control point will generally destroy the smoothness of the surface and introduce sharp edges (Fig. 5 (top)), movement of a triangular B-spline control point will also alter the shape of the surface, but will preserve the overall C^1-continuity of the surface throughout (Fig. 5 (bottom)).

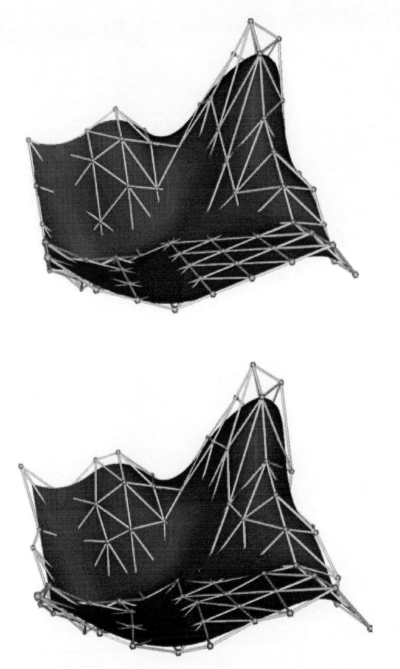

Figure 4: A quadratic C^1-continuous piecewise polynomial test surface with Bézier control net (top) and B-spline control net (bottom).

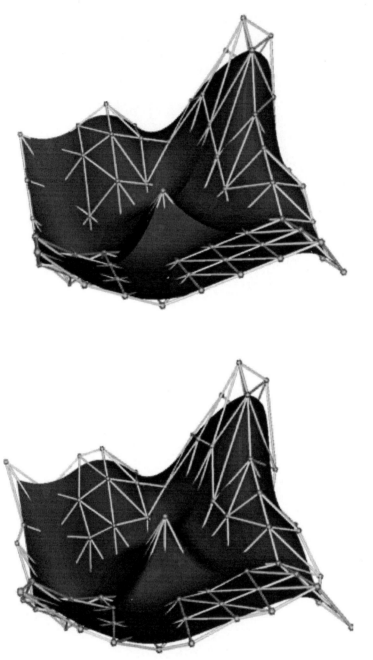

Figure 5: Influence of moving a single control point: If a Bézier control point is moved, the C^1-continuity of the surface is destroyed, and a sharp edge is introduced (top). If a B-spline control point is moved, the C^1-continuity of the surface is preserved (bottom).

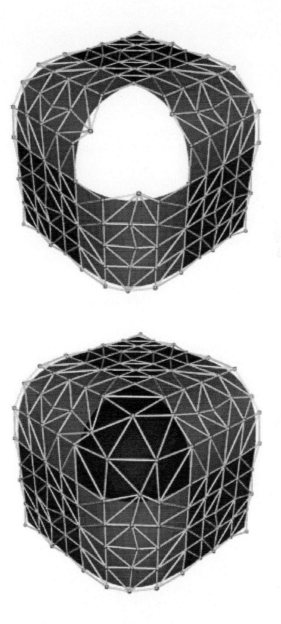

Figure 6: Solving the polygonal hole problem using triangular B-splines: First, the piecewise polynomial surface around the hole is represented as linear combination of B-splines (top). This B-spline surface can then be extended to produce an overall C^{n-1}-continuous fill of the hole (bottom). Note that this method can achieve C^1-continuity with piecewise quadratics, and C^2-continuity with piecewise cubics.

3.3. Smooth Blends

Another consequence of Theorem 3.1 is a method for the construction of smooth blends and for the filling of polygonal holes: Suppose that two primary piecewise polynomial surfaces F_1 and F_2 of degree n are given. Theorem 3.1 allows the representation of both F_1 and F_2 as linear combinations of triangular B-splines over different regions A_1 and A_2 of the parameter domain. Any extension of the resulting triangular B-splines to a domain $D \subset \mathbb{R}^2$ satisfying

$$A_1 \cup A_2 \subseteq D \tag{11}$$

will then produce a smooth blend F between F_1 and F_2. The analogous procedure works for the polygonal hole problem.

If F_1 and F_2 are piecewise polynomial of degree n, then the above method produces a C^{n-1}-continuous blend F that is piecewise polynomial of degree n as well. Given the desired order of continuity, this is the lowest degree possible.

The application of this method to the filling of a triangular hole is illustrated by Fig. 6: First, the piecewise polynomial surface around the hole is represented as linear combination of triangular B-splines (Theorem 3.1). This B-spline surface can then be extended to produce an overall C^{n-1}-continuous fill of the hole. Note that this method can achieve C^1-continuity with piecewise quadratics, and C^2-continuity with piecewise cubics.

4. Conclusion

The new B-spline scheme offers a method for modeling complex irregular objects over arbitrary triangulations and exhibits many features that are desirable for applications in graphics and robotics. An implementation of the new scheme at the University of Waterloo has demonstrated the practical feasibility of the fundamental algorithms underlying the new surface scheme. Quadratic and cubic surfaces over arbitrary triangulations can be edited and rendered in real-time. Applications like the filling of polygonal holes or the construction of smooth blends demonstrate the potential of the new scheme when dealing with concrete design problems. Further improvements to our editor that simplify user input, intersection computations, and additional applications are currently under way.

References

[1] S. Auerbach, R.H.J. Gmelig Meyling, M. Neamtu, and H. Schaeben. Approximation and geometric modeling with simplex B-splines associated with irregular triangles. *Computer-Aided Geom. Design*, 8:67–87, 1991.

[2] W. Dahmen and C.A. Micchelli. On the linear independence of multivariate B-splines I. Triangulations of simploids. *SIAM J. Numer. Anal.*, 19:993–1012, 1982.

[3] W. Dahmen and C.A. Micchelli. Recent progress in multivariate splines. In *Approximation Theory IV*, pages 27–121. Academic Press, 1983.

[4] W. Dahmen, C.A. Micchelli, and H.-P. Seidel. Blossoming begets B-splines built better by B-patches. *Math. Comp.*, 59:97–115, 1992.

[5] P. de Casteljau. *Formes à Pôles*. Hermes, Paris, 1985.

[6] P. Fong. Shape control for B-splines over arbitrary triangulations. Master's thesis, University of Waterloo, Waterloo, Canada, 1992.

[7] Ph. Fong and H.-P. Seidel. An implementation of multivariate B-spline surfaces over arbitrary triangulations. In *Proc. Graphics Interface '92*, pages 1–10. Morgan Kaufmann Publishers, 1992.

[8] R.H.J. Gmelig Meyling. *Polynomial spline approximation in two variables*. PhD thesis, University of Amsterdam, 1986.

[9] T.A. Grandine. The stable evaluation of multivariate simplex splines. *Math. Comp.*, 50:197–205, 1988.

[10] K. Höllig. Multivariate splines. *SIAM J. Numer. Anal.*, 19:1013–1031, 1982.

[11] C.A. Micchelli. On a numerically efficient method for computing with multivariate B-splines. In W. Schempp and K. Zeller, editors, *Multivariate Approximation Theory*, pages 211–248, Basel, 1979. Birkhäuser.

[12] M. Neamtu. *A Contribution to the Theory and Practice of Multivariate Splines*. PhD thesis, University of Twente, Enschede, 1991.

[13] L. Ramshaw. Blossoming: A connect-the-dots approach to splines. Technical report, Digital Systems Research Center, Palo Alto, 1987.

[14] L. Ramshaw. Blossoms are polar forms. *Computer-Aided Geom. Design*, 6:323–358, 1989.

[15] H.-P. Seidel. Polar forms and triangular B-Spline surfaces. In *Blossoming: The New Polar-Form Approach to Spline Curves and Surfaces, SIGGRAPH '91 Course Notes #26*, pages 8.1–8.52. ACM SIGGRAPH, 1991.

[16] H.-P. Seidel. Symmetric recursive algorithms for surfaces: B-patches and the de Boor algorithm for polynomials over triangles. *Constr. Approx.*, 7:257–279, 1991.

[17] H.-P. Seidel. Representing piecewise polynomials as linear combinations of multivariate B-splines. In T. Lyche and L. L. Schumaker, editors, *Curves and Surfaces*, pages 559–566. Academic Press, 1992.

[18] C.R. Traas. Practice of bivariate quadratic simplicial splines. In W. Dahmen, M. Gasca, and C.A. Micchelli, editors, *Computation of Curves and Surfaces*, pages 383–422, Dordrecht, 1990. NATO ASI Series, Kluwer Academic Publishers.

Blending Surfaces
with Minimal Curvature

Günther Greiner
Universität Erlangen, IMMD IX, Graphische Datenverarbeitung,
Am Weichselgarten 9, 91058 Erlangen, Germany

1. INTRODUCTION.

Both in Graphics and Robotics one often faces the problem to construct "optimal" curves and surfaces subject to certain constraints. Here optimal typically means that the curve or surface minimizes length, area, curvature or other geometric properties.

In Graphics for example, scattered data interpolation as well as blending surfaces lead to such problems. In scattered data interpolation one has to construct a surface which does not oscillate too rapidly and goes through a sampled set of points in the space. Finding a blending surface (i.e. a rather smooth transition between primary surfaces) amounts to construct a (nice-looking) surface which satisfies certain boundary conditions determined by the primary surfaces.

In Robotics, path planning can be considered as a problem of the above type. One has to find a curve which connects two points and optimizes a mixture of length, curvature and the distance to obstacles.

All these problems can be solved by finding a surface and curve respectively, which satisfies two conditions:
— it has to fulfill certain constraints and
— it has to minimize an appropriate functional, which measures the
   total curvature and surface area (arc length).

This optimization problem is highly nonlinear, a direct solution (if possible at all) will be very involved. We present an iterative procedure. Instead of investigating the nonlinear problem, we consider a sequence of quadratic variational problems. Thus, in each step of the iteration, one has to solve a linear system. In each step one obtains a curve or surface which satisfies the constraints. The smoothness of the curve/surface will increase progressively.

In this paper we describe in detail the method for constructing blending surfaces. These surfaces are needed to construct a smooth transition between two primary

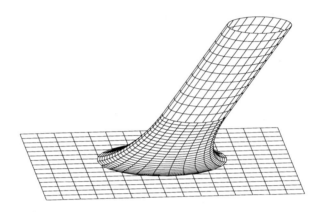

Figure 1:

surfaces or to close a hole in a single surface. One may think of a cylinder which intersects a plane (not necessarily perpendicular), cf. Fig. 1. In a neighborhood of the intersecting ellipse one removes part of the surface and the cylinder. Then the problem is to find a surface which gives a rather smooth transition between the cylinder and the plane. Such a surface is called "blending surface". In this paper we concentrate on surfaces which have continuous tangent planes at the joints. Equivalently, we require that the normal vector varies continuously across the boundary to the primary surfaces. Of course, there are many possibilities to generate such a blending surface, the rolling ball method [8], the potential method [6], the pde method [2] and many more. The idea of our approach is to choose the surface with minimal curvature in mean square sense from among the many surfaces which yield tangential continuous transition to the primary surface. More generally, one minimizes a combination of surface area and curvature. In order to apply the method in geometric modeling we construct the surface as tensor product spline surface.

Mathematically, the problem is the following:
Given closed curves γ_0 and γ_1 in $\mathbb{R}^3$, and vector fields Γ_0 and Γ_1 along γ_0 and γ_1 respectively. Find a tensor product spline surface (briefly TP spline surface) $F : [0, 2\pi] \times [0, 1] \to \mathbb{R}^3$ which is periodic with respect to the first variable and satisfies the following boundary conditions:

$$F(u,0) = \gamma_0(u) , \qquad\qquad F(u,1) = \gamma_1(u) ,$$
$$\frac{\partial F}{\partial v}(u,0) = \Gamma_0(u) , \qquad\qquad \frac{\partial F}{\partial v}(u,1) = -\Gamma_1(u) . \qquad (1.1)$$

γ_0 and γ_1 describe the boundary curves of the primary surfaces. Γ_0 and Γ_1 represent tangential fields of the primary surfaces along γ_0 and γ_1 respectively. In addition to the boundary conditions we require that F minimizes a combination of curvature and surface area. More precisely, we require that the following functional attains a minimum at F :

$$J(F) := \int_{[0,2\pi]\times[0,1]} H_F(u,v)^2 \, d\omega_F(u,v) + a \int_{[0,2\pi]\times[0,1]} d\omega_F(u,v) \qquad (1.2)$$

Here H_F denotes the mean curvature of F and $d\omega_F$ the surface element of F .

The functional J is highly nonlinear, not even convex. Thus a numerical solution will be rather involved. We are going to describe how functionals can be choosen which are very close to the one defined in (1.2) and whose minimum can be determined very easily. Actually we determine iteratively a sequence of such functionals. The corresponding sequence F_n of minima is likely to converge to the solution of (1.2). Examples show, that already after a few steps $(2 - 4)$ one obtains fairly good blending surfaces (cf. Fig. 2 and Sec. 5).

2. PRELIMINARIES.

We have to recall some notation and results from differential geometry. Let $F : \Omega \rightarrow \mathbb{R}^3$ be a parametrized C^2-continuous surface. The components are denoted by F_1 , F_2 , F_3 . The first fundamental form I_F corresponding to F , (also known as the Riemannian metric induced by F) is given by the following 2×2 matrix (more precisely, matrix-valued function over the parameter space Ω).

$$\begin{pmatrix} g_{F11}(u,v) & g_{F12}(u,v) \\ g_{F21}(u,v) & g_{F22}(u,v) \end{pmatrix} \quad \text{with} \quad g_{Fij}(u,v) := (\partial_i F(u,v) | \partial_j F(u,v))$$

Here ∂_1 and ∂_2 denote the partial derivative with respect to u and v respectively. "$(\cdot|\cdot)$" denotes the usual inner product in Euclidean space. Thus for example

$$(\partial_2 F(u,v) | \partial_1 F(u,v)) = \sum_{k=1}^{3} \frac{\partial F_k}{\partial v}(u,v) \frac{\partial F_k}{\partial u}(u,v) .$$

In the following we will omit the surface parameters "(u,v)" (having in mind that we are dealing with functions!). Also the subscript $_F$ will be omitted as long as we deal with just a single surface. Thus instead of $g_{F12}(u,v)$ we simply write g_{12} . This also applies for the quantities defined subsequently.

The determinant of the matrix (g_{ij}) will be denoted by g . Thus g is a real valued, differentiable function on Ω . We have $g = \|\partial_1 F \times \partial_2 F\|_2^2$ where "$\times$" denotes the vector product and $\|\cdot\|_2$ the Euclidean norm in $\mathbb{R}^3$. Thus the surface element $d\omega_F$ is given by

$$d\omega_F(u,v) = \sqrt{g(u,v)}\, du dv \ .$$

The second fundamental form II_F corresponding to F is defined as follows

$$\begin{pmatrix} h_{11} & h_{12} \\ h_{21} & h_{22} \end{pmatrix} \quad \text{with} \quad h_{ij} = (n_F | \partial_i \partial_j F) \ .$$

where $n_F(u,v) := \dfrac{1}{\sqrt{g(u,v)}} \cdot \partial_1 F(u,v) \times \partial_2 F(u,v)$ is the (normalized) normal vector of the surface given by F . The principal curvatures κ_1 and κ_2 are given by

$$\kappa_1 := \quad \max\{II_F(X,X) : I_F(X,X) = 1\} \quad \text{and}$$
$$\kappa_2 := \quad \min\{II_F(X,X) : I_F(X,X) = 1\}$$

The mean curvature of F is the arithmetic mean of the principal curvatures, i. e.:

$$H_F := \tfrac{1}{2}(\kappa_1 + \kappa_2) \ .$$

It can be described by $\quad H_F = \tfrac{1}{2}\text{trace}(II_F \circ I_F^{-1}) = \tfrac{1}{2g}(h_{11}g_{22} - 2h_{12}g_{12} + h_{22}g_{11}) \ .$ For our considerations another characterisation of H_F is more important. First we have to introduce the Laplace–Beltrami operator Δ_F induced by the Riemannian metric (g_{ij}) . It is a second order differential operator defined as follows:

$$\Delta_F f = \sum_{j,k} \partial_j (g^{jk} \partial_k f) + \tfrac{1}{2g} \sum_j \left(\sum_k g^{jk} \partial_k g \right) \partial_j f \ . \tag{2.1}$$

Here (g^{ik}) denotes the inverse of the matrix (g_{ik}) , i.e.,

$$g^{11} = \tfrac{g_{22}}{g} \qquad g^{12} = g^{21} = -\tfrac{g_{12}}{g} \qquad g^{22} = \tfrac{g_{11}}{g}$$

Essential for our considerations is the following fact: The Laplace–Beltrami operator of F applied to F (componentwise) yields a scalar multiple of the normal vector. The scalar is twice the mean curvature. I. e.

$$\Delta_F F(u,v) = 2H_F(u,v)n_F(u,v) \ , \tag{2.2}$$

where $n_F(u,v)$ the normal vector defined above. It follows that

$$H_F(u,v)^2 = \tfrac{1}{4}(\Delta_F F(u,v) | \Delta_F F(u,v))$$

and hence

$$\int_\Omega H_F(u,v)^2 \, d\omega_F(u,v) = \frac{1}{4} \int_\Omega (\Delta_F F(u,v) | \Delta_F F(u,v)) \sqrt{g_F(u,v)} \, du dv \quad \textbf{(2.3)}$$

A (rather complicated) description of the surface area can be obtained as follows. We have $2 = \mathrm{trace}(Id) = \mathrm{trace}(I_F^{-1} \circ I_F) = \sum_{jk} g^{kj} (\partial_j F | \partial_k F)$. It follows that the surface area of F is given by

$$\int_\Omega 1 \, d\omega_F(u,v) = \frac{1}{2} \int_\Omega \sum_{jk} g_F^{kj}(u,v)(\partial_j F(u,v) | \partial_k F(u,v)) \sqrt{g_F(u,v)} \, du dv \; . \; \textbf{(2.4)}$$

3. THE ALGORITHM.

First we have to fix a suitable subspace of parametrizations. In order that the expressions considered in the previous paragraph make sense, the components F_i of a parametrization have to allow square integrable partial derivatives of order ≤ 2 . Thus it is reasonable to consider subspaces of the Sobolev space $H^2(\Omega, \mathbb{R}^3)$ (see [1]). For practical purposes one will choose finite dimensional spaces. For example, bicubic or biquadratic TP spline surfaces (see the next section). The subspace is denoted by $\mathcal{H}$. Moreover, we define two subspaces of $\mathcal{H}$ as follows:

$$\mathcal{H}_0 := \{ F \in \mathcal{H} : F_{|\partial\Omega} = (\partial_1 F)_{|\partial\Omega} = (\partial_2 F)_{|\partial\Omega} = 0 \}$$

$$\mathcal{H}_1 := \{ F \in \mathcal{H} : F \text{ satisfies the boundary conditions (1.1)} \}$$

$\mathcal{H}_0$ is a linear subspace, $\mathcal{H}_1$ an affine subspace obtained from $\mathcal{H}_0$ be translation.

The problem which we would like to solve (at least approximately) then can be formulated as follows:

Find the minimum of the functional

$$F \mapsto J(F) := \int_{[0,2\pi]\times[0,1]} H_F(u,v)^2 \, d\omega_F(u,v) + a \int_{[0,2\pi]\times[0,1]} d\omega_F(u,v)$$

in the set $\mathcal{H}_1$.

From the considerations in the previous section (see (2.3) and (2.4)), we conclude that a solution G (provided it exists) is also a solution to the following quadratic problem:

Minimize in $\mathcal{H}_1$ the functional

$$F \mapsto J_G(F) := \int_\Omega (\Delta_G F | \Delta_G F)\, d\omega_G + 2a \int_\Omega \sum_{jk} g_G^{kj} (\partial_j F | \partial_k F)\, d\omega_G \ . \quad \textbf{(3.1)}$$

At the first glance this does not help very much, since the solution is necessary to define this functional. On the other hand, we point out that this functional is quadratic (G is fixed!), hence rather easy to solve. Moreover, in case $\tilde{G}$ is close to the solution G, then the functional

$$F \mapsto J_{\tilde{G}}(F) := \int_\Omega (\Delta_{\tilde{G}} F | \Delta_{\tilde{G}} F)\, d\omega_{\tilde{G}} + 2a \int_\Omega \sum_{jk} g_{\tilde{G}}^{kj} (\partial_j F | \partial_k F)\, d\omega_{\tilde{G}} \ .$$

will be close to (**3.1**).

The algorithm which yields a sequence of quadratic variational problems which approximate (**3.1**) is as follows.

3.1 The Algorithm.

1. Initialization.   Define $F_0(u,v) := (1-v)\gamma_0(u) + v\gamma_1(u)$.

2. Iteration.   Given F_n , consider the functional

$$J_n(F) := \int_\Omega (\Delta_{F_n} F | \Delta_{F_n} F)\, d\omega_{F_n} + a \int_\Omega \sum_{jk} g_{F_n}^{kj} (\partial_j F | \partial_k F)\, d\omega_{F_n} \ .$$

Define $F_{n+1} \in \mathcal{H}_1$ to be the solution of the quadratic variational problem

$$J_n(F_{n+1}) = \min\{J_n(F) : F \in \mathcal{H}_1\} \ . \quad \textbf{(3.2)}$$

3.2 Remark.   In every step of the iteration one has to solve a quadratic variational problem. This can be done rather easily. In fact, the minimum is characterized by the fact that the gradient of J_n vanishes. Since J_n is quadratic, its gradient is linear. Thus one only has to solve a linear system. For the finite dimensional case we briefly outline the procedure. More details can be found in [4]. Let $B_n(.,.)$ be the bilinear functional associated with the quadratic functional $J_n(.)$.

- Choose a basis $\{e_m : 1 \le m \le M\}$ of $\mathcal{H}_0$.

- Add vectors $\{e_m : M < m \le P\}$ such that $\{e_m : 1 \le m \le P\}$ form a basis of $\mathcal{H}$.

- Choose an arbitrary surface $\hat{F} = \sum_{m=1}^{P} \xi_m e_m$ which satisfies the boundary condition, i. e. $\hat{F} \in \mathcal{H}_1$.   For $n \ge 1$ one simply chooses $\hat{F} = F_n$!

- Solve the $M \times M$ linear system

$$\left(\sum_{i=1}^{M} B_n(e_j, e_i)x_i = -\sum_{i=1}^{P} B_n(e_j, e_i)\xi_i \right)_{j=1,\dots,M} \ .$$

Then $F_{n+1} = \sum_{m=1}^{M}(x_m + \xi_m)e_m + \sum_{m=M+1}^{P} \xi_m e_m$ yields the next surface.

If no degenaracies occur, this algorithm converges to a solution of our problem. Degeneracies may occur due to the following fact. So far we tacitly assumed that the parametrizations are *regular*, meaning that $\partial_1 F$ and $\partial_2 F$ are linearly independent (at each point $(u, v) \in \Omega$). Equivalently, (g_{ij}) is positive definite. If this is not the case, (g^{ij}) does not exist. Therefore both Δ_F and J_F are not defined. F_0 is regular (provided that γ_0 and γ_1 are regular curves). However it is not clear whether all parametrizations F_n obtained by iteration are regular as well.

3.3 Proposition. If the algorithm yields in each step a regular parametrization F_{n+1} and if the sequence F_n converges with respect to the norm induced by $H^2(\Omega, \mathbb{R}^3)$. Then $F := \lim_{n \to \infty} F_n$ is a local minimum of J_F in $\mathcal{H}_1$.

Note that in case $\mathcal{H}$ is finite dimensional, convergence of (F_n) with respect to any norm is OK.

Proof.   Before proving the proposition we recall what convergence in $H^2(\Omega, \mathbb{R}^3)$ means:

$F = H^2\text{-}\lim_{n \to \infty} F_n$ if and only if

$$F_n \xrightarrow{L^2} F \; , \; \partial_i F_n \xrightarrow{L^2} \partial_i F \; (i = 1, 2) \text{ and } \partial_i \partial_j F_n \xrightarrow{L^2} \partial_i \partial_j F \; i = 1, 2 \, , j = 1, 2 \, .$$

Here "$\xrightarrow{L^2}$" denotes convergence in mean square sense, i.e.,

$$G_n \xrightarrow{L^2} G \quad \Leftrightarrow \quad \lim_{n \to \infty} \int_\Omega |G_n(u, v) - G(u, v)|^2 \, du dv = 0 \, .$$

We briefly write Δ_n instead of Δ_{F_n}, $d\omega_n$ instead $d\omega_{F_n}$ and g_n^{kj} instead of $g_{F_n}^{kj}$. We define a sequence of bilinear mappings B_n on $\mathcal{H}$ as follows.

$$B_n(G, H) := \int_\Omega (\Delta_n G | \Delta_n H) \, d\omega_n + a \int_\Omega \sum_{jk} g_n^{kj} (\partial_j G | \partial_k H) \, d\omega_n \, .$$

Then $F_n \xrightarrow{L^2} F$ implies that for every $G, H \in \mathcal{H}$,

$$\lim_{n \to \infty} B_n(G, H) = B(G, H) :=$$
$$= \int_\Omega (\Delta_F G | \Delta_F H) \, d\omega_F + a \int_\Omega \sum_{jk} g_F^{kj} (\partial_j G | \partial_k H) \, d\omega_F \, .$$

Moreover, $F_n \in H^2(\Omega, \mathbb{R}^3)$ implies that B_n is continuous (with respect to the H^2-norm). B is continuous as well. The principle of uniform boundedness [7] then implies that there is a real constant c such that

$$|B_n(G, H)| \leq c \|G\|_{H^2} \|H\|_{H^2} \quad \text{for every} \quad n \quad \text{and every} \quad G, H \in \mathcal{H} \, .$$

Thus from the estimate

$$|B_n(F_n, H) - B(F, H)| \leq |B_n(F_n, H) - B_n(F, H)| + |B_n(F, H) - B(F, H)|$$
$$\leq c \|F_n - F\|_{H^2} \|H\|_{H^2} + |B_n(F, H) - B(F, H)|$$

we conclude that for arbitrary $H \in \mathcal{H}$

$$\lim_{n \to \infty} B_n(F_n, H) = B(F, H) . \tag{3.3}$$

It is known (e.g. [4]), that the minimum F of a quadratic variational principle corresponding to a symmetric bilinear functional B can be characterized as follows

$$G_0 = \min\{B(G, G) : G \in \mathcal{H}_1\} \quad \Longleftrightarrow \quad B(G_0, H) = 0 \quad \text{for all} \quad H \in \mathcal{H}_0 .$$

Thus we have the implications

$$F_n = \min\{B_n(G, G) : G \in \mathcal{H}_1\} \Leftrightarrow B_n(F_n, H) = 0 \; \forall \; H \in \mathcal{H}_0$$
$$\stackrel{(3.3)}{\Longrightarrow} B_F(F, H) = 0 \; \forall \; H \in \mathcal{H}_0 \Leftrightarrow F = \min\{B_F(G, G) : G \in \mathcal{H}_1\}$$

Since $J_F(\cdot) = B_F(\cdot, \cdot)$ we have shown, that F minimizes the functional J_F . $\square$

4. TENSOR PRODUCT SPLINE SURFACES.

In geometric modeling, one often uses TP spline surfaces. In case the primary surfaces are given as TP splines, the boundary data γ_i and Γ_i $(i = 0, 1)$ will be closed periodic spline curves of degree n say. Note that TP splines surfaces of degree ≥ 2 are contained in $H^2(\Omega, \mathbb{R}^3)$. In fact, the first order derivatives are continuous, second order derivatives are piecewise continuous, thus square integrable.

As parameter space we choose the rectangle $[0, 2\pi] \times [0, 1]$. We identify points $(0, v)$ and $(1, v)$, thus the boundary consists of the two sets $\{(u, 0) : 0 \leq u \leq 2\pi\}$ and $\{(u, 1) : 1 \leq u \leq 2\pi\}$. Without loss of generality we can assume that the parameter interval for the four curves γ_1 , Γ_i , $(i = 0, 1)$ is $[0, 2\pi]$. We choose a partition of the interval $0 = t_0 < t_1 < \ldots < t_N = 2\pi$ which contains all the knots of the four spline curves. Furthermore choose an equidistant partition of $[0, 1]$ consisting of $M + 1$ points, $M \geq 3$. That is, $s_j := \frac{j}{M}$, $j = 0, 1, \ldots, M$.

As space $\mathcal{H}$ we consider all TP spline surfaces of degree n which are periodic with respect to the first variable and are subordinated to the partition $\{(t_i, s_j) : 1 \leq i \leq N , 0 \leq j \leq M\}$. A basis can be obtained as follows: Choose a basis $\{\mathbf{b}_1, \ldots, \mathbf{b}_N\}$ of the real-valued, 2π-periodic spline functions on $[0, 2\pi]$ subordinated to the partition $0 = t_0 < t_1 < \ldots < t_N = 2\pi$. In addition choose linearly independent real-valued spline functions $\{\mathbf{d}_1, \ldots, \mathbf{d}_{M+n-4}\}$ on $[0, 1]$ of degree n , subordinated to $0 = s_0 < \ldots < s_M = 1$ which satisfy in addition $\phi(0) = \phi(1) = \phi'(0) = \phi'(1) = 0$. Add $\{\mathbf{d}_{M+n-3}, \mathbf{d}_{M+n-2}, \mathbf{d}_{M+n-1}, \mathbf{d}_{M+n}\}$ in order to get a basis of all spline functions ($M + 1$ knots, degree n).

If e_i , $i = 1, 2, 3$ denotes the canonical basis in $\mathbb{R}^3$, then $\{e_i \cdot \mathbf{b}_j \otimes \mathbf{d}_k : 1 \leq i \leq 3 , 1 \leq j \leq N , 1 \leq k \leq M + n - 4\}$ forms a basis for $\mathcal{H}_0$ and $\{e_i \cdot \mathbf{b}_j \otimes \mathbf{d}_k :$

$1 \leq i \leq 3$, $1 \leq j \leq N$, $1 \leq k \leq M + n\}$ is a basis of $\mathcal{H}$. Here $e_i \cdot \mathbf{b}_j \otimes \mathbf{d}_k$ denotes the TP spline function given by $(e_i \cdot \mathbf{b}_j \otimes \mathbf{d}_k)(u, v) := \mathbf{b}_j(u)\mathbf{d}_k(v)e_i$.

For the quadratic and cubic case we give in the following proposition an explicit form of a surface which satisfies the boundary data. This may serve as surface $\hat{F}$ for the first step in the iteration described in Section 3 (cf. Remark 3.2).

4.1 Proposition. Assume γ_i and Γ_i , $(i = 0, 1)$ are spline curves of degree $n \in \{2, 3\}$ defined on the interval $[0, 2\pi]$. Then the following TP spline surfaces satisfy the boundary conditions.

$n = 2$ (quadratic case):

$$
F_0(u, v) := \begin{cases}
\begin{aligned}
&\gamma_0(u)(1 - 2v)^2 + (4\gamma_0(u) + 2\Gamma_0(u))v(1 - 2v) \\
&\quad + (2\gamma_0(u) + 2\gamma_1(u) + \Gamma_0(u) - \Gamma_1(u))v^2
\end{aligned} & 0 \leq v \leq \tfrac{1}{2} \\[2em]
\begin{aligned}
&(2\gamma_0(u) + 2\gamma_1(u) + \Gamma_0(u) - \Gamma_1(u))(1 - v)^2 \\
&\quad + (4\gamma_1(u) - 2\Gamma_1(u))(2v - 1)(1 - v) + \\
&\quad + \gamma_1(u)(2v - 1)^2
\end{aligned} & \tfrac{1}{2} \leq v \leq 1
\end{cases}
$$

$n = 3$ (cubic case):

$$
F_0(u, v) := \gamma_0(u)(1 - v)^2(1 - 2v) + \Gamma_0(u)v(1 - v)^2 +
$$
$$
+ \Gamma_1(u)v^2(1 - v) + \gamma_1(u)v^2(3 - 2v) .
$$

<u>Proof.</u>   Differentiate (with respect to v) and evaluate at $v = 0$ and at $v = 1$.

$\square$

5. IMPLEMENTATION AND FINAL REMARKS.

For plane curves the analogue problem is implemented. In case the angles between the line through the endpoints of the primary curves and the (outward) tangents at these endpoints are accute, the algorithm converges rapidly to a smooth blend. Already after 2-3 steps visually the blend curves do not change very much. Actually, two iterations yield satisfactory blend curves.

For surfaces an implementation has been tested which yields blend surfaces between an elliptic cylinder and an ellipsoid or a plane. Also in this case, for most configurations the algorithm becomes stationary after a few steps. For practical applications, the surface F_2 , obtained after the second iteration may serve as a nice-looking blend. In Fig. 2 blend surfaces between a plane (with an elliptical hole) and an oblique cylinder are shown. The two figures at the top show two different views of $\hat{F}$. Intentionally, $\hat{F}$ has been chosen weird in order to show that this a priori blend, which is needed to start the iteration, can be

Figure 2: Blend surfaces between a cylinder and a plane. Top to bottom: two views of $\hat{F}, F_1$, F_2 and F_3 resp.

anything satisfying the boundary conditions. The six close-ups show F_1 , F_2 and F_3 , two views of each of them. It is hard to recognize differences between F_2 and F_3 . The blend surfaces consist of bicubic TP spline surfaces over a knot set of 12×9 points.

Successive refinement of the knot set will yield a sequence of surfaces obtained by the algorithm described above. The problem, whether this sequence will converge to the solution of the infinite dimensional problem in $H^2(\Omega, \mathbb{R}^3)$ is not discussed. For theoretical reasons this might be an interesting problem, probably also very difficult. For geometric modeling problems this is not a crucial point, since one always deals with some kind of spline surfaces. However, the implementation shows that doubling the knot set does not change the obtained blend surfaces very much.

We conclude pointing out two possible extensions of the procedure described in this paper. First of all one can use the same ideas in order to construct blends with higher degree of smoothness, e. g. blends which yield G^2 continuous transition to the primary surfaces. In this case, one should consider functionals J which also average on third order derivatives of the parametrization (cf. [5]). A typical example would be

$$J_G(F) := \int \Big(\mathbf{grad}_G(\mathbf{div}_G(\mathbf{grad_G}))) \big| \mathbf{grad}_G(\mathbf{div}_G(\mathbf{grad_G}))) \Big)$$

where $\mathbf{grad}_G$ and $\mathbf{div}_G$ denote the gradient and divergence with respect to a given parametrization G. Such a functional may be seen as measuring somehow the variation of the curvature. For curves this has been tested with promising results.

Another important extension concerns the implementation. So far there are severe restrictions on the toplogical nature of the blending problem. The reason for this: we work with TP spline surfaces. In order to handle blending problems of a more delicate nature (e. g. blending three or more cylinders) one has to work with other classes of spline surfaces. For example, with triangular spline surfaces (cf. [3]) one can handle arbitrary topologies.

References

[1] R. A. Adams, *Sobolev spaces*, Academic Press 1975

[2] M. I. G. Bloor, M. J. Wilson, Generating blend surfaces using partial differential equations. CAD 1989, pp. 165–171

[3] W. Dahmen, C. A. Micchelli, H.-P. Seidel, Blossoming begets B–Spline bases built better by B–Patches, Math. Comp.**59** (1992), pp. 97–115.

[4] G. Greiner, Blending techniques based on variational principles, Curves and Surfaces in Computer Vision and Graphics III, J. D. Warren, Editor, Proc. SPIE 1830, 174–183 (1992)

[5] G. Greiner, H.-P. Seidel, Curvature continuous blend surfaces, Modeling in Computer Graphics, B. Falcidieno, T. L. Kunii (eds.), pp. 309–318, Springer–Verlag, Berlin 1993

[6] C. Hoffmann, J. Hopcroft, The potential method for blending surfaces, in G. Farin (ed.), Geometric modelling: algorithms and new trends, SIAM, Philadelphia 1987, pp. 347–364.

[7] M. Reed, B. Simon, *Methods of Modern Mathematical Physics*, Vol. 1 (Functional Analysis), Academic Press, New York 1972.

[8] J. R. Rossignac, A. A. G. Requicha, Constant–radius blending in solid modelling, Compu. Mech. Eng. **3** (1984), pp. 65–73.

[9] J. R. Woodwark, Blends in geometric modelling, in R. R. Martin (ed.), The mathematics of surfaces II, Oxford University Press, Oxford 1987, pp. 255-297.

Surfaces In An Object-Oriented Geometric Framework [1]

Reinhard Klein
Universität Tübingen
Wilhelm-Schickard-Institut für Informatik
Graphisch-Interaktive-Systeme (WSI/GRIS)
Tübingen, F.R.G.

Abstract

To use the advantages of different surface representations, such as tensor-product surfaces, surfaces over triangular regions, implicitly defined surfaces, etc., it is necessary to integrate these surface types with a large variety of algorithms into one programming environment.
Inheritance and polymorphism of object-oriented languages offer the opportunity to realize an implementation, which is not bound to a certain representation of the surface. The most reasonable way to benefit from such an object-oriented approach is to use existing algorithms and if necessary to develop new algorithms that are based on the functionality provided by as many surface representations as possible.
An object-oriented design for surfaces is presented and the advantages of such a design are illustrated by examples.

1 Introduction

We present the integration of parameterized surfaces into an object-oriented framework together with the C++ implementation that starts from an abstract class of general differentiable surfaces and in turn refines this design to surfaces that are given in a parametric form.

---

[1]The basis of this framework and a first version were developed in cooperation with Philipp Slusallek, Universität Erlangen, IMMD IX, Graphische Datenverarbeitung, Am Weichselgarten 9, 91058 Erlangen, Germany, during his time in Tübingen and presented at the SPIE-conference on Curves and Surfaces [17].

On one hand the framework is used as a testbed for our research in the area of computer-aided design and on the other hand as the basis for our students to implement their own algorithms. It frees the user from the burden to reimplement many of the techniques which are well-known, however, difficult to implement and which are needed for example to interrogate curves and surfaces, to approximate surfaces by triangles or to visualize 3D-objects. Many of the techniques used in our object-oriented implementation may also be interesting in the area of research towards robotics.

In object-oriented design, the main issue is to identify the operations that can be applied to a certain class of objects. These operations, often called methods, describe objects of a class completely, when seen from its environment – the internal structure is hidden from the user of an object (*encapsulation*). A class can be 'derived' from another class allowing it to inherit all the methods of its superclass (*inheritance, code sharing*). An object of a derived class can be substituted for one of its superclasses and respond to the same set of methods. In this case, derived classes may use different algorithms to implement the same method (*polymorphism*, virtual methods in C++). For further information see e.g. [19] or [23].

An overview of our class hierarchy is shown in fig. 1. To clarify the approach only the most important abstract classes together with some classes of special curves and surface types are presented. Solid arrows mark derivations from superclass to subclass. Dotted arrows mark references between classes. Such an arrow either signifies a pointer to a class that implements a certain part of an object (e.g. `ParmeterRegion` for a surface) or a reference to the class of objects the specified class may operate on (e.g. `Composite Surface` has `ParamSurface` as a subclass).

Furthermore there is a large set of meta classes, that do not define any actual curves or surfaces by themselves, but that are associated with other curves or surfaces and visualize some of their properties. For instance, the class `CurvaturePlot` is a planar curve that plots the curvature of the associated curve over its arc length. Since `CurvaturePlot` itself is a `ParamCurve`, any method of the class `ParamCurve` works on it. Thus it is simple to apply a `CurvaturePlot` to a `CurvaturePlot`. This concept of meta classes provides so much flexibility and functionality – while being simple and quick to implement – that we have used it throughout the framework. Another example: When facing the

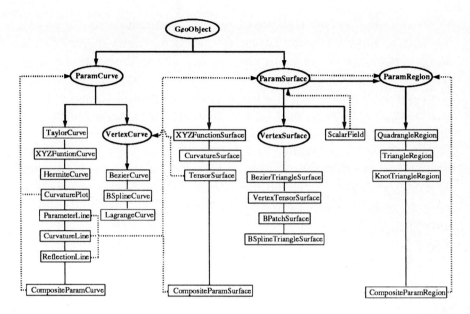

Figure 1: Schematic view of the class hierarchy. Solid arrows mark inheritance, dotted arrows mark references to other classes.

problem, whether we would need a method for a curve that returns the derivative over the whole parameter range as a curve itself, we used a meta class instead. When a point of this curve is queried, it evaluates the derivative of the original curve and returns it. Thus, hodographs [6],[11] are available for any curve type.

In section 2 we briefly sketch the implementation of parameterized curve and turn in section 3 to a more detailed description of the implementation of parameterized surfaces. In section 4 examples that illustrate the approach and its advantages are given. Section 5 summarizes the achievements of this object-oriented approach and discusses extensions and further research areas.

2 Parameterized Curves

A detailed description of the implementation of parameterized curves in the framework is given in [17] and [12]. Therefore here we present only a brief overview on the class-design. A parameterized curve is a mapping of an interval I to $\mathbb{R}^3$. The most fundamental method for this type of curves is to evaluate the curve at a given parametervalue

$t \in I$ to derive a point $C(t)$ on the curve. Additionally methods are required to obtain the derivatives $C^r(t)$. Using these methods it is possible to compute the curvature, torsion, or the Frenét Frame at a given parameter value t.

Assuming sufficient differentialbility of the curves, all these methods can be implemented using only the point evaluation method of the curve together with proper numerical methods to compute derivatives. To offer all this functionality for any curve that at least knows how to evaluate a point $C(t)$ for a given parameter value t, the corresponding methods are implemented for the abstract class `ParamCurve`. If a subclass of `ParamCurve` provides better or faster algorithms to obtain these results, these methods can always be overwritten. For example, because for Béziercurves it is easy to compute derivatives explicitly, in the class `BezierCurve` the methods to compute derivatives are also implemented and these methods overwrite the methods implemented in its parent class `ParamCurve`. On the abstract level of the class `ParamCurve` there is also a method to output the curve to a graphics display.

3 Parameterized Surfaces

Parameterized surfaces are a bit more difficult. They are a mapping of a subset $D \subset \mathbb{R}^2$ to $\mathbb{R}^3$ and they are implemented in the classes `ParamSurface` and `CompositeParamSurface`. All methods that evaluate the surface at a single point, or near a single point in the case of numerical approximation, are nearly identical to the curve methods, except that we have to calculate partial derivatives, etc. Problems arise when a nonlocal method needs to be applied to a surface, since the method needs knowledge about the whole parameter region over which the surface is defined. This is more difficult than in the one-dimensional case for curves.

3.1 Parameter Region

An important part of a parameterized surface is its domain that we will briefly discuss. Let D be a multiple-connected domain in the plane $\mathbb{R}^2$ that is defined by a set $B = b_0, b_1, \cdots, b_M$ of closed boundary curves. The set B includes the exterior boundary b_0 and interior boundaries $b_1, \cdots, b_M$. Each boundary b_i is a Jordan curve, i.e., it

separates $\mathbb{R}^2$ into two disjoint regions, and comprises a finite number
(≥ 2) of generally curved domain edges. Each domain edge $S[p,q]$
with endpoints p and q, is described as a parametric curve in two dimensions. The start and end points of the boundary curves belong to
the set $P = p_0, \cdots, p_N$ of nodes, that includes also interior nodes, i.e.
nodes lying on the boundary curves $b_0, \cdots, b_M$. We assume that the
boundary curves only intersect in a finite number of nodes $p \in P$ and
that the interior boundaries $b_1, \cdots, b_M$ lie in the interior of the domain
with respect to the exterior boundary b_0.

The domain itself is implemented as an own class which we called
`ParamRegion`. To mention only some of the most interesting methods,
this class contains a method to determine if a point p lies inside the
domain, methods to triangulate the domain according to a given net
criteria, for example a maximum edge length of the triangles in the
triangulation, a method to get the boundary of the domain, to manipulate the domain, e.g. adding and deleting parts, etc. A domain and
triangulations of it are shown in figure 2 and figure 3. The methods we
used for the triangulation of domains are described in detail in [16].

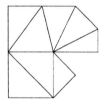

Figure 2: Constrained delaunay
triangulation of a parameter region without inner points.

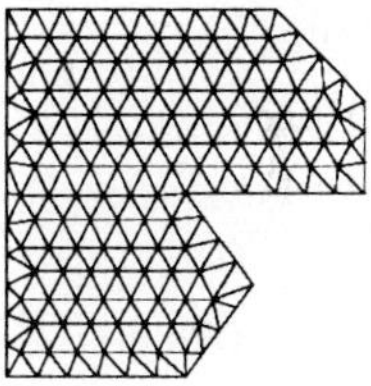

Figure 3: Constrained delaunay triangulation of the same
parameter region with inner
points.

To accelerate the methods that require a point in region test, a constrained delaunay triangulation [18] together with a quadtree datastructure is used as an internal representation of the domain.

3.1.1 Derived classes

To handle the standard cases of tensorproduct surfaces and triangular Béziersurfaces we implemented the subclasses `QuadrangleRegion` and `TriangleRegion` of the class `ParamRegion` as well as a special class `KnotTriangleRegion` for the domain of triangular B-Spline patches. In these cases the methods to triangulate the domain and the point in region tests are much simpler and therefore the correspondent methods of the class `ParamRegion` are overwritten.

For the case of domains $D = \cup D_i, i = 0, \cdots, K$ which are the disjunct union of subdomains D_i we implemented the class `CompositeParam-Region`. This class is derived from the class `ParamRegion` and therefore it inherits all the functionality of this class. The main additional method is to determine for a given point $p \in \mathbb{R}^2$ the subdomain to which the point belongs.

3.2 Subclasses of the class `ParamSurface`

There are a lot of subclasses of the class `ParamSurface` that implement different kinds of surface types, e.g. `BezierTriangleSurface`, `BPatchSurface`, etc. Among these specific classes there is a class to manage composite surfaces and there are meta classes that implement special functionality on surfaces. Two selected classes shall be presented here in more detail.

3.2.1 Composite ParamSurface

In many applications models are built from several surface patches, such as nets of B-Spline-tensorsurfacepatches or Bézier-trianglepatches. To get a closed linear approximation of such surfaces, e.g. for visualization purposes, we have to consider the neighbourhoods between the patches to avoid holes in the approximative net, caused by different accuracy of the linear approximation on the patches. To handle such and even more complicated cases we implemented a class `Composite-ParamSurface`. Given a domain $\Omega = \cup_{i=1\ldots N} \Omega_i$ as the disjunct union of domains Ω_i and a set of parameterized functions $f_i : \Omega_i \mapsto \mathbb{R}^3$, $i = 1 \cdots N$ a composite parameterized surface $F : \Omega \mapsto \mathbb{R}^3$ is defined by $F(p) = F_i(p)$ if $p \in \Omega_i$. The functions f_i are allowed to be of different types, for example, a `CompositeParamSurface` can contain a B-spline-tensorproduct surface, a Bézier-triangle surface and a B-spline-triangle surface at the same time. The `CompositeParamSurface` is derived from the class `ParamSurface` and therefore a `CompositeParamSurface` can even contain other CompositeParamSurfaces. All methods available for the class `ParamSurface` are inherited, for example all surface interrogation tools. The implementation of the *getPoint-method* overwrites that of the parentclass `ParamSurface` and uses the special acceleration datastructure of the domain-triangulation to find the corresponding Ω_i. There are also methods to query the differentiability of the surface at points where the patches are joined together, to get information about the neighbourhood relations between the patches, etc.

3.2.2   ScalarField2D

The class `ScalarField2D` is a special class for scalar fields on surfaces, that is for functions $f \colon \mathbb{R}^3 \supset S \mapsto \mathbb{R}$, where S is a given parameterized surface. Examples of such fields are mean and gaussian curvature on a surface, the distribution of heat and pressure on the surface, etc. The class possesses several methods to visualize the scalar field, such as colour-coded maps [2], offset-surfaces [10], focal-surfaces [20], etc. The class is also derived from the class `ParamSurface` and therefore it is possible to visualize for example one scalar field as an offset surface over the given surface and a second scalar field on that offset surface as a colour-coded map.

3.3   Special methods

3.3.1   Derivatives

In the abstract classes methods to numerically calculate derivatives for curves and surfaces are required. It is well-known that numerical differentiation is a complicated process. For a function $f \colon \mathbb{R} \mapsto \mathbb{R}$ it is not possible to compute the limit $\lim_{h \to 0} \frac{f(x+h)-f(x)}{h}$, because we loose accuracy due to the restricted number of digits. With decreasing h the relative error becomes larger.

One way to overcome this problems is to approximate the function in a neighbourhood of x with a polynomial of degree n. The derivative of this polynomial in the corresponding parameter x is then used as an approximation for the desired derivative. The higher the order of the polynomial the better we expect the approximation of the derivative to be. However the computational cost also increases. It turns out that approximation with cubic polynomials for the first and second derivatives delivers a good compromise between accuracy and computational costs.

This leads to the following formulas for the first and second derivatives used in our implementation.

$$f'(x_m) \approx \frac{1}{24h}(f(x_0) - 27f(x_1) + 27f(x_2) - f(x_3))$$
$$f''(x_m) \approx \frac{1}{2h^2}(f(x_0) - f(x_1) - f(x_2) + f(x_3)),$$

where $x_i = x_0 + i \cdot h$, $i = 0, \cdots, 3$ are equidistant knots, $x_m = \frac{1}{2}(x_0 + x_3)$ and h is a user defined constant.

For higher order derivatives, it is necessary to use higher degree polynomials for the approximation, or to use recursive application of the above formulas.

3.3.2 Meshing

In addition to the tesselation of parameter regions, there is a special meshing method for composite surfaces. This method has knowledge of all composing surfaces and can therefore implement different resolutions for the different surface patches. It uses bounds on the second derivatives of the patches to compute a maximum length of the triangle sides in the corresponding tesselation of the parameter region of a subpatch, see also [22]. In contrast to structured grids with a global refinement the amount of data of the resulting mesh is reduced using such a technique.

On the abstract level this method is implemented by using a method of the `ParamRegion` to triangulate itself by inserting new nodes, and then constructing the surface approximation using this triangulation of the parameter region.

In the case of the `BezierTensorProductSurface` class, the `BSpline-Tensorproductsurface` class as well as for the `BezierTriangleSurface` class there are additional methods to get adaptive linear approximations of the surfaces using the well-known subdivision techniques, see e.g. [9].

4 Applications

4.1 Differential Geometry

For a regular surface S, $S_u = \frac{\partial S}{\partial u}$ and $S_v = \frac{\partial S}{\partial v}$ are linear independent and define a local coordinate system for the tangent plane in the corresponding point on the surface. Together with the normal n on the tangent plane and the values E, F, G of the first and L, M, N of the second fundamental form [3], they deliver the essential information to implement the methods for differential geometry used in our framework.

The normal n is given by

$$n = \frac{S_u(u,v) \times S_v(u,v)}{||S_u(u,v) \times S_v(u,v)||}.$$

Further the coefficients of the fundamental forms are given by

$$\begin{aligned} E &= (S_u|S_u),\ F = (S_u|S_v),\ G = (S_v|S_v) \\ L &= (S_{uu}|n),\ M = (S_{uv}|n),\ N = (S_{vv}|n). \end{aligned}$$

The family of planes containing the normal n at a given point p cuts the surface in a family of normal section curves $\alpha(t) = (u(t), v(t))$ with $\alpha(0) = p$. For the tangent vector t of these curves in p we have due to the chain rule

$$t = \alpha'(0) = S_u u'(0) + S_v v'(0).$$

$u'(0)$ and $v'(0)$ are the coordinates of the tangent vector t in the local coordinate system S_u, S_v of the tangent plane.

The curvature κ_d of the normal section curve in the direction of $d = (u', v')$ is given by

$$\kappa_d = \frac{L u'^2 + 2M u'v' + N v'^2}{E u'^2 + 2F u'v' + G v'^2}.$$

The maximal and minimal curvature of the surface in a given point are defined as the extremum values of the curvature κ_d of the normalsection curve in direction d as a function in d. The corresponding directions are called principal directions d_{min}, d_{max}.

Further interesting quantities are the Gaussian curvature K and the mean curvature H defined by

$$K = \frac{LN - M^2}{EG - F^2}, \quad H = \frac{2FM - (EN + GL)}{2(EG - F)^2}.$$

Normal section curvature is visualized through curvature circles. To visualize the variation of the curvature as a function of direction we can use animation of the curvature circles.

The variation of the scalar values Gaussian and mean curvature as well as minimal and maximal curvature over the surface can again be visualized by means of a colour-coded map. There are a lot of elaborate techniques to gain good results [2]. The realization of these techniques uses the meta class `ScalarField2D`. Visualizing a scalar field as an offset surface can often be helpful. In figure 4 and 5 the gaussian curvature of a surface patch is displayed in the first case as an offset surface over the patch itself, in the second case as a surface over a plane.

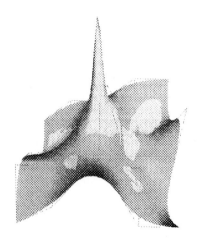

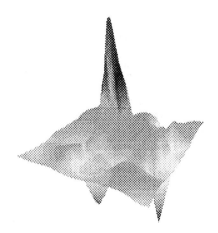

Figure 4: The Gaussian curvature of a surface is visualized as an offset surface over the surface itself. The offset surface is displayed in darker colours. In the intersection points of the two surfaces the gaussian curvature vanishes.

Figure 5: The gaussian curvature of the same surface is visualized as a offset surface over the plane. In addition the absolut value of the gaussian curvature is colour-coded.

An informative way to analyze the variation of the principal directions across the surface is to integrate a family of lines of curvature [7]. A curve on the surface is a line of curvature if its tangent direction coincides in every point with the same principal direction.

A usefull tool to visualize the fairness of surfaces are reflection lines.

Reflection lines on a surface are defined as the image of a given straight line on the ideal reflecting surface seen from a fixed eye-point [14]. Both, the lines of curvature and the reflection lines are themselves parameterized curves, and their differential geometrical properties can be visualized by the methods available for curves described above.

4.2 Rolling-ball blends

The rolling ball blend is perhaps the most popular blend type in CAGD [21], [25], [24]. One of the reasons is, that here the points of two contact curves (see below) of the blend surface mutually correspond in a direct way, which makes easy computations possible.
First we need some notations. The surfaces to be blended shall be denoted by $S_i(u_i, v_i)$ $(i = 1, 2)$. The rolling ball blend surface will be denoted by $G(s, t)$. r denotes the radius of the ball and C the so-called spine curve, that is the curve the center of the ball is describing. The contact curves C_1 and C_2 are defined by the following equations:

$$(S_i - C)^2 - r^2 = 0,$$

$$< S_i - C, \frac{\partial S_i}{\partial u_i} > = 0,$$

$$< S_i - C, \frac{\partial S_i}{\partial v_i} > = 0$$

for $(i = 1, 2)$ and where $<, >$ denotes the scalar product. If we parametrise the curve C by a parameter t, then we get three parametric curves: The spine curve $C(t)$ and the two contact curves $C_i(t) = S_i(u_i(t), v_i(t))$, $i = 1, 2$. To compute the blendsurface $G(u, v)$ we use a modified version of the algorithm of Klass/Kuhn given in [15] combined with ideas of Hermann described in [13]. Setting the radius of the rolling ball to zero the same algorithm can be used to calculate surface-surface intersections between parameterized surfaces. To compute the contact curve in that approach the functions $u_i(t), v_i(t)$ $i = 1, 2$ are computed by solving two linear differential equations derived from the defining equations above. When the spine curve together with the contact curves are available the resulting blendsurface can be computed. For the blendsurface we use a representation as a G^1-piecewise continuos `CompositeParamSurface` of Bézier-tensorproduct surfaces. Because the algorithm only needs the values of the first and second fundamental form of the surfaces at certain points in the domain, the whole method can be implemented on the abstract level of the class `ParamSurface`. That means that the blending algorithm can be applied to each type of surface in our framework derived from the abstract class `ParamSurface`, especially for all surfaces of type `CompositeParamSurface`.

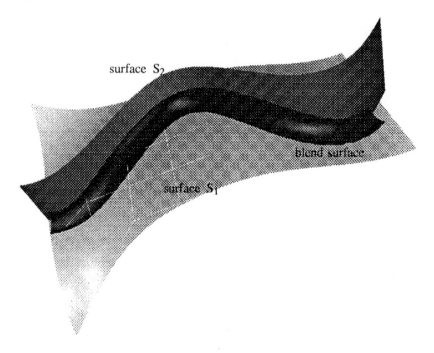

surface S_2

Blend surface

surface S_1

Figure 6: A rolling ball blend between a G^1-continuous `CompositeParamSurface` and a `XYZFunctionSurface`. The composite surface consists of a Bezier-tensorproduct-surface-patch (left side with controlnet) and of a `XYZFunctionSurface`.

In figure 6 an example of a rolling ball blend between two surfaces is shown. In the example the primary surface S_1 is a C^1-continous composite surface containing a Bézier-tensorproduct patch and a `XYZ-FunctionSurface`. The `XYZFunctionSurface` is a class for parameterized surfaces defined by three functions $f_x, f_y, f_z : \mathbb{R} \longmapsto \mathbb{R}$, each for one of the three coordinate axes.

5 Conclusion and further Work

We have shown a way to integrate parameterized surfaces into an object-oriented framework. It was shown that new parametrized surface types can easily be added. Only the most fundamental method, point evaluation, must be supplied. All other methods are already implemented in abstract base classes. We have further seen for the case of rolling ball blends that algorithms operating on parameterized surfaces must be implemented only for the abstract base classes and can then operate on all surface types available in the framework. This result in a much smaller amount of implementation effort for the integration of new techniques, since the algorithms must not be supplied for all surface types.

At the moment we are working on an optimized, adaptive general tesselation algorithm for parameterized surfaces based on the triangulation algorithms for parameter regions. We are also integrating visualization techniques for vector fields and tensor fields on surfaces. Future work aims for the full integration of implicitly defined surfaces into the framework.

.

References

[1] Gershon Elber an Elaine Cohen. Hybrid symbolic and numeric operators as tool for analysis of freeform surfaces. In B. Falcidieno and T.L. Kunii, editors, *Modeling in Computer Graphics*, pages 275–288. Springer-Verlag, 1993.

[2] J. Beck, R. Farouki, and J. Hinds. Surface analysis methods. *IEEE Computer Graphics and Applications*, 6(12):18–36, 1986.

[3] M. P. do Carmo. *Differentialgeometrie von Kurven und Flächen.* Vieweg, Braunschweig/Wiesbaden, 1976.

[4] Gershon Elber and Elaine Cohen. Hidden curve removal for free form surfaces. In Forest Baskett, editor, *Computer Graphics (SIGGRAPH '90 Proceedings)*, volume 24, pages 95–104, August 1990.

[5] Gershon Elber and Elaine Cohen. Second-order surface analysis using hybrid symbolic and numeric operators. *ACM Transactions on Graphics*, 12(2):160–178, 1993.

[6] Gerald Farin. *Curves and Surfaces for Computer Aided Geometric Design*. Academic Press, 1990.

[7] R. Farouki. Graphical methods for surface differential geometry. In R. Martin, editor, *The Mathematics of Surfaces II*, pages 363–386. Oxford University Press, 1987.

[8] R.T. Farouki. Concise piecewise-linear approximation of algebraic curves. *IBM Research Division*, 1988.

[9] D. Filip, R. Magedson, and R. Markot. Surface algorithms using bounds on derivatives. *Computer Aided Geometric Design*, 3(4):295–311, 1986.

[10] Thomas A. Foley, David A. Lane, Gregory M. Nielson, and Ramamani Ramaraj. Visualizing functions over a sphere. *IEEE Computer Graphics and Applications*, 10(1):32–40, January 1990.

[11] A. Forrest. Interactive interpolation and approximation by bezier polynomials. *Computer Journal*, 15:71–79, 1972.

[12] G. Greiner, R. Klein, and P. Slusallek. Design of blending-surfaces in an object-oriented framework. In P.-J. Laurent and A. Le Méhauté, editors, *Curves and Surfaces*. Academic Press, 1993.

[13] T. Hermann. Rolling ball blends, self-intersection. In J. Warren, editor, *Curves and Surfaces in Computer Vision and Graphics III*, chapter 4, pages 204–211. SPIE - The Invernational Society for Optical Engineering, Nov. 1992.

[14] R. Klass. Correction of local surface irregularities using reflection lines. *Comput. Aided Des.*, 12:73–77, March 1980.

[15] R. Klass and B. Kuhn. Fillet and surface intersections defined by rolling balls. *Computer Aided Geometric Design*, 9(3):185–193, August 1992.

[16] R. Klein and J. Krämer. Delaunay triangulations of planar domains. Technical report, Wilhelm-Schickard-Institut, Graphisch Interaktive Systeme, Universität Tübingen, 1993.

[17] R. Klein and P. Slusallek. Object-oriented framework for curves and surfaces. In J.D. Warren, editor, *Curves and Surfaces in Computer Vision and Graphics III*, pages 284–295. SPIE, november 1992.

[18] D. T. Lee and A. K. Lin. Generalized Delaunay triangulations for planar graphs. *Discrete Comput. Geom.*, 1:201–217, 1986.

[19] S.B. Lippman. *C++ Primer*. Addison Wesley, 2 edition, 1991.

[20] H. Pottmann, H. Hagen, and A. Divivier. Visualizing functions on a surface. *J. Visualization and Animation*, 2(2):52–58, Apr./June 1991.

[21] A. Rockwood and J. Owen. Blending surfaces in solid modeling. In G. Farin, editor, *Geometric Modeling: Algorithms and New Trends*, pages 367–383. SIAM, Philadelphia, 1987.

[22] X. Sheng and B. E. Hirsch. Triangulation of trimmed surfaces in parametric space. *Computer Aided Design*, 24(8):437–444, August 1992.

[23] B. Stroustrup. *The C++ Programming Language*. Addison Wesley, 2 edition, 1991.

[24] T. Varady, J. Vida, and R. Martin. Parametric blending in a boundary representation solid modeller. In D. C. Handscomb, editor, *The Mathematics of Surfaces III*, pages 171–198. Clarendon Press, 1989.

[25] J. Woodwark. Blends in geometric modelling. In R. Martin, editor, *The Mathematics of Surfaces II*, pages 255–298. Oxford University Press, 1987.

An Active Stereometric Triangulation Technique Using a Continuous Colour Pattern

A. Knoll[1] and R. Sasse[2]

[1] University of Bielefeld, Faculty of Technology, Postfach 10 01 31, D-33501 Bielefeld
[2] Technical University of Berlin, Computer Science Department, Sekr. FR 2-2, Franklinstr. 28, D-10587 Berlin

1 Overview

We present a novel method for obtaining dense range maps, which is based on the combination of two (or more) colour cameras and the projection of a continuous colour pattern. The technique offers several advantages for use in robotics including the potential for very high speed of operation and for higher accuracy than achievable with other active triangulation techniques that employ discrete coloured light stripes or sequential binary-encoded monochrome patterns. The high speed makes the range image generation of fast moving objects in highly dynamic environments possible and thus enables a sensor based on this method to perform both coarse navigational tasks and the fine control of gripper operations. In this approach a continuous colour pattern with uniform brightness is projected onto the objects in the scene.

The objects so illuminated are seen by the two cameras. Corresponding points in both images are then searched for in a manner similar to passive stereo. The criterion to be met by correspondences is that they have the same (relative) colour in both images. Knowledge or recognition of the absolute colours (which were emitted by the projector) is therefore never needed; this makes the method insensitive to colour changes caused by the object and prevents false matches at object discontinuities. Moreover, the method is quite insensitive to geometric distortions and reflectance variations. A working prototype system based on this principle has been realised using standard low cost optical components. Our findings indicate that distance resolutions on the order of 1% of the measured distance are easily achievable. It was shown experimentally that this is true for most materials with different reflectance functions used for technical products (metals, all kinds of plastics, foams).

1.1 Problem Definition

Active triangulation techniques for measuring distances or for generating range images have been in widespread use in the computer vision and robotics research community for a long time [Altschuler 79, Boissonat 81]. Successful applications in industry have also been reported, e.g. [Pritschow 91]. Various designs with different numbers of cameras and lighting patterns are conceivable to match the most diverse range of applications (see [Vuylsteke 90] for an overview and [Sasse 93] for further introductory notes). Besides this flexibility, the advantages of all of these methods include the potential for high measurement accuracy and resolution, independent of the ambient lighting conditions. The common disadvantage of these methods are their limited distance range and, if they are used to generate dense depth maps, their slowness. While the former disadvantage is a direct consequence of the need for active lighting and can be removed when the target application is known, the latter results from the use of mechanical scanners, which direct the lighting pattern over the scene.

This problem of slow data acquisition can be overcome by projecting lighting patterns consisting of many elements, e.g. a multitude of points or lines, and thereby illuminating more points or areas of the scene [Echigo 85]. As the number of simultaneously illuminated areas increases, their spatial distance on the object surface decreases and it is no longer possible to recognise the elements of the pattern individually. Moreover, the spatial order of the elements seen by the camera does not necessarily correspond to the order which was projected. The resulting danger of misinterpretation, particularly at object discontinuities, gives rise to the need of *coding* the pattern elements in a unique manner. Coding can refer to time (by sequentially projecting a series of different patterns on the scene), to structure (by projecting a pattern consisting of individually recognisable elements of different brightness or shape), to frequency (by projecting a colour pattern), or any combination of the three.

Probably the most well known of the time-sequential methods is binary encoded structured light [Altschuler 79, Gutsche 91]. In this approach a series of patterns masks is projected, each of which consists of a different spatial sequence of alternating black and white stripes. Thus, every point on the object receives a different time-sequence of black and white intensity values, which marks it unambiguously for identification. If a sequence of n pattern masks is used, this corresponds to 2^n-1 projected stripes. The problems with the method are the exact alignment of the stripes in all masks and the need for objects that do not move while the n images are recorded. The former problem has been alleviated by the advent of LCD-shutters used in recent designs (which need about one second to record 8 projections), but the difficulties arising from the need for taking n pictures remain. However, since every line must have a minimal spatial extent, the resolution of the range image is limited.

These difficulties can be eliminated if a binary pattern is constructed in such a way that a great number of arrays are projected, each containing, for example, 3×3 dots. The distribution of black and white dots within each array is different from the constellation in all other arrays. Thus, if an appropriate coding scheme with a large

Hamming-distance is used, a great number of areas can be marked unambiguously in the scene. A sophisticated implementation of this structure-based approach is described in [Vuylsteke 90b]. Here, the resolution of the range image is also limited because every block must have a minimal spatial extent. Moreover, problems exist with surfaces that exhibit strong textures.

1.2 Advantages of the Approach

With the method described in this paper, a special *continuous* non-repetitive pattern of hues illuminates the entire scene. The object so illuminated is seen by two colour-cameras. Correspondences of all points visible in both cameras can be found from a single pair of images. The search process is similar to the process employed with passive stereo. This obviates the need for scanning and makes the generation of dense range images from a single snap-shot possible. Thus, the acquisition time is only dependent on the shutter speed of the cameras. This is in contrast to all serial triangulation techniques and enables the range image generation of fast moving objects. Consequently, a sensor based on the technique is immune to motion problems.

Since two cameras in a stereoscopic configuration are used, the criterion to be met by corresponding points is that they have the same colour in *both* images. This colour is not necessarily equivalent to the colour that was emitted from the light source. This is the reason, therefore, that the method is perfectly well suited to non-structured scenes of uniform intensity (a search for edges or prominent object features is never necessary) but sets it apart from other colour-based techniques that employ a sequence of colour stripes whose absolute colour must be identified in an image recorded with a single camera [Boyer 87, Plaßmann 91, Monks 92]. Unlike these, the proposed method is insensitive to colour changes caused by the object (provided they evenly affect both cameras) and does not depend on special cameras with high response stability over a large dynamic range (such as the method described in [Tajima 87]). Preliminary findings (see sec. 3) indicate that this is true for most materials with different reflectance functions, which are used for technical products (metals, all kinds of plastics, foams). Moreover, this point-based method does not depend on the identification of object features. Once the correspondence search is accomplished, the distance of the image points can be calculated by simple triangulation. This implies that the accuracy of the method is only limited by the ability of the cameras to differentiate between colours and their spatial resolution. There is no principal lower limit to accuracy inherent to all methods relying on discrete patterns. The experiments undertaken with inexpensive single-CCD colour cameras show an accuracy that is slightly lower than achievable with a scanned laser light sheet and the same recording hardware. It is, however, more than sufficient for assembly operations and was obtained without any preprocessing of the data. On average, about 70% of all points in the image were matched.

Furthermore, due to the recording of the scene with two cameras, the position and the orientation of the light source are irrelevant; this minimises the amount of calibration required before measurements can be taken. Other than for the cameras, there is no calibration necessary. In particular, this makes it possible to move the cameras (mounted, for example, on a robot end effector) between the measurements with the projector remaining in place. Lastly, the areas (if any) on the object where no results can be obtained (e.g. due to occlusions) can be identified easily from the measured data. Assignments of non-corresponding points in the two images or, conversely, missing assignments of corresponding points, i.e. false matches such as familiar from passive stereo, are unlikely.

2 The Principle of Operation

The basic principle of operation is depicted in fig. 1.1: The projector illuminates the scene (of which only a single arbitrary object point O is shown in the figure) with the colour pattern.

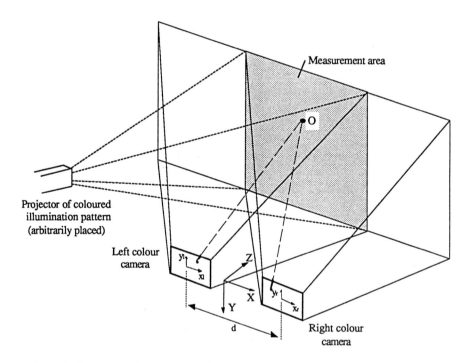

Fig. 1.1 This shows the basic setup for implementing the method.

In fig. 1.1 the measurement area is the intersection of the viewing areas of the two colour cameras and the area illuminated by the projector. The coordinate system

(X,Y,Z) is the world system; d is the baseline of the cameras. The systems (x_l, y_l) and (x_r, y_r) are the internal camera coordinate systems. The pattern consists of a multitude of colour hues in the horizontal direction, in the vertical direction the individual colour does not change. In other words: the colour values change only in one dimension, i.e. they vary continuously as we move over the projection plane from left to right (X-direction in fig. 1.1) but remain constant when we move vertically (in the Y-direction). Thus, from the projector's point of view, every vertical line (ideally an infinitesimally small stripe) of the object is marked with a unique colour. All of these coloured object lines are seen by the left and right camera. Depending on the object geometry, reflectance and colour, these lines are, however, distorted (or even interrupted) and the colour that is recorded may no longer be the colour that was projected. While the distortion of the lines is the basis for calculating the distance Z of objects points by all triangulation techniques, the object-induced shifts in colour are an unwanted, yet inevitable, effect encountered in all practically relevant scenes. For a detailed analysis of the dichromatic colour reflectance model justifying the methods of both the correspondence search and the colour correction outlined below, we refer the reader to [Klinker 90, Sasse 93].

Since the goal is to identify an individual object point by the colour received from it, the criterion for the correspondence search is the value of the received colour, no matter how it compares with the projected colour. Nevertheless, since the correspondence search relies on the comparison of the colours in both cameras, it is necessary that the colour shift due to the object colour result in the same colour in both cameras. In the course of our experiments we have found that this precondition is met in most cases, whereas in accordance with the dichromatic reflection model the absolute colours frequently change dramatically between projection and recording (this precludes the use of single–camera techniques as described in [Tajima 87], which recover colour-stripes on the object from the knowledge of the exact position of the projected hues).

Other than for the fact that the projector must be able to project a colour pattern and the cameras must record colour images, there is no essential difference from standard stereo setups. This makes it particularly easy to fuse the results obtained from (colour) images recorded with ambient lighting (passive stereo) and the results from the active coding technique. We shall now detail the possible colour patterns and subsequently describe the correspondence search.

2.1 The colour pattern

There is an unlimited number of colour coding patterns conceivable, all of which can be specified by defining the intensity distribution functions of the three colour components (i.e. red-green-blue, RGB) over the projection plane. Depending upon the application, one can think of colour-sequences obtained from varying the three colour components according to a simple function (e.g. three phase-shifted sine-functions of the same spatial frequency) or a system of orthogonal functions (e.g. Walsh-functions of different frequencies) as most appropriate for constructing the pattern. Although a full discussion would go beyond the scope of this paper, we would like to mention that it is not necessary to restrict the pattern to structures that vary only in one dimension, i.e. in the X-direction in fig. 1.1. One can also think of patterns whose colour component intensities follow superposed two-dimensional spatial wave-fields of colour patches with random colour, random structure (or both) and of coloured pseudo noise sequences similar to the coding pattern in [Vuylsteke 90b]. Random patterns hold some promise for scenes with completely unknown object structures, but have not yet been examined in this context.

No matter what structure seems most appropriate for a given application, the pattern should be so designed as to facilitate the correspondence search process even in the case of a low signal-to-noise ratio by providing additional hints about the most likely colour value of the object point under consideration (see below). Making use of such redundancies or a priori knowledge can obviously increase the "hit rate" of the search process and speed it up considerably. Although we feel that the exploration of the advantages and disadvantages of different classes of patterns is an interesting subject for further research, we have restricted ourselves to the class of line patterns, i.e. patterns whose colour changes only in one dimension (as outlined above).

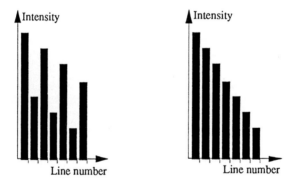

Fig. 2.1 High contrast (left) and low contrast (right) illumination. Both diagrams show the intensity of one colour channel (e.g. red) for seven consecutive lines of the colour pattern.

In principle, these patterns fall into two categories: High contrast and low contrast line sequences (see fig. 2.1). With high contrast sequences the colour changes rapidly from line to line (and returns almost to the original value one or two lines later) whereas with low contrast illumination the colour changes smoothly over the whole pattern plane. In the first case the individual lines may easily be differentiated between on smooth surfaces while at object discontinuities (e.g. edges, corners or object boundaries) the contrast may become very low. Obviously the reverse is true for low contrast illumination with a continuous change in colour: Here, the distinction between the lines may be more difficult on smooth surfaces but an object discontinuity will always produce a high colour contrast in the image. It should be pointed out that the width of the lines is one of the limiting factors of the distance resolution and must therefore be chosen very carefully.

In practice the high contrast approach yields acceptable results only if the image of every line is projected on exactly one pixel column of the image plane of the camera. For general geometries and with a fixed pattern this requirement can only be met for a fixed distance. Otherwise, adjacent lines are mapped to one pixel or, on the contrary, one line is mapped to several pixels. In either case of misalignment the contrast in the image is lost. Moreover, if an ordinary light projector with a small depth of focus is used, a satisfactorily sharp image of the colour pattern can be projected only within a small range of depth. As the scene object moves too close or too far away from the projector, the pattern becomes blurred, which also reduces the contrast. Obviously, this problem also occurs when low contrast illumination is used, but the deterioration in resolution is much severe.

In order to make maximum use of the ability of the camera to distinguish between colours, the pattern should have the highest possible colour range, i.e. it should consist of all the colours the camera can recognise. In other words: from the left to the right end of the projection plane the entire visible spectrum should be run through.

2.2 Colour Correction, Noise Elimination and the Search for Correspondences

If the intensity response of the cameras were uniform over the entire frequency spectrum, arbitrary patterns would be reproduced without distortion. However, inexpensive single-chip CCD cameras, such as used in our experiments, frequently exhibit a much lower sensitivity to blue than to red and green hues. It is therefore mandatory to equalise the outputs of the colour channels of both cameras before searching for corresponding points. This process will be referred to as *colour correction*.

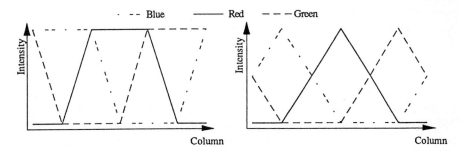

Fig. 2.2 These are compositions of the colours for low contrast sequences. Left: At any pixel one of the three colour components equals zero. Right: In addition to one component being zero, the intensity of the pattern is uniform.

There are two other main difficulties related to the cameras: Perspective distortion and the superposition of random observation noise generated in semiconductor recording devices. While perspective distortions can be sufficiently reduced by applying standard camera calibration techniques, observation noise becomes a severe problem when areas in the image are examined in which one or more colour channels produced a low signal (superposed by a more or less constant noise level), i.e. in areas of a low signal-to-noise-ratio. An elegant way of circumventing this problem is the exploitation of redundancy or additional a-priori information built into the pattern, e.g. by restricting the full choice of colours or by letting colour values rise and fall over the projection plane in a well-defined manner. We now look at two possible patterns which contain information enabling both noise suppression and colour correction.

The values of the three basic colours of these special patterns as a function of the pixel column are shown in fig. 2.2. With both patterns, at any image column either of the three colour components is zero while the other two are anywhere between zero and their maximum intensity. For the purpose of *noise suppression*, the weakest component in the image can therefore be set to zero in the vicinity of the object point even if the recorded image due to noise effects suggests the contrary. More formally:

$$I(j;x) := \begin{cases} 0 & \text{if } I(j;x) = \min[I(R;x), I(G;x), I(B;x)] \\ I(j;x) & \text{otherwise} \end{cases}$$

where $I(j;x)$ is the intensity of an image point, $j \in \{R, G, B\}$ and x is the column number of the image line under consideration. This is obviously a very simple, nevertheless quite useful strategy. More elaborate schemes may employ redundancy checks, such as familiar from coding theory, or matched filters.

In the experiments colour compositions according to the right function shown in fig. 2.2 were used. Not only is either of the three components zero, in addition the intensity (brightness) of the resulting projected pattern is uniform over the entire plane. This enables the application of very simple scaling operations to the recorded image: After setting the smallest colour component to zero, the two remaining components are multiplied by a common factor. This factor is so chosen as to make the sum of the two match the required brightness, i.e.:

$$I(j;x) := \lambda \frac{I(j;x)}{I(R;x) + I(G;x) + I(B;x)}$$

where λ is the maximum intensity value of a colour channel, which equals the (uniform) sum of all three components R, G and B. For an eight bit quantizer, $\lambda = 255$. Although the following step of *correspondence search* relies only on the relations between the colours at (or around) the pixel under consideration, the scaling, which does not alter these relations, helps to simplify the search procedure.

We conclude this section by briefly introducing the procedure of correspondence search which we found most useful in the experiments (although much more complicated colour metrics are conceivable, they do not necessarily justify their increased complexity by the obtained results). Our pragmatic approach is centred around an intensity based comparison of colour value relations over the two epipolar lines of the left and right image (with the appropriate local and global disparity limits). Since, due to different observation angles, the intensity of the colours in the two images may be different, the basic idea underlying the procedure is that the colour reflected off a certain pixel is determined mainly by the largest of the three colour components. We assume that the colour vectors at an arbitrary pixel in the left and right image are linearly dependent, i.e. they are multiples of each other:

$$\begin{pmatrix} R_l \\ G_l \\ B_l \end{pmatrix} = s \begin{pmatrix} R_r \\ G_r \\ B_r \end{pmatrix}$$

In order to scale the two colour vectors before applying the similarity measure, the factor is determined as follows:

```
m   := max(R₁, G₁, B₁)
IF      m = R₁ THEN s := R₁ / Rᵣ
ELSIF m = G₁ THEN s := G₁ / Gᵣ
ELSE               s := B₁ / Bᵣ
END
```

Subsequently, to determine the similarity between two pixels to be compared at column positions x_l and x_r, the squared vector distance between the two individually scaled vectors of all correspondence candidates is computed according to:

$$Q(x_l, x_r) = \sum_{i=-N}^{N} \left[\left(R_l(x_l + i) - s_i R_r(x_r + i) \right)^2 + \left(G_l(x_l + i) - s_i G_r(x_r + i) \right)^2 + \left(B_l(x_l + i) - s_i B_r(x_r + i) \right)^2 \right]$$

where i runs over a window of size $2N+1$ (two-dimensional windows are also possible, but at the expense of higher algorithmic complexity). The candidate for which $Q(x_l, x_r)$ reaches a global minimum within the considered image line is chosen as the corresponding point (for x_l).

The reader is referred to [Sasse 93] for further details on colour models, colour correction, noise elimination, image smoothing, correspondence search and colour interpolation for imaging setups with converging optical axes, i.e. for geometries with epipolar lines not corresponding to pixel lines or columns. In the following section practical issues will be examined and measurement results will be presented.

3 Implementation and Experimental Results

A large number of different scenes with different objects were evaluated using a simple experimental setup with two single-chip colour CCD cameras. Their resolution was 512×512 pixels, their focal length f = 8mm, the base width was d = 200mm. The angle of convergence (the angle the optical axis of the camera makes with the imaginary optical axis of a setup for parallel line stereo) was $15°$.

To illustrate the quality of the image data produced by our setup, fig. 3.1 shows the output of the three colour channels when the camera sees a uniform white reflector illuminated by a pattern according to fig. 2.2 (right). The colour correction algorithm was already applied to the output, equalising severe slowly varying changes in the intensity amplitudes (resulting in peaks of different heights).

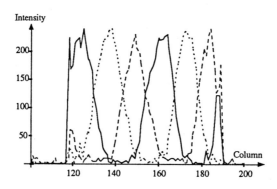

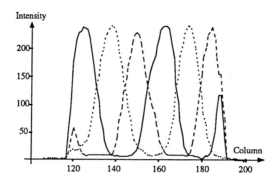

Fig. 3.1 Real intensity data of the three colour channels along one image line produced from a test scene. Top: Intensity after colour correction (scaling). Bottom: Result after application of a smoothing operator.

The remaining disturbances were removed (fig. 3.1, bottom) by a smoothing operator on the colour-corrected data. This obviously leads to somewhat "blurred" intensity data and thus limits the local spatial resolution of the distance measurement. It speaks for the robustness of the approach that the distance measurements are of a more than acceptable accuracy despite the low quality of the acquired data.

An analysis of the geometrical arrangement of our setup [Ottink 89; Ottink 90] yields a principal distance error of about 2mm over a distance range of $z = 100...$ 550mm. This accuracy can be obtained only if the correspondence search is error-free, which in turn presupposes cameras of higher quality than we could afford. Nonetheless, using only the comparatively simple relations given in the previous section, an absolute error in distance of better than 1% of the measured distance was achieved. The number of pixels for which the correct distance was computed was on average 75%. Note that this holds despite the low quality of the input data.

Table 3.1 Absolute distance errors for white reflector

Distance Z [mm]	Error ΔZ [mm]
250	1,5
300	2,3
350	2,0
400	1,9
450	3,0
500	2,6
550	4,0

Table 3.2 Absolute distance errors for different reflectors, Z=350 mm

Material	Error ΔZ [mm]
White Cardboard	1,46
Wood	1,67
Plastics, bright	1,72
Steel	2,80
Aluminium	2,80
Plastics, dark	3,74
Brass, polished	3,84

Table 1 lists the mean absolute distance error for different distances. The values were obtained by evaluating several hundred measurements of a known distance Z. In table 2 the absolute error is given for different materials of the reflector. These values were recorded to justify our claim of the method working independently of the reflectance properties of the reflector. Note that the error increases as the reflection grows. Note further, however, that the value for polished brass was obtained although a human observer due to the optical properties, which much resemble that of a mirror, would only see specular reflections, if anything.

To increase the precision of the measurements further, the distance may be computed with sub-pixel accuracy. This was not done to obtain the readings listed in tables 1 and 2, but is straightforward to implement: upon completion of the search process, the position of the corresponding point and the position of that of the two neighbours on the epipolar line which has the lower value of the similarity function Q are interpolated. The weights of the interpolation are the two values of Q for the corresponding point and its neighbour.

In the remaining part of this section we present two examples of range maps obtained from real world objects and in a real world environment. The ambient lighting conditions were those of a normal office room with the brightness changing continuously. The objects which were not used for calibration purposes were all taken from real assembly processes and not modified.

To illustrate the method's insensitivity to varying reflection due to oblique surfaces, in the first example an object with a triangular surface was measured. The object was so positioned as to avoid occluding contours. For evaluation, a rectangular area was selected in the recorded images, which was completely illuminated with the pattern. Within this area the correspondences were determined using the procedure outlined above. The range map produced with the distances computed based on these correspondences is shown in fig. 3.2.

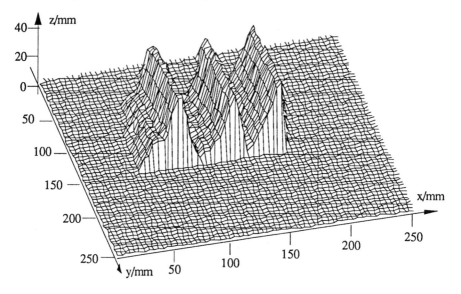

Fig. 3.2 Three dimensional plot of the range map obtained from the object mentioned in the text. All distances are given in mm. The maximum error is about 2mm over the entire area.

The second example is much more complex. It contains all the difficulties one is faced with when measuring distances with either active or passive stereo vision systems. The object (fig. 3.3) has a uniform diffuse surface, it has smooth curvatures as well as sharp edges, it produces shadows and has occluding contours. Lastly, in spite of the diffuse surface, it generates specular reflections.

Fig. 3.4 shows the digitised recorded image of the left camera before colour correction. It shows quite well the irregular distribution of the colour intensities due both to the locally different frequency response of the camera and to the geometrical distortions introduced by the pattern projector. This effect is well visible at the left upper transition from green to red. Points of equal intensity are mapped to ovals instead of parallel vertical lines.

Fig. 3.5 shows the range map of the object in fig. 3.3. Due to the high density of points for which distances were obtained, a three dimensional black-and-white plot was inadequate. Instead, a false colour picture was produced with the colours representing the distances. The scale bar on the left side indicates the distance: It is purple at its lower end and orange at its upper end. This change in colour corresponds to a linear change in distance between $Z = 310mm$ and $Z = 230mm$.

Fig. 3.3 View of the object used in the second example.

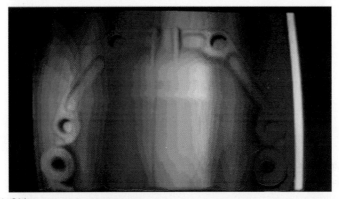

Fig. 3.4 Object as seen by one camera.

Fig. 3.5 Range map obtained for the object. See text for explanations.

A black dot represents a pixel of unknown distance, i.e. an image point for which no corresponding point was found (positive false match). All the points displayed in the range map were extracted from the original image data (fig. 3.4) during the initial search, no interpolation or iterative search was performed, which would provide values for the points that were not assigned a distance in the first step. A window size of 9 pixels was used for correspondence search, the global disparity limit was the interval [230mm, 310mm], the number of pixels under investigation was 102960, of which 73375 were found after 2 hours of computation on a VAXstation.

There are about 10% negative false matches, of which about 75% are in the area of the particularly weak blue channel. This means that for this particularly difficult object about 71% of the pixels were assigned the correct distance (with an absolute error of much less than 1mm), 10% a more or less deviating distance and the rest of 19% no distance at all. It is obvious that even simple iterative strategies like hierarchical search or hypothesis-test procedures may considerably improve these figures in the environment of a false match. However, even without such elaborate schemes, a hit rate of 71% is acceptable given in particular the shortcomings of the physical setup. A further discussion of the residual errors and the remaining problems can be found in [Sasse 93].

4 Conclusions

We have presented a fast and accurate method for generating range images of objects of arbitrary shape and surface. Its potential reaches far beyond the standard applications of active stereo vision. Since there is no principal lower physical limit of its size, it can be miniaturised using fiber optics for providing the necessary light at the point of measurement or for picking up the images, or both. This would enable the method to be employed for measuring the environment of small artificial anthropomorphic hands. Moreover, since only standard hardware is used, the method lends itself to the combination with passive (colour) stereo, such a combination would bring together the advantages of both approaches without trading in their deficiencies.

As far as the improvement of the accuracy and of the hit rate are concerned, the following lines of research can easily be identified:

- Modelling and compensation of the non-linearities of the cameras, parameterisation to account for differences between left and right camera.
- Extension of the camera calibration, which should consider non-linear errors.
- Different coding of the pattern to improve the redundancy and to increase the signal-to-noise ratio and the contrast between two columns of the pattern. This would allow the filtering algorithms to be adapted and to exploit this a priori knowledge.

- Inclusion of subpixel techniques.
- Improvement and miniaturisation of the light pattern source.
- Development of appropriate processor architectures to obtain video-frequency generation of range maps.

Even without a realisation of these advanced topics, the method can be utilised for solving several of the problems encountered whenever computer vision systems are intended to help perform recognition tasks on the factory floor.

5 References

Altschuler 79 Altschuler, M., Altschuler, B., Taboada, J.
Measuring Surfaces Space-Coded by a Laser-Projected Dot Matrix
Proc. SPIE, Vol. 182, 1979

Boissonat 81 Boissonat, J., Germain, F.
A new Approach to the Problem of Acquiring Randomly Oriented Workpieces out of a Bin
Proc. 7th Int. Conf. on Art. Intell., IJCAI–81, 1981

Boyer 87 Boyer, K., Kak, A.
Color-Encoded Structured Light for Rapid Active Ranging
IEEE Trans. on Pat. Anal. and Mach. Intell., Vol. PAMI-9, No. 1, Jan. 1987

Echigo 85 Echigo, T., Yachida, M.
A fast method for extraction of 3-D information using multiple stripes and two cameras
Proceedings of the Int. Joint Conf. on Art. Intell. 1985

Gutsche 91 Gutsche, R., Stahs, T., Wahl, F.
Path Generation with a Universal 3d Sensor
Proc. 1991 IEEE Conf. on Robotics and Autom.

Klinker 90 Klinker, G. J., Shafer, A., Kanade, T.
A Physical Approach to Color Image Understanding
International Journal of Computer Vision, Nr. 4 (1990), pp. 7-38

Monks 92 Monks, T., Carter, J., Shadle, C
Colour Encoded Structured Light for Digitisation of Real–Time 3D Data
Int. Conf. on Image Process. and its Applications, Maastricht, April 1992

Ottink 89 Ottink, F.
Kalibrierung eines Roboter-Kamera-Systems
Studienarbeit, Institut für Techn. Informatik der TU Berlin, 1989.

Ottink 90 Ottink, F.
Grundlagenuntersuchung zur Laserstereoskopie
Diplomarbeit, Institut für Techn. Informatik der TU Berlin, 1990.

Plaßmann 91	Plaßmann, P. *Measuring the Area and Volume of Human Leg Ulcers Using Colour Coded Triangulation* Proc. 1. Conf. on Advances in Wound Management, Cardiff, 1991
Pritschow 91	Pritschow, G., Horn, A. *Schnelle adaptive Signalverarbeitung für Lichtschnittsensoren* Robotersysteme, No. 4, 1991, Berlin: Springer–Verlag
Sasse 93	Sasse, R. *Bestimmung von Entfernungsbildern durch aktive stereoskopische Verfahren* Dissertation, TU Berlin, Fachbereich Informatik, 1993
Tajima 87	Tajima, J. *Rainbow range finder principle for range data acquisition* Proc. IEEE Workshop Ind. Appl. of Mach. Vision and Mach. Intell., Feb. 1987
Vuylsteke 90	Vuylsteke, P., Price, C., Oosterlinck, A. *Image Sensors for Real-Time 3D Acquisition* ASI Series F, Vol. 63: Traditional and Non-Traditional Robotic Sensors, Berlin: Springer-Verlag, 1990
Vuylsteke 90b	Vuylsteke, P., Oosterlinck, A. *Range Image Acquisition with a Single Binary-Encoded Light Pattern* IEEE Trans. on Pat. Anal. and Mach. Intell., Vol. PAMI-12, Feb. 1990

Automatic Model–Generation for Image Analysis

A. Winzen and H. Niemann
Lehrstuhl für Mustererkennung (Informatik 5), Universität Erlangen,
Martensstraße 3, D–91058 Erlangen, F.R. of Germany

1   Introduction

A model–based vision system for industrial applications like object recognition and localisation consists of three components and two data structures, Fig. 1:

- *segmentation*: extracts an initial symbolic description from the image, i.e., a set of *segmentation objects (segments)* found in the image such as lines, contours, surface–patches and relations between these elements.
- *initial symbolic description (segmentation data)*: data structure containing results from the segmentation module, e.g., a set of straight lines with 3D–coordinates.
- *knowledge base*: contains knowledge about scenes and objects which is used for interpreting the initial symbolic description from the segmentation component. Objects are described by models representing their parts and their attributes.
- *image analysis*: performs tasks of object recognition, localisation, and scene analysis by comparing the initial symbolic description of the image with models from the knowledge base.
- *model–generation*: generates models from samples of images. Some vision systems use CAD data for models and do not have a component for automatic learning of models. Advantages of a model–generation component are shown in the next sections. During model–generation, segmentation data of several images has to be integrated. So the problem of matching segments is also important for model–generation.

The following sections describe a 3D–model–generation component for polyhedral models generated from samples of 3D–lines of an object. A solution for the problem of effciently matching segments and parts of a model (3D–lines), which can also be used in an image analysis component, is described in section 4.

2   Image Data and Segmentation

Fig. 2 shows two examples for 3D–image data used for automatic model–generation. 3D–Line segments can be obtained from stereo vision or coded

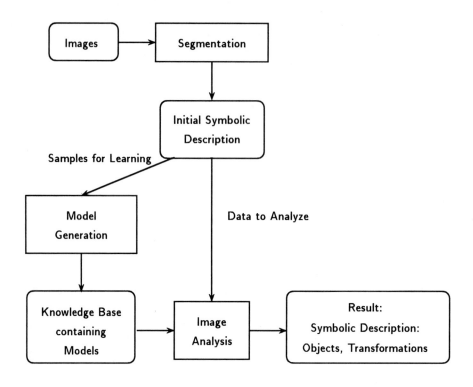

Fig. 1. Data flow in a model–based vision system

light[11]. Segmentation results shown in this text are results from line–based stereo vision[8]. For purposes of model–generation each image contains one view of a single object. The sample (for one object) used for model–generation is a sequence of several views of the object from different viewpoints and rough estimations of the relative movement of the camera (transformation parameters) from one view to the next. Such a sequence can be acquired from cameras moved around the object by a robot or a vehicle.

Because of inaccuracies of segmentation data and transformation estimation, data from different views has to be matched and more accurate transformation parameters have to be computed from corresponding segments.

The views in a sample need not give complete information about all visible parts of the object if this is not required for the application. If some parts of the object are not reachable or hidden, they may not be present in the sample and are not integrated in the model (which is an integration and

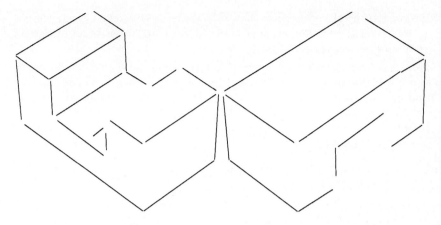

Fig. 2. 3D–views of an ⊔–shaped object in perspective projection

generalization of the data from the sample). Models are generated using the assumption that views in the sample are representative for the application of the models, i.e., they represent those views which are relevant for the image analysis task.

3 Goals of Model–Generation

3.1 Information represented in Models

Because image analysis recognizes objects by comparing parts of models and segments found in the image, the time needed for object recognition depends on the number of parts represented in a model. So parts of a model which are rarely found in images unnecessarily énlarge search–space (and time for recognition) during image analysis should not be included in a model.

An image analysis component has to judge comparisons between segments found in the image (distorted by noise and geometric transformations) and parts of a model, so information about the reliability of parts and their attributes is also useful. This information can be provided by models which were generated from image data: The frequency of a part in the sample can be used to measure its stability. Statistical parameters of numerical attributes, such as mean values and standard deviations of lengths or positions of line ends, can be computed from the sample. This kind of information is not represented in models generated from CAD data and also geometric data from segmented images differs from ideal geometric data in a CAD–model, Fig. 10(a).

With respect to the restriction that only stable parts should be represented in the model, models should be as complete as possible, i.e., contain all stable parts found in the samples. A selection of subsets of parts and attributes sufficient for object recognition (and distinction of different objects) is not done by model–generation, because knowledge about the entire set of objects that should be recognized is necessary for such operations.

Models meeting these criteria depend on the choice of segmentation methods and on the environment where the vision system is applied (lighting conditions, position of cameras) and on image acquisition hardware.

3.2 Model–Generation

The operation of model–generation is illustrated in Fig. 3. Input data for model–generation is the sequence of views and transformation parameters $< s_1, t_1, s_2, t_2, \ldots, s_n >$, where s_i is a segmented image with one view of the object and t_i is the set of 3D–transformation parameters of the relative movement between object and camera moving from the viewpoint of s_i to the viewpoint of s_{i+1}. The views of the sample are integrated into one sample–description representing all views: This is done by matching and fusing data from views and sample–descriptions. Matching and fusing views 1 and 2 yields a sample–description representing the first two views of the sample. This sample–description is matched and fused with the data from the third view giving a sample–description representing views 1 to 3. The 'Matching and Fusing' step is iterated for the whole sample, generating a sample–description of all views.

Matching, described in section 4, determines correspondences of parts of the sample–description and segments from next view. The initial estimation of transformation parameters is used to determine a complete set of all corresponding elements and to resolve ambiguities (due to symmetries of the object). 'Corresponding elements' are parts of the sample–description and and segments from the next view, which are images of the same part of the object and thence should be integrated. An improved estimation of transformation parameters is computed from the set of all corresponding elements.

Fusing integrates data of the current sample–description and the next view into a new sample–description using matching results: Corresponding elements were integrated, elements without matching partners were added to the new sample–description. E.g., corresponding lines l_1 from the sample–description and l_2 from the next view are integrated into one line l by adding the attribute values of l_2 (ends, length, strength, ...) to the attribute statistics of l_1 and defining attribute values of l as mean values of its attribute statistics.

The final sample–description contains all parts from the sample and also all segmentation errors from the sample. The *processing* step, described in section 5 uses the statistical information gathered by the 'Matching and Fusing' step for an improvement of the quality of the sample–description, e.g., by removing parts which are likely caused by segmentation errors.

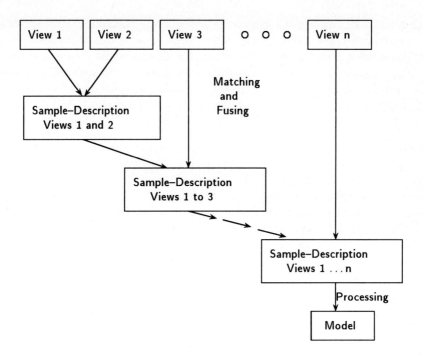

Fig. 3. Operation of model–generation

4 Matching

4.1 Matching–Problems

The *matching–problem* for image analysis can be described as follows:
Given a set of segments P, found in the image, a set of models of objects $\mathcal{M} = \{O_1, \ldots, O_m\}$ and for each model $O_i \in \mathcal{M}$, the set of its parts M_i; the set of models found in P, and for each model O_i recognized in P, a correspondence between parts in M_i and segments found in the image have to be determined.

For the definition and computation of correspondences, the distinction between different M_i is not necessary, so M is written instead of M_i. A *correspondence* $K \subset M \times P$ can be defined as a relation containing *associations* $(m, p) \in M \times P$ representing corresponding elements. Without any restrictions, K is the relation of a partial function $k : M \rightarrow 2^P$. The following restrictions of 'correspondence' are often used:

1. $k : M \rightarrow P$, assuming that parts of the model and segments found in images are robust enough for finding unique matching partners for all elements (if existing).

2. k : M$\rightarrow$2^P, with im(k) containing pairwise disjoint sets, which allows a restricted correction of errors: a part of the model can be matched with a set of segments found in the image. For geometric data, such as surface patches or line segments this correction is useful, because splitting one line or surface of the object (which is also represented as one line or surface in the model) into several segments is a frequent segmentation error.

In the case of matching during model–generation the current sample–description is used as a 'model'; the segmentation data from the next view has to be matched with this 'model'. So the 'model' is already known and need not be determined from a set of models M. Estimations of transformation parameters $t_1, \ldots, t_{n-1}$ facilitate computation of corresponding elements. In image analysis, especially for recognizing single objects, the computation of some corresponding elements is sufficient for recognition, but model–generation tries to integrate corresponding elements from different views, thus complete correspondences are needed for this purpose.

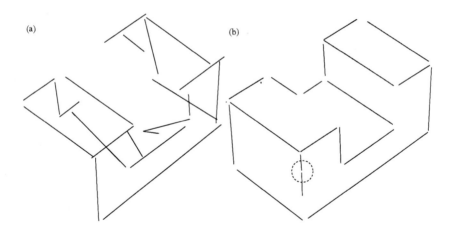

Fig. 4. Data to be matched: (a) sample–description of $< s_1, t_1, s_2, t_2, s_3 >$ transformed with t_3, (b) segmentation of the next image s_4

Results of the 'Matching and Fusing' step are shown in Fig. 4 and Fig. 5. Fig. 4 shows input data for the matching step: a sample–description, Fig. 4(a), generated from three views $< s_1, t_1, s_2, t_2, s_3 >$ transformed with the estimated transformation parameters t_3 which is matched with segmentation data of s_4, Fig. 4(b). Lines from Fig. 4(b) with corresponding lines in Fig. 4(a), are shown in Fig. 5(a). The correction of a segmentation error (one line has been splitted into two segments) in Fig. 4(b), indicated by a circle,

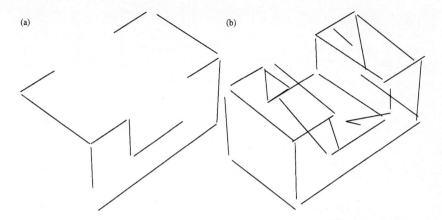

Fig. 5. Results of matching and fusing: (a) matching result: corresponding lines, (b) sample–description of $< s_1, t_1, s_2, t_2, s_3 >$ fused with s_4, using the result from (a)

can also be seen in Fig. 5(a). Based on this result, corresponding lines are integrated into a new sample–description and lines without matching partner are added, giving the result shown in Fig. 5(b).

The following subsections describe methods for the computation of correspondences.

4.2 Tree Search

The problem of computing a matching function is often described by NP–complete problems, like subgraph–isomorphism or CLIQUE–problems for matching relational structures, or optimization problems. They have often been solved by application of (heuristic) search methods, such as branch– and bound–techniques[5] or A*–Algorithm[7]. Such techniques have been widely used for image analysis[4, 9, 2]. A model–generation component using an A*–Algorithm for matching has also been built and tested for a 2D–vision system[6]. This subsection describes the application of an A*–Algorithm for the computation of the matching function and the problems involved.

Fig. 6(c) shows a complete search tree generated for matching two 2D–triangles with unknown 2D–translation and 2D–rotation parameters. In this case, the correspondence is a bijective mapping beween the two sets of lines M and P in Fig. 6(a) and Fig. 6(b). Each node consists of the associations of its predecessor enlarged by one additional association; leaves of the tree contain complete associations.

The generation of the tree during the search is guided by a cost function and terminates when a leaf with minimal costs is reached. The cost $\psi(v)$ of

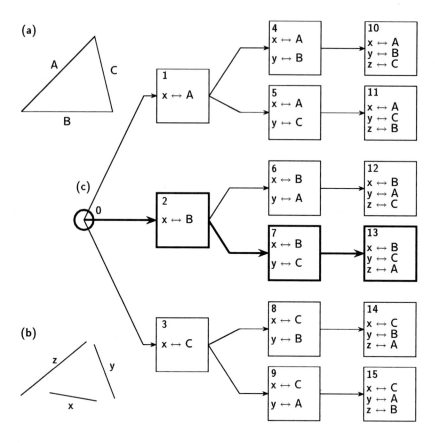

Fig. 6. Search tree generated for matching 2D–triangles

a node v is defined as an inverse quality measure of the correspondence K_v represented in this node, e.g., the sum of distances $d(m, p)$ of lines $m \in M$ and $p \in P$ associated in the correspondence. A* tries to find a leaf of the tree with minimal costs using a cost function $\hat{\phi}(v) := \psi(v) + \hat{\chi}(v)$, where $\hat{\chi}(v)$ is an optimistic estimate of the minimal costs $\chi(v)$ of a path from the node v to a leaf. So the problem of efficiently searching a correspondence becomes the problem of defining an optimistic cost estimation which is close enough to the real costs to prevent A* from generating nodes not on a path to an optimal solution, thus not requiring an exponential amount of storage and time.

In the first level of the tree, associations between one line of one triangle and each line of the other triangle are used as hypotheses. In each node 1– 3, hypotheses for transformation parameters are computed. We assume that the orientation of each line segment is unique, the transformation parameters computed from each hypothesis are unique, otherwise there would be two choices of transformation parameters for two possible orientations of the line giving six nodes on the first level. Transformation hypotheses for nodes 1–3 of Fig. 6 are shown in Fig. 7(1)–(3).

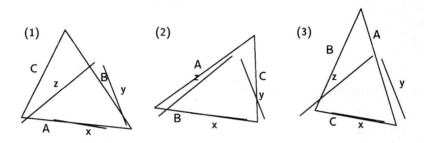

Fig. 7. Hypotheses from the first level of the search tree

Using these parameters $\hat{\chi}(v)$ can be computed by assuming that each line x without matching partner in K_v, gets a matching partner y with minimal costs, regardless wether y has already been matched or not. Unfortunately, such simple heuristic cost estimations are not strong enough to limit the set of nodes to be searched to a size not exponentially growing with $|M|$ and $|P|$. Inaccurate segmentation results, cluttered image data and symmetries in the objects complicate this task. For 3D–matching with unknown translation and rotation parameters, the situation is worse, because the first hypothesis for transformation parameters can be computed on the third level of the tree, after generating $O((\max\{|M|, |P|\})^3)$ nodes. Grimson shows in [3] that the efficiency of such search methods crucially depends on the choice of the termination criterion, i.e., the correspondences generated should be only as large as necessary for recognition and not complete. So applications depending on complete correspondences should not use such techniques.

4.3 Hypothesis–Generation and Verification

The matching–algorithm used for 3D–model–generation also uses A*, but for searching a different tree, Fig. 8. Nodes on the first level contain hypotheses, these are sets of three assocations, computed using the initial transformation estimate. Each of the nodes 2–11 contains also an improved transformation estimate computed from the three line associations of that node. Nodes on the second level are verified (or falsified) hypotheses. A node $v \in \{12, 13, 16, 21, 22\}$ represents a correspondence $k_v : M \rightarrow P$, where k_v is injective, and an improved estimation of transformation parameters (estimated from all corresponding lines defined by k_v). Nodes on the 'correction' levels are derived from the verified hypotheses by enlarging the correspondence to injective functions $k_v : M \rightarrow 2^P$ thus correcting errors like splitting of single lines into multiple parallel or collinear lines. Because almost all matching partners have been determined in the nodes on the second level of the tree, alternatives rarely occur during the correction steps. So most branches were generated during hypothesis generation.

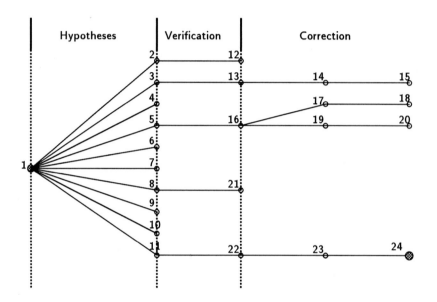

Fig. 8. Search tree, nodes were generated by an A^*–Algorithm in sequence of their numbers

The reason for using this kind of search tree is the existence of efficient methods for computing the verification in polynomial time.

4.4 Bipartite Matching used for Verification

Verification is performed by the computation of a maximal weigthed matching in a bipartite graph (V, E) with a vertex set $V := M' \cup P'$ and an edge set $E := M' \times P'$. A *matching* $H \subset E$ in a bipartite graph, shown in Fig. 9, is a set of edges with no common vertices:

$$\forall (a, b) \in H \ \forall (c, d) \in H : (a, b) \neq (c, d) \Rightarrow (a \neq b \land c \neq d)$$

A non negative *weight function* w : $E \longrightarrow \mathbb{R}_{\geq 0}$ is defined for the edge set and the *weight of a matching* H is $\sum_{(m,p)\in H} w(m,p)$.

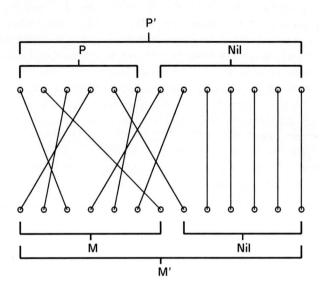

Fig. 9. Bipartite graph matching used as verification method

This result can be used to compute an optimal correspondence in $O((|M|+|P|)^3)$ time: The *weigthed bipartite matching problem* is the problem of computing a matching with maximal weight in a bipartite graph, with $|M'| = |P'|$. It can be solved in $O(|M'|^3)$ (the computation of $w(m,p)$ is assumed to take constant time) by the Hungarian Method[10]. The amount of storage used by this method is a linear function of $|M'|$. M' is defined as M plus a set of $|P|$ dummy elements representing missing matching partners for elements from P: 'Nil' in Fig. 9. The definition of P' is analogous. The weight w is defined as $w(m,p):=D-d_v(m,p)$ where d_v is the distance of the two lines (regarding the transformation hypothesis of node v) and D is an upper limit for d_v. For 'Nil'–elements, w is defined as a threshold for the minimum weight of an association[12]. A maximal weighted matching in this graph is a correspondence k_v : M→P minimizing the sum of distances of its associations. The distance measure $d_v(m,p)$ was defined as $d_v(m,p):=\min\{d_e(m',p), d_e(p,m')\}$, where $d_e(m',p)$ denotes the maximum of the Euklidian distances of the ends of line m' to (all points of) line p and m' is m, transformed with the transformation estimation of node v.

5 Final Processing and Results of Model–Generation

Fig. 10(a) shows the result of data integration from a sample of nine pairs of stereo–images. Clusters of 3D–points indicate the positions of line ends found in the sample. The final procssing of the sample–description (Fig. 3) includes thresholding operations for the removal of lines which were not stable and operations for closing gaps between lines. A polyhedral object can be constructed by finding approximately planar contours and approximating these contours with planar patches, thereby recalculating the positions of lines and vertices. During all these operations the statistical information gathered from the sample is preserved. Fig. 10(b) shows the result of these operations applied to the data in Fig. 10(a), numbers indicate centers of planar patches. This result can be used, if polyhedral objects are needed for image analysis, in other cases, where 3D–wireframe models are sufficient, the operations of contour–finding and patch–approximation can be skipped.

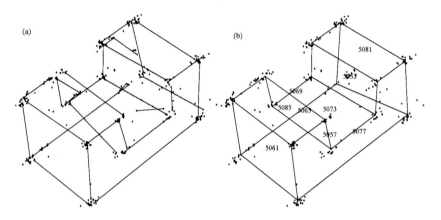

Fig. 10. Results of model–generation: (a) corrected sample–description, vertex clusters shown, (b) result (a) with planar surfaces

The accuracy of models depends on the accuracy of segmentation data: Using the stereo vision approach[8], the lengths of most lines are about 1cm shorter (max. 2.3cm) than the corresponding edges of the object. With image data from the coded light approach[11] and samples containing more than 20 images, the maximum inaccuracy is 3mm, in most cases less than 2mm. The size of the ⊔–shaped object is 14cm×8cm×7cm, other objects used for experiments are about of the same size.

The reconstruction of planar surfaces (and the surface normals) is not unique in all cases and also segmentation errors in the thresholded sample–description may cause the construction of wrong polyhedral objects. To resolve such ambiguities or errors, additional information, such as labeled lines[1, p. 296] or information about surface normals near lines has to be provided by the segmentation component. The use of such information and the extension of model–generation from straight lines to 3D–polygons, used as approximation for arbitrary 3D–curves, and definitions of distance functions for 3D–polygons are topics of current research.

References

1. D.H. Ballard and C.M Brown. *Computer Vision*. Prentice-Hall, Englewood Cliffs N.J., 1982.
2. R.C. Bolles and P. Horaud. 3DPO: A three–dimensional part orientation system. In T. Kanade, editor, *Three–Dimensional Machine Vision*, pages 399–450. Kluwer Academic Publishers, Boston, MA, 1987.
3. W.E.L. Grimson. The combinatorics of heuristic search termination for object recognition in cluttered environments. *IEEE Trans. on Pattern Analysis and Machine Intelligence*, 13(9):920–935, September 1991.
4. W.E.L Grimson and D.P. Huttenlocher. On the verification of hypothesized matches in model-based recognition. In O. Faugeras, editor, *European Conference on Computer Vision 1990, Springer LNCS 427*, pages 489–498, Heidelberg, 1991. Springer.
5. K. Mehlhorn. *Data Structures and Algorithms*, volume 2: Graph-Algorithms and NP-Completeness. Springer, Heidelberg, 1984.
6. H. Niemann, H. Brünig, R. Salzbrunn, and S. Schröder. Interpretation of industrial scenes by semantic networks. In *IAPR Workshop on Machine Vision Applications*, pages 39–42, Tokyo, 1990.
7. N.J. Nilsson. *Problem Solving Methods in Artificial Intelligence*. McGraw-Hill, New York, 1971.
8. S. Posch. *Automatische Bestimmung von Tiefeninformation aus Grauwert-Stereobildern*. Deutscher Universitäts Verlag, Wiesbaden, 1990.
9. P. Rummel and W. Beutel. Workpiece recognition and inspection by a model–based scene analysis system. *Pattern Recognition*, 17(1):141–148, 1984.
10. A. Sultan. *Linear programming, An Introduction with Applications*. Academic Press, Boston, 1993.
11. F. Wahl. Benutzerhandbuch für die PC–basierte Implementierung des codierten Lichtverfahrens. Technical report, Institut für Robotik und Prozeßinformatik, TU Braunschweig, 1991.
12. A. Winzen. Efficient methods for hypothesis verification paradigms. In *Proc. Int. Conf. on Pattern Recognition*, pages 558–561, The Hague, Netherlands, 1992. IAPR, IEEE Computer Society Press.

Navigation Through Volume Data by Active Vision Methods

Hans-Heino Ehricke
Universität Tübingen
Wilhelm-Schickard-Institut für Informatik
Graphisch-Interaktive Systeme (WSI/GRIS)
Tübingen, F.R.G.

Abstract

Recently, the interactive exploration of volume data has received increasing attention in Scientific Visualization research. In this context one of the key problems is the machine perception of object surfaces prior to their three-dimensional rendering. We present an active vision approach exploiting interactivity features of modern visualization systems. By the integration of Computer Vision methods into the visualization pipeline immediate user control of the highly complex machine perception process becomes possible. On the basis of this concept we propose the vision camera, a tool for interactive vision during volume data walkthroughs. This camera model is characterized by a flexible front-plane which, under the control of user-specified parameters and image features elastically matches to object surfaces, while shifted through a data volume. Thus, objects are interactively carved out and can be visualized by standard volume visualization methods. Implementation and application of the model are described. Our results suggest that by the integration of human and machine vision new perspectives for data exploration are opened up.

1   Introduction

The navigation of robots through 3D space has been an issue of constant research in Robotics during recent years. In this context a great number of object recognition approaches related to the Computer Vision (CV) area have been proposed for obstacle detection and collision prevention. Similar problems are encountered in scientific visualization (SV) systems. Here the efficient exploration of volume datasets by walkthroughs requires the detection of object surfaces which are to be visualized. Regarding the complexity of volume datasets it becomes obvious that by the use of local voxel-based models [1] discrimination between relevant and obscuring voxels is often not possible. Thus, visualization results often fail to reveal relevant properties of the dataset. We describe an extension of the visualization pipeline, allowing for the merging of the disciplines SV and CV. In CV over certainly more than twenty years now, a variety of model-driven approaches for the interpretation of image data have been proposed [2]. Their primary deficiency, perhaps is the lack of interfaces in order to easily adapt the models to new application areas. The goal of the concept proposed here is to provide the user of a visualization system with vision tools for interactive data exploration.

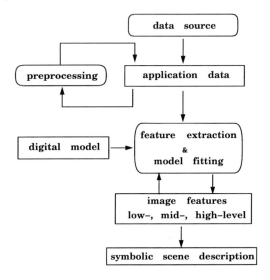

Figure 1: Principles of Computer Vision demonstrating the concept of machine perception.

2   The Vision by Visualization Concept

"Visual perception is the relation of visual input to previously existing models of the world" [3]. The primary goal of SV is the conversion of unstructured input data into a representation which allows visual perception of relevant information. This stepwise analysis process has led to a conceptual model for scientific visualization systems, the visualization pipeline [4]. Unfortunately this model does not adequately address one of the key problems in SV, the object recognition dilemma. Most visualization methods which have been proposed so far, require a pre-interpretation of the input data in order to discriminate between objects of interest and background voxels. This is not an easy task and therefore, highly complex object recognition approaches have been described in the CV literature [2]. Figure 1 presents the primary elements of object recognition systems. In CV digital models are fitted to application data. In an iterative manner features of higher and higher semantical level are derived leading finally to a symbolic description of the scene. Since the models are unflexible as compared to mental models of a human being, computer vision systems are designed for very specific applications.

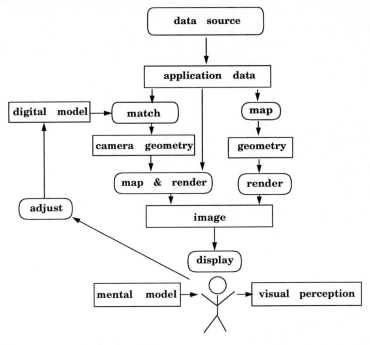

Figure 2: The Scientific Visualization pipeline extended by Computer Vision concepts. The diagram illustrates the integration of the vision camera.

Dependance on specific types of input data and scene objects is an undesirable feature for visualization systems. One way to get out of this dilemma is to interactively adapt the digital models used in CV to the mental models a visualization system user applies when exploring volume data. This means integration of the CV and SV pipelines, leading to the concept of vision by visualization. If we approach SV with these aspects in mind new perspectives open up, which can be expressed by questions like:

- How can we extend CV methods by interaction and visualization interfaces?

- Having in mind the potential of interactive visualization systems, what novel CV methods can we think of?

CV approaches may be introduced not only at the application data level (data pre-interpretation), but the vision by visualization concept addresses all levels of the SV pipeline. Here we focus on the map & render element and propose an original extension, the vision camera (see fig. 2).

3   The Vision Camera

Based on the vision by visualization concept, with the vision camera (Visi-Cam) we propose a tool for data exploration with integrated vision capabilities. The idea is to use a flexible camera front-plane which adapts to surfaces within the dataset. The physical model consists of a rectangular rubber frame which carries an elastic grid. The visualization system user pushes the camera through the scene and the flexible grid adapts to object surfaces via an elastic matching method (see fig. 3). 3D visualization is achieved by ray-casting, using the camera front-plane as a clipping plane. Any of the available illumination methods, e.g. semi-transparent volume rendering, threshold-guided greylevel gradient shading or maximum intensity projection may be used. Since the front-plane adapts to surface structures, object discrimination can be easily carried out during rendering. When the user pushes the camera further into the scene the rubber grid finally gets off the current object surface and tends to become planar again. When the next surface is met the adaptation process becomes active again.

For the implementation of this physical model we use elastic matching, a technique from the CV area. The method has been widely used for the adaptation of geometric models to actual image data, thus recognizing objects and their boundaries. Our initial geometric model is a planar and regular grid which is fixed to a flexible frame, located at the initial camera position within the volume. The goal is to match this model to relevant surface structures in a stepwise manner. During one step each node of the grid is investigated and one of the alternatives, (1) shift one voxel in camera motion direction, (2) shift one voxel in opposite camera motion direction, (3) keep current position in 3D space, is selected (see fig. 4).

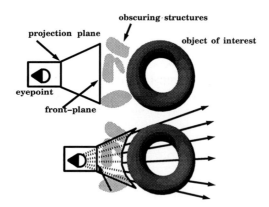

Figure 3: The VisiCam model and the way it approaches an object surface.The front-plane is used as a clipping plane.

In order to arrive at a decision, which of the three possibilities to carry out, we use a cost function. This is evaluated for each of the three alternative node positions and the minimum cost position is chosen. Similar to the approach proposed in [5] the costs are determined according to the following formula:

$$C_i(x, y, z) = a_0 b_i D_i + a_1 I(x, y, z) + a_2 T_i \tag{1}$$

where:
$C_i(x, y, z)$ is the cost of node i at position (x, y, z),
D_i is a driving force which pushes nodes in camera motion direction,
$I(x, y, z)$ is an image feature function,
T_i is a topology evaluation function,
a_0, a_1, a_2, b_i are weighting factors.

The *driving force* D_i is a term responsible for the pushing of a node in camera motion direction. For linear motion we use a simple ramp function with a slope of 0.5.

By the *image feature function* $I(x, y, z)$ nodes are attracted to object surfaces. $I(x, y, z)$ has the form $1.0 - G(x, y, z)$, where $G(x, y, z)$ is a local greyvalue gradient, normalized to 1.0. We use the Zucker-Hummel operator in a 3*3*3 voxel neighbourhood. In order to get rid of local minima problems we previously apply a median filter with a kernel of 5*5*5 voxels.

The *topology function* T_i prevents the flexible rubber grid from collapsing, dragging it to a more or less planar shape. The positions of the eight orthogonal neighbours of a node (two in each of the four directions) on the grid are averaged and the distance between the nodes position and the neighbour's average is calculated. From this value the minimum distance within the three alternative node positions is subtracted and the resulting value is multiplied by the maximum distance.

By the weighting factor b_i the motion speed of the flexible frame is augmented, as compared to the speed of the grid nodes: $b_i > 1.0$ for nodes on the frame, $b_i = 1.0$ for other nodes. So, when the user pushes the camera in a certain direction the force is transmitted mainly to the frame which passes it to the flexible grid. After each step the eyepoint(camera) position is updated, based on the average node position within the grid. When an object surface is met, the camera motion speed is decreased by the influence of the image feature function and the flexible grid as well as the rubber frame adapt to it. The user has to increase the motion force to penetrate the surface and drag the front-plane into the object where other surfaces may be detected. In this way camera motion is controlled by the user as well as image data properties.

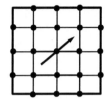

for each node n

> **for each possible node position i**
> **(as is, one step forward, one step backward)**
>
> **calculate cost C_i**
>
> **determine minimal cost C_j among the three**
>
> **set position of node n to j**

Figure 4: Example grid and adaptation algorithm.

4 Results

We have implemented the vision camera on a Silicon Graphics Indigo work-station as a C++ class structure with an X11/Motif interface. Although the program does not provide realtime response it can be used as an interactive testbed for our algorithms. We have used it for the exploration of various volume datasets from medicine and biology. Figure 5 presents example images from an exploration study with a Magnetic Resonance Imaging dataset of a patient's head. The left column demonstrates how the grid adjusts to the skin surface. We used a grid with 128 * 128 nodes. Each node represents a pixel of the resulting projection image. For a better understanding we have integrated the result into an overview image of the head which has been generated by threshold guided raycasting with greylevel-gradient shading. After adaptation to the skin surface we kept the shape of the camera front-plane fixed and pushed the camera forward for another 10 mm. Then the matching process was enabled again. The right column in fig. 5 illustrates the result. We have been able to carve out the brain surface and display it by Z-buffer shading (top), as a wireframe (middle) and with Gouraud-shading (bottom).

5 Conclusion

In spite of our promising results several issues deserve a deeper investigation: (1) The cost function possesses a great number of parameters which have to be tuned to a special recognition situation.

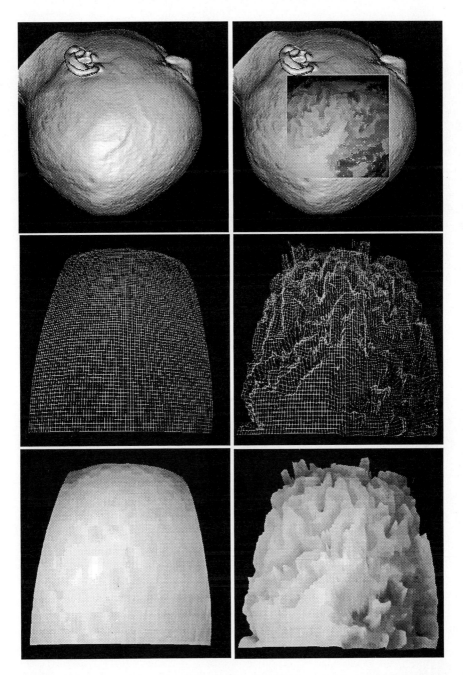

Figure 5: Exploration of a medical volume dataset. Adaptation of the grid to the skin surface of a patient's head (left column) and to the brain surface (right column).

For this task a great deal of experience is necessary. Here an intuitive user interface with realtime response to parameter modifications seems to be the best solution. By the pre-computation of the gradients used by the image feature function and the reduction of the number of grid nodes by an interpolation strategy, we are currently trying to achieve interactive feedback on an SGI Indigo.

(2) Although we use a cost function which employs global characteristics (topology) our algorithm performs merely a local evaluation. This may lead to non-optimal solutions in a global sense. Globalization of the cost function and grid movement along the steepest gradient may lead to better results, as explained e.g. in [6].

(3) So far only linear motion of the camera is supported by the algorithm. The implementation of camera rotation facilities requires modification of the cost function evaluation strategy and of the shape of the driving force component.

We have demonstrated that the vision by visualization concept leads to the development of new interaction tools in the area of SV. VisiCam is only one possibility. We are convinced that with this concept in mind a variety of new techniques will be proposed, bringing together machine and human vision.

References

[1] M. Levoy. Display of surfaces from volume data. *IEEE Comp. Graph. Appl.*, 8(3):29–32, 1988.

[2] P. Suetens, P. Fua, and A.J. Hanson. Computational strategies for object recognition. *ACM Computing Surveys*, 24(1):5–61, 1992.

[3] D.H. Ballard and C.M. Brown. *Computer Vision*, chapter 1, page 6. Prentice Hall, Englewood Cliffs, 1982.

[4] R.B. Haber. Visualization in engineering mechanics: Techniques, systems and issues. Siggraph'88 Course Notes, 1988. Visualization Techniques in Physical Science.

[5] J.V. Miller, D.E. Breen, W.E. Lorensen, and R.M. O'Bara and M.J. Wozny. Geometrically deformed models: A method for extracting closed geometric models from volume data. *Computer Graphics*, 25(4):217–226, 1991.

[6] Michael Kass, Andrew Witkin, and Demetri Terzopoulos. Snakes: Active contour models. *International Journal of Computer Vision*, 1:321–331, 1988.

TOWARDS A VISION SYSTEM FOR A DOMESTIC ROBOT

A. Gagalowicz

INRIA - Rocquencourt

Domaine de Voluceau

BP. 105

78153 Le Chesnay Cedex

email : ag@bora.inria.fr

Résumé

We shall discuss a way to set up a reliable 3D office scene recognition and interpretation scheme for a home robot with the use of articicial vision only. It is a very difficult problem which has been studied by numerous scientists for many years. We do not pretend to describe the solution of this problem in the present paper, but simply to express our state of mind. Our efforts are concentrated on the manner to produce a well posed problem and on the use of an analysis/synthesis feedback loop in order to solve it. It is expected to produce a more robust solution than the visual open loop solutions already available in the literature.

Keywords : Analysis/synthesis collaboration, computer vision, computer graphics, learning, polyhedral world.

1 Introduction

This document relates the activity of the INRIA Syntim Laboratory which has been studying the problem of artificial vision for a domestic robot in an Analysis/Synthesis framework for several years. I, therefore would like to associate all its members to this document as all this work is a team one. The basis of the approach is described in [7, 1]. I invite the reader to consult these documents before this one as I will consider them as a prerequisite.

Our desire is to study only the "vision" problem of a domestic robot. We would like this robot to understand perfectly his workspace in order for him to perform all kinds of tasks such as bring coffee, clean up, switch lights on, off, etc... We have in our mind a "versatile" robot, a true house assistant.

We are aware of the fact that the achievement of this dream is still far away and requires not only big progress in artificial vision but also in other domains.

Interface with such a robot must be easy. We do think that the best one should be an oral one. Progress in speech analysis and synthesis is already very significant in the literature and if it is still not possible to think of the use of our own language to communicate with the robot, it is already conceivable to do it with key words, separated or bound by syntax and semantics of the type "switch on green light".

Control problems for a robot are very serious as well, but are also very thoroughly studied by the scientific community. Such a home robot should be able to move at its own will in a flat or a factory: robots with wheels or legs are already well mastered by roboticians [13]. A home robot may be only useful if it is interacting with its environment. It must therefore have one (or two) arms. Unfortunately, to our knowledge, though the control of a robot arm seems to be achieved in a satisfactory way [14], robots with wheels and arms are still not much studied and the control problem of such robots is much more difficult due to the increased number of degrees of freedom [15]. Nevertheless it is reasonable to conceive that this problem will be solved in a near future.

Finally, the last but not the least problem is that of the autonomy and the real time aspect of the robot action. Very complex programs will have to be run by the robot himself. It is impossible to imagine that computers such as a connection machine or a CRAY (which would be necessary today!) could be embarked on the robot. But the technology improvements are so rapid that such a computing power will be very soon available in small spaces as those which are tolerated by a robot. Numerous efforts were also devoted to specialized architectures for vision tasks. For example, at ETCA, a French military research institute, the perception systems laboratory directed by B. Zavidovique [3] has already produced some circuit boards computing mainly all the low level vision techniques presented in this paper in real time and it is conceivable that these researchers could solve the high level ones in the future. We are ourselves only interested by the vision problem and especially by a reliable methodology. We do believe that, there too, achieved results seem to allow a certain optimism though enormous problems remain. The steady progress of the various mentioned disciplines and their combination seem to become a reasonable perspective so that it seems already possible to dream of this home robot for the beginning of the next century.

In this paper, we restrict ourselves to the static case, where we study a single stereo pair (coming from the two eyes of the robot!). The target is to try to understand and interpret the perceived scene by the two cameras of the robot. To interpret a scene at a certain position of a robot, means also, to do it in a discrete set of positions. It is foreseen to associate, in the future, measures and results obtained from a sequence of stereo images in order to treat the dynamical case of a robot moving in a room and thus to take advantage of the accumulation of evidences from the various positions.

2 Acquisition of knowledge for a robot

We desire that a domestic robot "understands" what is a table, a chair, a coffee machine..., ultimately all the objects which are in our flat, in order for him to be able to interact with them. Suppose that a human being were born in a deep forest far from contacts with any other humans (even parents) and that he spent all his life there. It is obvious that he would not be capable to "understand" and recognize these objects. What makes us recognize them is that we LEARNT what they are, living with them, touching them, and being taught how they are called, what is their use and so on. We recognize our world through the accumulation of knowledge which was our main activity in the childhood and which is continuing even afterwards. It took us many many years, FULL TIME, to come up to this level of knowledge which permits to evolve in our world with a certain comfort. How would one require a robot to perform better than humans, being only a set of electronic boards and programs which are not including this knowledge? A robot will never (at least in a forecastable future) be able to invent knowledge. We then have to give it to him!

The way the knowledge of objects (table, chair, ...) is stored in our brain is still completely unknown. It seems difficult to be inspired by our own procedure. Instead, we have chosen to proceed in a very primitive way. We are certain that it is not the method used in our brain; but it is easy to understand and allows to produce a good, well-posed recognition process. The idea is to put the precise geometrical description of all objets of the robot workspace into its memory. It could be the architecture drawing of the house plus the industrial drawing of the objects of the house, for example.

There could be very complex objets in the house (human beings, plants, animals,...). We have decided to skip these objects from the scene for the moment. Their modelling, recognition and reconstruction represent themselves some of the major research problems in the literature. If we eliminate these complex objects, we may point out that usual objets are manufactured and mostly polyhedral. We shall restrict ourselves to a polyhedral robot workspace for the moment. Of course, this apparent restriction is not so crucial if we remark that it is very common to approximate complex objets by polyhedral ones in computer graphics.

How to transfer this geometric knowledge to the robot? As the nature and variety of the objects of a flat or house are of an infinite complexity, it is nonsence to try to think of a general solution to the problem. We think that it is, in a first step, better to produce a strategy adapted to the particular environment of each individual robot (his house!). The idea is the following: when a particular person will buy a robot, on top of the normal vision (analysis/synthesis) programs which will be necessary for its proper work, he will also receive a knowledge acquisition program. How will it run? The robot will have naturally one or two color cameras but it will be necessary to add a control screen to the system where the images perceived by the robot will be visualized. The knowledge acquisition program will have to be run by the user at home. As the user will not be a specialist in computer science, this program will have to be easy to run (some notice may be available). This program will be the way for the user to TEACH his own robot his workspace in a similar way to parents are teaching their child. The solution which we advise is to produce a totally interactive program.

This knowledge acquisition program is in fact subdivided in two parts. The first one is dedicated to the camera calibration. We utilize a simple pinhole model for the cameras. This calibration allows us to estimate quantitatively the perspective transform between a 3D point and its locations on the focal planes of the cameras. For each camera, we determine the intrinsic parameters (zoom, angle, image sampling coefficients) and the extrinsic ones (position, orientation). The first calibration technique tested was Toscani's [8]. He proposes a linear solution minimizing a mean square error criterion without constraints. The necessary data of the program are the 3D coordinates of N no coplanar points ($N > 5$) and their projections on both images. This method happened to be too sensitive to noise. We used our own method which is initialized by Toscani's solution. Our solution minimizes the mean square position error between the projections of the 3D points found and their 2D locations. It is more intuitive than Toscani's criterion but is non linear with regard to the calibration coefficients. It is a gradient type solution which enhances Toscani's results. The measure of 3D points in a unique coordinate system happens to be fastidious, constraining and subject to noise: it requires the talents of a geographer. We are now studying a new calibration technique that we call "weak metric calibration". The idea is to measure only lengths (1D values) but no 3D coordinates. We already have a solution based upon the use of rectangles parallel to a fictious coordinate system which produces results similar to Toscani's. We are now trying to improve the precision of our method while including non parallel rectangles or segments. This method requires very few interactions with the 3D world and could be compared to the non metric approach proposed by O. Faugeras [9].

When the cameras are calibrated, the second step consists in constructing the object models themselves. For these purposes, it is possible to take advantage of the great expertise of computer graphists who already produce software for object construction which is called modeler by the community. With the aid of SOGITEC, a French company specialized in the field, we designed such a modeler called ACTION 3D. ACTION 3D allows to construct completely interactively objects of various shapes, to animate them and give them various types of material or texture. To produce an object geometry, it is possible to start from simple primitives (for example, parallelepipeds, spheres, cones, cylinders, pyramids...) and to create more complex objects through the assembly of such primitives and their deformations. It is also possible to create their surface from a deformable skeleton and from a curve which slides along it (generalized cylinders), or simply by the connection of various curves. The tools available in ACTION 3D are so numerous that they produce infinite possibilities for objet conception while preserving compact representations. The problem is: how to use ACTION 3D? We were inspired by an idea presented by Bernard Peroche and Philippe Jaillon which consists in using ACTION 3D as a counter-drawing which is superimposed over the stereo pair (figure 1) coming from the two cameras. The user sees this superposition on the control screen of the robot. Each object coming from ACTION 3D is projected and superimposed in a white wireframe drawing over the two images (see figure 2). The target is here to construct each object of the scene (for example, the table), primitive after primitive (top part, body, legs...) starting from a simple polyhedral primitive, that is displaced first in the center of the 3D space and then moved towards the desired position while using the various displacement tools available in the modeler (the user will use a mouse and/or buttons). It is also possible to stretch each primitive

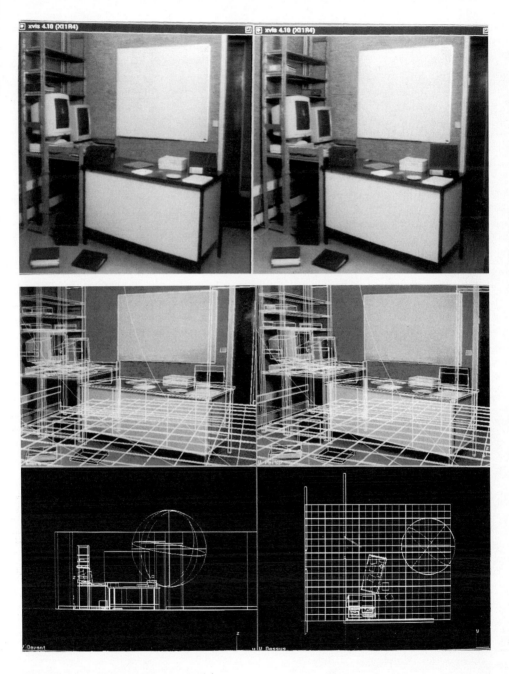

Figure 1: Office stereo view

Figure 2: Interactive acquisition of the scene model: superposition of figure 1 and of Action 3D construction

and deform it interactively using other functions until the two projections of this primitive coincide visually with the real part of the scene available on the stereo image pair.

The procedure is, of course restricted to the portion of 3D space perceived by the robot. In order to avoid projection errors due to depth, we may always display the complete scene model and modify the relative object positions a posteriori. Each new primitive is inserted only if it has a common face with an object already positioned. A particular function of the knowledge acquisition program performs this, which also improves considerably the interaction (matching with the data). We still have to write the software which allows the transition from the construction of one part of the robot workspace to the next one in order to obtain the full (360°) workspace database. The advantage of this interactive technique is that the user knows perfectly his house and all objects inside it, and how he calls them; he may transmit his names to the robot. The user also solves the hidden surface, shadow problems, and coherence bookkeeping (no objects sharing the same 3D space!).

It is also given to the user the difficult decision of the choice of the refinements of the description of each object, depending on his own needs. The modeler allows him to easily place several instances of the same object in the scene and start from a given one and modify it (by deformations) in order to create new ones (for example: chairs of different types). It would be straightforward to load a previously built object database to allow a robot to work in different universes and of course, it is always possible to associate this interactive system to other modeling tools such as laser range finder systems, for example.

Figure 1 shows the example of an office scene sensed by a robot. To simplify the scene, we threw away most objects on the shelf and the desk so that we have a rather fair approximation of a polyhedral world. The reader may verify that both images are not textured, as existing ones on the floor, the walls, the shelf, were filtered out by the camera. Figure 2 presents the overlap between the stereo pair and the result of the use of the interactive data base acquisition program. All objects are already reconstructed, which took several days of work, but it has to be done only once, and it is so much less than the time you would have spent to raise your child!

3   Geometric analysis of the scene

We now suppose that the robot fully acquired all his environment and that he has to perform a specific task. To do so, he must interpret the scene in front of himself in order to go to the place where he has to act. We propose a new scheme coupling computer vision and computer graphics to perform this visual interpretation. For more details, consult [1, 7].

First, we analyze the first stereo pair corresponding to the starting position of the robot. It may be a pair like figure 1. Before anything, the cameras have to be calibrated in a way similar to that proposed in the knowledge acquisition part. Then, a segmentation algorithm is run in both images which partitions them in regions of similar color distribution. Numerous techniques, either bottom-up or top-down were tried. We evolve towards non parametric methods, which are fully data driven.

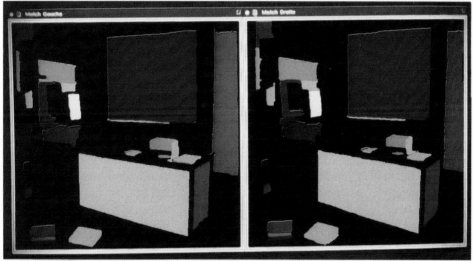

Figure 3: Segmentation of figure 1

Figure 4: Results of the region matching from figure 5

The method described in [4] seems to produce interesting results. It minimizes a global criterion which is some weighting between a mean square approximation error and the total frontier length obtained, inspired by Mumford and Shah (see [4]). On figure 3, segmentation of figure 1 is displayed. Each segmented region received a different color.

The next step consists of the region matching of the two images. We have to find out what are the region pairs which come from the same 3D region (facet). Our experimental conditions are the following : the distance between the two cameras is small with respect to the camera to objets distances and the angle between the two optical axes varies from 5 to 10 degrees. Thus both images are very similar (see figure 1) as we have almost two parallel projections. Thus, all physical 3D facets must have very similar projections on both images. Of course, both segmentations are very noisy. The procedure proposed consists in only keeping very similar region pairs, as the probability that two badly segmented regions may be matched nevertheless, because of similarity, is very low. In that sense, this region matching provides a filter against bad segmentations. Figure 4 shows region matching results from figure 3. Everything which is black was not matched, considered as badly segmented. Matched regions get the same color on the stereo pair.

The third phase is a 3D reconstruction one : given previous region pairs and calibration data, it is possible to compute the 3D position of the planar facet, from which, each region pair is the projection [10, 5]. The originality of our method relies on the use of the coherence of the region data and the epipolar constraint to perform the reconstruction and eliminate, once again, region pairs which reveal a too big epipolar average error. Figure 5 shows the projection of the 3D facets obtained, reprojected on both images.

The fourth and final step is the recognition step. We compare the 3D facets obtained from step 3 with the set of all facets of the database describing the total robot workspace. The problem is to find what are the correspondances between these two sets.

Remark

The solution proposed here is a restriction of the recognition and interpretation problem that we should solve. We suppose here that we dispose of a global data base describing the full geometry of the 3D scene. This solution is therefore called global. It requires that no object may have moved between the time when the robot learnt his environment and the present one, except for objects that the robot will have moved himself (and registered their move in the database). No new object should appear (for example, a human being!). This type of constraints may be, far too restrictive.

In the global case, the solution we came up with (see [10]) uses a hashing technique [11] to perform a first pruning of the model facet candidates to the matching with each of the scene ones.

The algorithm then looks for the maximum number of matches compatible with the fact that these matchings must correspond to a rigid transform between the two sets of facets: we use a displacement error threshold to evaluate this property. If several solutions exist, we take the solution which minimizes the mean square error between the scene facet vertices and the rigidly displaced model ones. For these purposes, we utilize the classical algorithm described in [12], which gives us the best displacement (R,T) fitting the database model with the observed scene. Finally the scene interpretation is obtained by windowing and clipping the displaced model so as to show only what is perceived by each camera. Such an interpretation of figure 1 is shown in figure 6, where the clipped and windowed data base is superimposed in white wireframe above the input images. We have also used a Z-buffer algorithm in order to retain only non-occluded facets. The reader may see that this classical

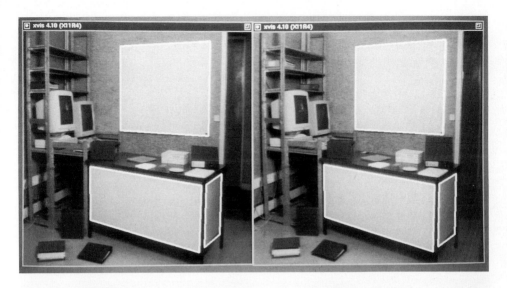

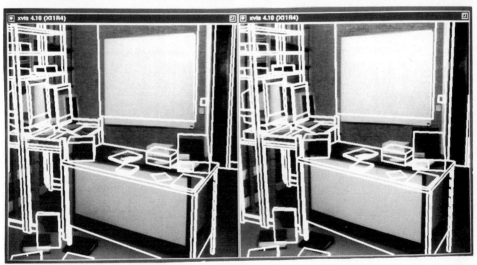

Figure 5: 3D Reconstruction results fom the best regions matches of figure 4

Figure 6: Interpretation of figure 1 obtained by minimizing a mean square error between corresponding scene and model facet vertices.

solution is not very accurate. Nevertheless, from this moment, the robot already "approximately" knows where are all the objects of the database, even those which are not seen!

We remark that the model facets (even those of figure 5 that we used for the interpretation) do not project well on the real scene. This comes from the rigidity constraint and the position errors due to the reconstruction procedure.

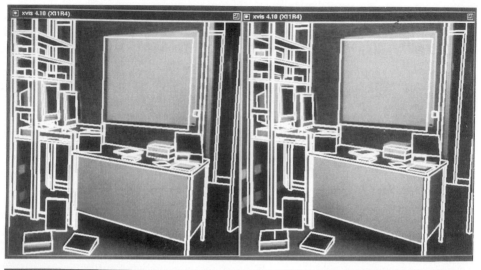

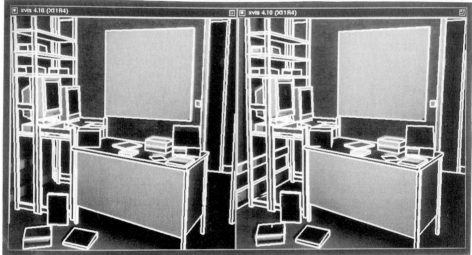

Figure 7: improved solution minimizing the projected mean square displacement error.

Figure 8: final interpretation result when 8 facets where utilized

We now use the analysis/synthesis feedback, by minimizing the mean square error between the projections of the model facets and the segmented regions used for the interpretation. More precisely, we look for an optimal displacement (R^*, T^*) which minimizes this projected mean square error. It is a non linear problem that we solved using a gradient type approach initialized by the result of the classical approach (figure 6). As the initial solution is not so far from the optimum, it has better chances to be reached by this local approach. We noticed a sensitive

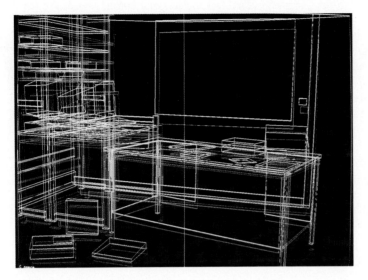

Figure 9: interpretation error: the green wireframe is the ideal scene position; the white wireframe is the final interpretation result.

improvement of the projection results, but there is still an important displacement with regard to the real data. The result of this algorithm is visualized in figure 7. There is a real improvement of the interpretation when compared to that of figure 6. But there is still a clear positioning error. We propose to continue the geometric analysis/synthesis feedback in order to improve the interpretation result.

The important residual error level forced us to continue the (geometrical) feedback loop. The next idea consists in using the segmentation induced by the interpretation: the Z-buffering procedure reveals only the facets of the model which are seen by the cameras. They are visualized by the white polygons of figures 6 and 7. These polygons create a partition of the two images which are, thus, two segmentations where each image pixel received the label of the 3D model facet, from which it is the projection (we also obtain an induced region matching of the two model driven segmentations at the same time).

We compare our original segmentations with the recognition driven ones and add to the list of initial region pairs of the scene (the 3 of figure 5 in our case), new region pairs which are also perfectly superimposed with the recognition driven ones, even if the regions are very small. In this new phase, we have obtained 8 matched regions (instead of 3 before) which produce 3D facets which are evidently matched to model facets (the segmentations retained are the projections of these facets!). The previous non linear interpretation algorithm is then run on the 8 facets (regions pairs). We obtained a satisfactory result presented in figure 8. If it would not be good enough, the procedure could be iterated. In our case, the only limitation of the interpretation improvement comes from the quality of the image segmentation. Figure 9 is also shown in order to appreciate the final 3D interpretation error. The green wireframe represents the real 3D scene (seen from the left camera) constructed by the use of the knowledge acquisition program. As a first approximation, we consider this construction as ideal (no error). The white wireframe is what the vision program produced. There is still some discrepancy between the interpretation result and the ideal solution. The remaining error is coming from various defects. The major defect is due to segmentation errors: we try to fit at best the projection of ideal facets on both images with segmented regions which are not exactly what they should be. We are now studying how to improve the segmentations using a model-based approach.

In conclusion, our results prove that this approach, at least in the restricted (global) case, allows to solve the interpretation problem, which enables the robot to move in this constrained environment. We are now studying the local case where the database will be only given by the local descriptions of object types. The interpretation has, then, to construct the scene geometry during the recognition process and an active method will probably be required.

4 Photometric analysis and analysis/synthesis feedback

A more innovative use of the analysis/synthesis cooperation occurs when we desire to study the photometric component of the scene model (see [7]).

The photometric analysis problem is the following: we dispose of a stereo pair (such as figure 1) and of the results of the geometrical interpretation of the observed scene (figure 6). From these inputs, we have to find the emittance function of the light sources and the reflectance functions of the visible object facets.

The various theoretical and practical aspects of the geometrical reconstruction of scenes have been widely studied, and now, as we have seen, it provides relatively good results. It is not the case for the photometric reconstruction of tri-dimensional surfaces, which are not so commonly studied in the framework of image analysis. Yet, this aspect of the real environment modeling has some success in the new research topics, and several recent papers prove that fact [16, 17, 18, 19, 20, 21].

Our aim is to propose methods to recover some parameters describing the photometrical behaviour of surfaces, considering this problem in the framework of robot vision. We are, thus, searching for passive methods which, for example, do not need to modify light sources (like switching off and switching on some of them). Moreover, we will see that some a priori information helps to handle this complex problem.

We intend to use as input the 3D geometric interpretation of the scene and the two images of the stereo pair. As output, we desire to determine the emittance values of the various light sources and the reflectance functions of all 3D facets (of the various polyhedra). The main simplifying hypothesis we use is that all objects are not textured. We also suppose that, to a given polyhedron, corresponds a single reflectance function (each object is supposed to be constituted of only one material!), but this constraint may be very easily overcome.

The study we started in our laboratory first considers a very simple photometric model: the lambertian one, which considers that any object facet receiving photometric energy, propagates it back in the half space uniformly: the energy bounced back in space has a constant value for all directions and may be represented by a hemisphere.

4.1 Point light sources at infinity

Analysis task

We shall suppose in a first step that the energy received by each facet is only due to the direct lighting from light sources (+ ambient light, if necessary). We shall neglect energy transfers between lambertian facets, but it will be possible to take into account occlusion of the light sources. We shall use a pointwise approximation for the light sources and suppose that light sources are "at infinity" with regard to all other objects. If we consider a unit surface element in any facet, then the amount of energy received by this element from all sources is constant as it the product of the light sources emittance multiplied by the cosine of the angle between the facet normal and the unit vector parallel to the light direction. So, when a facet is lambertian and not textured ($\rho(x,y) = constant$, $\forall(x,y) \in$ planar facet), its intensity is constant when it is projected on any image plane. We consider, first of all, non textured surfaces (which is a problem simplification) for which the reflectance may be approximated by a constant. This is often the case for objects in an office when they are sensed by conventional cameras!

We may show in this case that it is possible to produce a compatible solution with one ρ value per facet (and one emittance value E_i per light source), knowing the geometry of the scene and the mean of the intensity function of each region of both images.

The light intensity (radiosity) of a lambertian facet is of the form:

$$I(x,y) = \frac{\rho}{\pi} \sum_{i=1}^{n} E_i N_i . L_i \alpha_i \tag{1}$$

where ρ is the diffuse reflection coefficient (percentage of the incident energy reflected in the half space), E_i is the emittance of the light sources s_i, N is the unit normal vector to the facet, n is the number of light sources visible from the position of the facet, L_i is the unit vector lying on the line between the position of s_i and the center of the facet, and pointing towards the facet, and α_i is a visibility parameter equal to one if the facet "sees" source i, and equal to zero if it "does not see" source i ((.) is the scalar product). In this equation, we suppose that the size of the facet is small with regard to the distance beetween the light source and the facet so that L_i does not depend on (x,y): the grey level value I(x,y) of each pixel of the left and right regions which are the projections of the given facet are constant within each region and are constant from left to right (lambertian character).

If we analyze the former equation, we deduce that there is one constraint per facet (equation 1, where I (the average of the grey levels in the two matched regions), N, L_i are given). There are n + 1 unknowns (ρ and all E_i) as N and all L_i are available from the geometric interpretation. It is an under-constrained problem! If we do not have more information, we propose to fix all E_i to the value 1 (the whitest grey levels) which allows to compute ρ.

The solution may be refined if we have several facets coming from the same object because this brings new constraints (ρ is the same for all of them). Thus we need only n facet pairs (in fact n - 1) to obtain a more realistic solution. If two facets coming from the same object, are made of the same material, we suppose that they were polished uniformly so that their reflectance is constant. Each equation $\rho = \rho'$ produces and homogeneous equation with respect to all E_i.

$$I(x, y) \sum_{i=1}^{n} E_i N_i' . L_i' \alpha_i' = I'(x, y) \sum_{i=1}^{n} E_i N_i . L_i \alpha_i \tag{2}$$

As they are homogeneous, at most (n-1) of them may be independent, so that emittance E_i will depend linearly on one of them. This left degree of freedom could be only resolved by the use of a microdensitometer to fix such a value absolutely. This comes from the fact that ρ and E_i are always coupled (ρE_i) in equation 1.

Synthesis task

To any type of analysis task of the photometric interpretation, corresponds, in a dual mode, a synthesis algorithm. The feedback between computer vision and computer graphics appears in fact at this level.

Given the former assumptions that the world is lambertian, that light sources are pointwise and at infinity, and that the energy available at each facet comes mainly from the light sources, and given the geometry and photometry of the scene, the problem is to produce a picture (or a stereo pair) of the scene. We may apply equation 1 to each facet. This time ρ, E_i, N, L_i, α_i are known. We obtain a value $I_s(x, y)$ which is close to I (x,y) and not exactly equal, because of computation noise and of the lambertian approximation. The lambertian model projects constant intensity functions on each pair of matched regions of the image planes; this constant is the mean of the intensity functions of the input images (computed on the union of the two regions). If this error between I and I_s is too great, it may be due to two reasons: presence of texture which can be detected on the image planes themselves (spectral signature is high) or shading effects due to the mutual influence of lambertian facets (if they are lambertian!).

Figure 10 shows the result of the stereo pair photometric analysis followed by its synthesis. This reconstruction has been made using the lambertian model with one infinite light source, plus ambient light. Using the preceeding hypotheses on albedos, this leads to an underconstrained system, which is solved by mean square minimization.

The use of a Z-buffer algorithm run on the left and right image planes allowed to determine the left and right projections of each seen facet on these two planes (white wireframe of figure 8). For each facet, it is the possible to compute the red, green, blue means of the left and right regions, which produces $I_R(x, y)$, $I_G(x, y)$, $I_B(x, y)$ of equation 1 available for the red, green, blue components of the images. From these values we could compute ρ_R, ρ_G, ρ_B of each facet (supposing that E_1^R, E_1^G, E_1^B, are equal to one). These reflectance values finally fed a simple scan-line algorithm available in the ACTION 3D modeler and run for the position of the left and right cameras.

Figure 10 shows the natural stereo pair on top, and the synthesized one on the bottom. Each facet is synthetically projected on two regions of constant color, equal on left and right images. It is a <u>zero-order</u> approximation of the left and right

Figure 10: Comparison of the natural stereo pair (on top) and the synthetic one in the case of a lambertain model with pointwise light sources at infinity.

natural images. This zero-order approximation exhibits some defects. It seems very "flat" and has no shadows because of the use of a simple scan-line algorithm.
How could we improve this?
We have to design a more sophisticated synthesis algorithm capable of dealing with shadows. There are intensity gradients on a certain numbers of facets. So, the hypothesis that light sources are at infinity, which produces this "flat" aspect has to be removed. We have decided to study a more complex synthesisable model, which is the most general lambertian case, called the radiosity approach.

4.2 Radiosity solution

The best lambertian non textural solution consists of a choice of light sources at finite distance, and having a certain surface: we chose a rectangular light. We also consider that the energy arriving to each facet is coming from all others and not only from light sources. We came up with the radiosity solution where we had to compute the emittance and the reflectance values as in the previous case. The synthesis algorithm corresponding to this assumption has been described in details in the computer graphics literature.

We came up with the radiosity equation:
$[I - \rho F]R = E$, where:

- I is the N x N identity matrix, N is the number of facets in the scene, .

- ρ is an N x N diagonal matrix, where for each column i, ρ_i is the diffuse reflectance parameter of facet i,

- F is a form factor matrix, related to the solid angle from which each facet i "sees" facet j,

- R is the N x 1 radiosity vector, producing the value of the color of each facet,

- E is the N x 1 emittance vector; E_i is non zero only for light sources.

In the photometric analysis case, R and F are given by the two images and by the 3D geometric interpretation and we have to find out ρ and E. We have N + n (number of light sources) unknown and only N equations, which could bring us to think that this problem is under-determined. In fact, this problem is usually very over-determined as there are many constraints of the type $\rho_i = \rho_j$, for facets consisting of the same material. This problem was solved; the reflectance coefficients and the emittance values obtained were used as input to a radiosity synthesis algorithm. This algorithm is particular as it is a scan-line algorithm which should be an advantage for its speed... It is run in two passes.

In the first pass, independent of the viewpoint, the algorithm propagates light from all light sources to all facets which can be reached directly by them. The structure in which we store the energy received by each facet is fundamental: it is a quadtree in which the received energy for each leaf is equal to the sum of all energies stored in the tree nodes situated on the trajectory between this leaf and the tree bottom. The further and weaker the light sources are, the less, we will have to go down in the tree to store the energy that they send. When it is finished, each tree is then simplified: we suppress all leaves of a node if they correspond to similar energies and so on, climbing up the tree. We then obtain, for each facet, a very subdivided tree when the gradients of energy received are important, and the contrary where the energy does not change very much.

In the second pass, we start from the viewpoint and we follow the inverse trajectory of the light, like in a ray tracing algorithm. This algorithm looks for energy arriving on the intersected surface element and reflected in the considered direction. We stop after one or at most two diffuse reflections.

The interest of this algorithm is that it can be applied to the non lambertian case (facets having specular components), case that we intend to study in the future.

Figure 11 shows the results of the radiosity solution, for only the right image of Figure 1. The right image is the natural one and the left one is the synthetic image. The similarity with the natural picture is much better. Nevertheless there are still numerous defects: shadows do not have the correct position, which proves that the position we found for the light source is too low. Certain objects are still ill-positioned with bad colors, due to remaining geometrical positioning errors. Certain

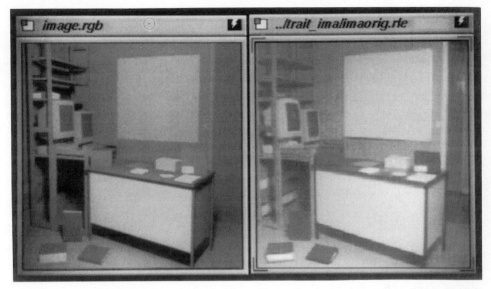

Figure 11: natural image on the right and synthetic image using the radiosity approach, on the left

surfaces of the natural stereo pair (door, computer screens) have specular spots that the lambertian approximation could not model. We are now trying to cope with these three defects.

But it is interesting to see that the radiosity approach is a good approximation for most facets. Is it necessary to consider the full lambertian situation? Perhaps a simpler lambertian model could be sufficient? We are now investigating the case of point light sources at a finite distance.

If we want to obtain a COMPLETE model, we have also to add specular components! How can we model them? We will have still probably to perform a certain number of feedback loops in order to obtain this desired complete model.

In conclusion, we have to stress that the way we set this vision problem makes it a well-posed one and that we may dream that, in a near future, using the analysis/synthesis feedback we will find a good choice of COMPLETE model for this type of office scenes. After the type of model will be determined (the main problem remains the photometric representation), we will move to the local approach, which is more useful in practice. After the global analysis will have determined which type of COMPLETE model is best suited, we will have only to focus on the strategy to construct the 3D geometry in the local approach, already knowing what is the correct photometry type. We do hope that the results obtained show the interest of the analysis/synthesis approach. We also think that such a strategy could be used in the visualization framework of other applications.

References

[1]   A. GAGALOWICZ - *"Collaboration Between Computer Graphics and Computer Vision"*, Progress in Image Analysis and Processing II, edited by World Publishing, pp. 229-258, 1992.

[2]   A. GAGALOWICZ - *"Comment Donner Le Sens de la perception Visuelle à un Robot Domestique"*, Numéro spécial du Courrier du CNRS sur l'Informatique, Février 1992.

[3]   B. ZAVIDOVIQUE, T. BERNARD - *"Generic Functions for On-chip Vision"*, Proc. of IEEE Int. Conf. on Pattern Recognition ICPR 92, The Hague, The Netherlands, pp 1-10, 1992.

[4]   A. ACKAH-MIEZAN, A. GAGALOWICZ - *"Discrete Models for Energy Mnimizing Segmentation"*, ICCV'93 Conference, pp. 200-207, 1993.

[5]   J. FELDMAR, G. JOURDAN - *"Vision Stéréoscopique: Reconstruction Géométrique et Reconnaissance de Modèles"*, Rapport de DEA, INRIA, 1992.

[6]   V. MEAS-YEDID - *"Construction Interactive de Modèles Géométriques de Scène"*, Rapport de Stage, ESIEA, 1992.

[7]   A. GAGALOWICZ - *"Coopération entre l'Analyse et la Synthèse d'Images"*, Invited Conference at RFIA 89, Paris, pp. 1727-1758, 1989.

[8]   G. TOSCANI - *"Système de Calibration Optique et Perception du Mouvement en Vision Artificielle"*, Thèse de Docteur de 3ème cycle, Paris, Orsay, 1987.

[9]   O. FAUGERAS - *"What Can Be Seen in Three Dimensions With an Uncalibrated Stereorig"*, Proceedings of the 2-nd European Conference on Computer Vision, G. Sandini (réd.), Springer Verlag, Lecture notes in Computer Science, 588, pp. 563-578, May 1992.

[10] J. FELDMAR, A. GAGALOWICZ, G. JOURDAN - *"Stereo Reconstruction and 3D Recognition of Polyhedral Occluded Scenes"*, in preparation.

[11] E. GRIMSON - *"Object Recognition by Computer"*, MIT Press, 1990.

[12] O. FAUGERAS, M. HEBERT - *"The Representation Recognition and Locating of 3D Objets"*, International Journal of Robotics Research, Vol. 5, No 3, 1986.

[13] N.A.M. HOOTSMANS S. DUBOWSKY - *"Large Motion Control of Mobile Manipulators Including Vehicule Suspension Characteristics"*, Proceedings of 1991 International Conference on Robotics and Automation. Sacramento, CA, pp. 2336-2341, April 1991.

[14]   S. DUBOWSKY, P.Y. GU, J.F. DECK - *"The Dynamic Analysis of Flexibility in Mobile Robotic Manupilator Systems"*, Proceedings of the Eight World Congress on the Theory of Machines and Mechanism. Prague Czechoslovakia, pp. 9-12, Vol. 1, August 1991.

[15]   V. KUMAR, X. YUN, E. PALJUG, N. SARKAR - *"Control of Contact Conditions for Manupilation with Multiple Robotic Systems"*, Proceedings of 1991 International Conference on Robotics and Automation, Sacramento, CA, pp. 170-175, April 1991.

[16]   E.H. ADELSON, A.P. PENTLAND - *"The Perception of Shading and Reflectance"*, Vision and Modeling Technical Report 140, MIT Media Laboratory, October 25 1990.

[17]   M.S. DREW, B.V. HUNT - *"Calculating Surface Reflectance Using a Single-Bounce Model of Mutual Reflection"*, Third International Conference in Computer Vision, Osaka, Japan, 394-399, Dec. 4-7 1990.

[18]   K. IKEUCHI, K. SATO - *"Determining Reflectance Parameters using Range and Brightness Images"*, Third International Conference in Computer Vision, Osaka, Japon, pp. 12-20, Dec. 4-7 1990.

[19]   S.K. NAYAR, K. IKEUCHI, T. KANADE - *"Determining Shape and Reflectance of Hydrid Surfaces by Photometric Sampling"*, IEEE Transactions on Robotics and Automation, Vol. 6, No 4, pp. 418-437, August 1990.

[20]   H.D. TAGARE, R.J.P. DEFIGUEIREDO - *"A Theory of Photometric Stereo for a Class of Diffuse non-Lambertian Surfaces"*, IEEE Transcations on Pattern Analysis and Machine Intelligence, 13(2): 133-152, February 1991.

[21]   Q. ZHENG, R. CHELLAPPA - *"Estimation of Illuminant Direction, Albedo, and Shape From Shading"*, IEEE Transcations on Pattern Analysis and Machine Intelligence, 13(7): pp. 680-702, July 1991.

[22]   A. ACKAH-MIEZAN, A. GAGALOWICZ - *"Energy minnimizing Segmentation of an Image"*, Processing of International Symposium on Computer and Information Science, ISCIS VII, Antalya, Turkey, pp. 631-634, 2-4 November 1992.

Springer-Verlag
and the Environment

We at Springer-Verlag firmly believe that an international science publisher has a special obligation to the environment, and our corporate policies consistently reflect this conviction.

We also expect our business partners – paper mills, printers, packaging manufacturers, etc. – to commit themselves to using environmentally friendly materials and production processes.

The paper in this book is made from low- or no-chlorine pulp and is acid free, in conformance with international standards for paper permanency.